Custer on Canvas

Race has, of course, been a characteristic American obsession—and the racial imagination has been at work on many different groups of people, Indians included.

(Deloria 1998, 5)

The Wild West Show . . . was a kind of reverse minstrel show, with its nonwhite members occasionally masquerading as white men to better persuade a largely white audience of their own superiority.

(Warren 2005, 405)

DATELINE:

Disneyland Resort Paris, February, 2011—Buffalo Bill's Wild West Show

An encounter with Buffalo Bill, Sitting Bull, Annie Oakley and the Rough Riders brings the audience back to the Old West. Guests will enjoy . . . the "Buffalo Bill's Store" souvenir shop and a western photo location for a memorable souvenir of this evening full of adventures and encounters.

Prepare to relive the fantastic epic of the Far West!

(http://disney-village.disneylandparis.co.uk/buffalo-bills-wild-west-show/index.xhtml#)

The aura or reverence for a work of art adheres not in the object itself, but in the meanings brought to it, those associated with religion, tradition, ritual, magic, bourgeois structures of power. With the advent of art's mechanical reproduction there is no actual original. The experience of art is now freed from time and place and instead brought under the gaze and control of the mass audience, art is emancipated from a dependence on ritual or aura. The meaning of art in the age of mechanical reproduction will inherently be based on the practice of politics.

(Benjamin 1968, 222–223, paraphrased, italics added)

Custer on Canvas

Representing Indians,
Memory, and Violence
in the New West

Norman K. Denzin

LONDON AND NEW YORK

First published 2011 by Left Coast Press, Inc.

Published 2016 by Routledge
2 Park Square, Milton Park, Abingdon, Oxon OX14 4RN
711 Third Avenue, New York, NY 10017, USA

Routledge is an imprint of the Taylor & Francis Group, an informa business

Copyright © 2011 Taylor & Francis

All rights reserved. No part of this book may be reprinted or reproduced or utilised in any form or by any electronic, mechanical, or other means, now known or hereafter invented, including photocopying and recording, or in any information storage or retrieval system, without permission in writing from the publishers.

Notice:
Product or corporate names may be trademarks or registered trademarks, and are used only for identification and explanation without intent to infringe.

Library of Congress Cataloging-in-Publication Data
Denzin, Norman K.
  Custer on canvas : representing Indians, memory, and violence in the new west / Norman K. Denzin.
     p. cm.
  Includes bibliographical references and index.
  ISBN 978-1-59874-598-6 (hardcover : alk. paper) -- ISBN 978-1-59874-599-3 (pbk. : alk. paper)
 1. Little Bighorn, Battle of the, Mont., 1876--Pictorial works. 2. Little Bighorn, Battle of the, Mont., 1876, in art. 3. Little Bighorn, Battle of the, Mont., 1876--Drama. 4. Custer, George, 1776-1833--Portraits. 5. Custer, George, 1776-1833--Drama. 6. Custer, George, 1776-1833--Anniversaries. 7. Indians in art. 8. Indians in popular culture--Montana--Little Bighorn Battlefield--Pictorial works. I. Title.
  E83.876.D46 2011
  973.8'2092--dc22
                            2011009011

ISBN 978-1-59874-599-3 paperback
ISBN 978-1-59874-598-6 hardcover

This book is a product of the author's ethnographic imagination. Names, characters, places, events, and incidents are used fictitiously. Any resemblance to actual events, locales, or persons, living or dead, is at least partially coincidental. The dialogue contained herein is intended as a stage play and should not be quoted or considered to be the actual words of the speakers unless contained in Quote marks. The opinions of the speakers are the conjecture of the author.

CONTENTS

Acknowledgments 7
Introduction 9
Dramatis Personae 27

CHAPTER ONE A Good Day to Die: The Battle of Many Names 31
CHAPTER TWO Whose Last Stand? The Early Paintings 63
CHAPTER THREE Whose Custer? 91
CHAPTER FOUR Killing Custer 117
CHAPTER FIVE Here Fell Custer
An Autoethnography of a Painting 151
CHAPTER SIX Custer's Last Rally 185
CHAPTER SEVEN The Last Stand 219

APPENDIX A *Timeline:* The Plains Indian Wars (1860–1890) and the Battle of Many Names (1876) 243
APPENDIX B *Timeline:* Paintings of the Battle of Many Names 247
APPENDIX C *Timeline:* William F. "Buffalo Bill" Cody 251

Notes 253
List of Plates and Credits 263
References 265
Index 273
About the Author 279
Section of color plates appears after page 128.

ACKNOWLEDGMENTS

I would like to thank Mitch Allen, Katherine E. Ryan, Michael Giardina, Art Bochner, and Carolyn Ellis for their quick and early support of this project. Mitch Allen is the editor of all editors, and his vision and fingerprints are all over this book.

I thank Carl and Dee Dee Couch for starting this project. In 1987 they invited us to their cabin on the Boulder River, south of Big Timber, Montana. We have been traveling West every year since. Robert Moran, retired librarian at the Red Lodge Carnegie Library, first pointed me in the direction of Custer and his Last Stand in the summer of 1990. I cannot thank him enough. My two granddaughters, Sylvia and Naomi Maehr, initiated the project when, during a family reunion in Montana in 2007, they asked me to explain the meaning of two Custer's Last Stand paintings in the Whitney Gallery of Western Art.

This project could not have been done without the generous support of the staff at the Buffalo Bill Historical Center (BBHC) and the Whitney Gallery of Western Art. I received invaluable assistance from Sean Campbell, Image Rights and Reproductions Manager; Christine Brindza, Acting Curator, Whitney Gallery of Western Art; and Marguerite House, Editor, *Points West: Magazine of the Buffalo Bill Historical Center*. I cannot thank them enough. I also received valuable assistance from Tammy Ryan, Business Manager, Publications Office of the Montana Historical Society (MHS) and the Permissions and Reproductions Department of the Research Center of the MHS.

I thank Lisa Scholder for giving me permission to reproduce images of Fritz Scholder's *Custer and 20,000 Indians* (1996) and *American Landscape* (1976). I thank Lou Lou Goss for permission to reproduce the image of

Earl Biss's *General Custer in Blue and Green* (1996). Allan Mardon and Ted Larsen were generous in their support, including giving me the rights to reproduce a portion of Allan's painting, *The Battle of Greasy Grass* on our cover. Caitlin von Schmidt was quick to give me permission to use the photographs made by her father, Eric von Schmidt, which are contained in Eric von Schmidt's "Sunday at the Little Big Horn with George" (*Montana The Magazine of Western History*, 1992, pp. 50–51). I thank Robin Taylor and the Philmont Museum-Seton Memorial Library for permission to reproduce images of White Swan's drawings.

I wish to thank Lisa Devenish for her book design and production skills, Anne K. Brown for copy editing, Sally Gregg for her meticulous reading of the page proofs and Jane Henderson for the production of the index. This project would not have been completed without the assistance, patience, and talents of James Salvo. I also thank the students at the University of Illinois who patiently sat through formal and informal seminars, listening to earlier versions of my arguments about performance ethnography, cultural studies, politics, and pedagogy. I especially thank Carol Rambo Ronai, editor of *Symbolic Interaction,* who published an early version of Chapter One.

Finally, I gratefully acknowledge the moral, intellectual, and financial support given this project by the late Dean Kim Rotzoll of the College of Media, as well as the past and current directors of the Institute of Communications Research: Clifford Christians, Paula Treichler, and Angharad N. Valdivia.

INTRODUCTION[1]

Most Americans know (or think they know) the basic story. On June 25, 1876, Custer and his Seventh Cavalry troopers attacked a large village of Sioux and Cheyenne people on the Little Bighorn River and were wiped out by a swarm of warriors. . . . Custer was an overweaning fool . . . [transformed into] a martyr at a time when this country . . . desperately needed a martyr.
—James Welch

The Battle of the Little Bighorn, Custer's Last Stand . . . has inspired scores of Hollywood films, over a thousand documented paintings,[2] and countless books, cartoons, and advertisements.
—Paul Stekler

The Last Stand pictures fascinate all beholders . . . [but] the scene is totally imaginary, for no white witness survived the Custer tragedy.[3] . . . Hence, as historical documents, pictures of Custer's Last Stand are admittedly worthless.[4]
—Robert Taft

Custer died for your sins.
—Vine Deloria Jr.

"Custer's Last Rally" appeared for the first time in Buffalo Bill's Wild West Show on January 4, 1887. Custer is the last man killed, and he dies after performing prodigies of valor.
—Louis S. Warren

The West is a tragedy relieved by interludes of comedy. It is a tale of good and evil, a morality play of personified abstractions.
—Dee Brown

This book could be called *Searching for Yellowstone, Part 2*, for it continues the project started in my 2008 book, *Searching for Yellowstone: Race, Gender, Family, and Memory in the Postmodern West*, namely the examination of race, minstrelsy, gender, Native Americans, and memory in the postmodern West. Instead, after Vine Deloria Jr. (1988), James Welch and Paul Stekler (1994), Philip J. Deloria (1998), William Kittridge (2007), and Sherman Alexie (2007), I have chosen to call it *Custer on Canvas: Representing Indians, Memory, and Violence in the New West*.

Lieutenant Colonel George Armstrong Custer's last stand at the Battle of the Little Bighorn,[5] also called the "Battle of Greasy Grass," signified a turning point in American history (Philbrick, 2010).[6] If Custer (1839–1876) died for our sins, as a popular bumper sticker reads, then the Battle of the Little Bighorn was "really the Indians' last stand" (Alexie, 2007, p. 70). After this battle, many Native American nations—Lakota, Ute, Cheyenne, Crow, Shoshone, Blackfeet, Nez Perce, Apache, Navajo—in the western United States were, in effect, populations of walking dead people, waiting only for the last battle at Wounded Knee to cement their fate (Brown, 1970). The resistances of Chief Joseph and Geronimo, the Ghost Dance movement of 1890, and the American Indian Movement (AIM), begun in 1968, could do little to reverse history.

After his death, Custer became the symbol of American military power for post–Civil War America, the symbol of white supremacy, the symbol of white men ruling the West. Native Americans were vilified because they killed America's national hero. They murdered innocent white Americans. They had to be erased from the Western landscape, placed on reservations. And they were.

Custer on Canvas is an exercise in the politics of representation. There is no single, authoritative account of this battle, or one agreed-upon painting. The representations of the battle in paintings by Lakota, Cheyenne, and Crow artists tell one story. The stories told in the paintings done by white painters tell another, and these differences cannot be reconciled. *Custer on Canvas* is about the places, events, and representations that keep this historical figure and the Battle of Greasy Grass alive. It is about memory, violence, and a museum—Buffalo Bill Historical Center—named after a man, Buffalo Bill Cody, who was a friend of Custer and performed re-enactments of Custer's Last Stand in his traveling Wild West Show. And, this book is about a set of paintings that represent that battle. From more than one thousand Last Stand paintings, I focus on only a few, just those that have reached canonical status in the Custer literature (Taft, 1954; Russell,1968; Brindza, 2010).[7]

In interpreting these paintings, I am less interested in figuring out what each one means. I am more interested in figuring out my response to them and other people's responses as well.[8] I have spent nearly five years moving around and inside the paintings, getting closer to them, studying them, standing in front of them and standing behind them, talking to them. I have wanted to write through them, get on the other side of them, to put them in play with one another, have their creators talk to me and to one another. As if I were a museum curator in the *Night at the Museum* movies,[9] I wanted the figures in the Custer paintings and their painters to step off the canvas and talk to me. (I have them do this in chapter 6.)

In this book, I am having a conversation with the paintings and with an event. It is a conversation that extends off the canvas into complex historical spaces, a dialogue that enlists a "Dramatis Personæ," a cast of characters that includes Cassilly Adams, Otto Becker, Adolphous Busch, Walter Benjamin, Dee Brown, Edward S. Curtis, Sherman Alexie, Ned Buntline, George Armstrong Custer, Vine Deloria Jr., Louise Erdrich, Richard Fox, Elizabeth Cook-Lynn, Henry Wadsworth Longfellow, John Mulvany, E.S. Paxson, Sitting Bull, Eric von Schmidt, Walt Whitman, and Howard Zinn.

A Last Stand painting is always more than a painting. A painter reaches you with a painting, and for an instant that painting diverts you from your day, for that instant it changes you, and it may change the course of history as well (Marcus, 2010, p. 217). You may try to forget the painting, but it won't let you; its imagery haunts you. So it is for me with the Last Stand paintings. I cannot get them out of my head.

The Custer paintings are performances, military dramas, stories of war, conflict, and violence. To understand what they mean, I must do more than locate them in their historical moment. I must read myself into them, as if I were looking in a mirror (Marcus, 2010, p. 189). What I see in the Custer paintings are people—Lakota, Cheyenne, Crow, men, women, children, Custer, his men—who are not free. They are trapped in a battle scene, players in a violent story they can't get out of. Some are prisoners of their vanity, their compromises, ego, cowardice, false bravery. Few, very few, are joyous and free. In studying these paintings, we find new ways to write and paint ourselves into history.

I have attempted to write myself into a shared space with the painters, with Custer, and with you. If we can share this space long enough, perhaps we can imagine how this tragic piece of nineteenth century history could have happened differently. And if so, maybe, just maybe, such events will never happen again. That is my goal.

My thesis is simple: The Custer paintings function as paradigmatic images of First Nations people and their place in Western history.[10] They represent nineteenth and twentieth century Western American art in the service of official governmental history.[11] I contest Taft's 1953 argument (included in an epigraph to the introduction) that the paintings of "Custer's Last Stand are admittedly worthless" (pp. 130–131). As cultural documents, these paintings celebrate military power. They reproduce prevailing racist views of Native Americans and their place in U.S. history[12] and contemporary popular Western culture (Lane, 1973; Dippie, 1974).

The Custer in these paintings symbolizes the fallen, if tarnished, post–Civil War military hero.[13] The military battle is presented as a massacre, a debacle. It is depicted in somber, melodramatic, violent, flag-waving detail. In painting after painting, the event is represented as an assault on brave, heroic soldiers by nearly naked, blood-thirsty Native Americans carrying guns, knives, bows and arrows, and tomahawks. As a historical group, the Custer paintings keep these negative images alive. At the same time they marginalize Lakota and Cheyenne representations of the battle.

I read these paintings back against themselves, placing them alongside Native American representations of the battle, including Lakota Chief Red Horse's forty-one ledger drawings made in 1881 and the artwork of White Swan, Kevin Red Star, Earl Biss, Fritz Scholder, John Nieto, and others. Chief Red Horse's representations of the battle[14] are not part of the official archive of Custer's Last Stand paintings (Taft, 1953; Lane, 1973; Dippie, 1974). In this reading, my intent is to do more than unsettle official versions of the Last Stand. The official history and public museum memories of this battle should no longer be allowed to exclude Lakota, Cheyenne, and Crow representations of this turning point event in American history. We should remember, too, that this was not solely a battle between Native Americans (Lakota and Cheyenne) and the American military. Crow Indian interpreters and scouts fought with Custer against the Lakota and Cheyenne.

*— * — *—

First memory: I begin with another time, another war. In 1968 I lived at 203 West Pennsylvania Avenue in Urbana, Illinois. My next door neighbor was Dee Brown (1908–2002), Western historian and head librarian at the University of Illinois. It was early spring; the Vietnam War was in full force. The Browns' son, Lt. Colonel J. Mitchell Brown, was home on a short leave from the war zone. Dee and I were both writing books. His book was *Bury My Heart at Wounded Knee* (1970); mine was *The Research Act* (1970). I was writing about how to study society. My neighbor was writing about how to change society. An HBO movie based on Brown's book debuted on May 27, 2007.[15]

The Browns asked me to have a drink with their son. Mitchell Brown and I sat together in the shade of the towering sycamore tree in their side yard and talked awkwardly about the antiwar movement in America.

Second memory: It took me until July 10, 2007, to get back to Brown's book, that is, to get back to the nineteenth century history of Native Americans and their treatment by American society. This happened because of a family visit to the Whitney Gallery of Western Art inside the Buffalo Bill Historical Center in Cody, Wyoming. I was standing in front of Allan Mardon's *Battle of Greasy Grass* (1996) with Naomi and Sylvia Maehr, two of our granddaughters. Mardon's 11-by-6-foot, oil-on-linen, mural-sized painting is modeled after Indian ledger art.[16] It tells the story of Custer's Last Stand from the Lakota and Cheyenne point of view. The story unfolds hour by hour, from 2:40 p.m. on Sunday, June 25, to 3 p.m. Monday, June 26, when Sitting Bull calls an end to the fighting. In vivid colors, the huge painting depicts Lakota and Cheyenne warriors on horseback and on foot, engaging Custer and his men in the Last Stand. The painting celebrates movement, energy, life itself; it shows only a few dead bodies and no apparent bloodshed. Naomi tugged at my hand and said, "Grandpa, come over here and look at this painting." She led me into another room in the gallery. We stopped in front of Edgar Samuel Paxson's 6-by-9-foot *Custer's Last Stand* (1899). "I'm confused," she said. "Are these two paintings about the same thing? They look so different."[17] I was confused, too.

E.S. Paxson's masterpiece, painted 107 years before Mardon's, is somber, sad, violent, with dead bodies everywhere, blood spilled on the ground, smashed skulls, arrows sticking out of necks, smoke filling the air. Custer, a noble figure in the center of the Paxson painting, is only one among many in Mardon's canvas. Naomi had good reason to be confused. Two paintings of the same event but with totally different representations. Upon returning to Urbana, I called the archivist at the Buffalo Bill Historical Center and asked about the exhibit. Her answer frames scene 3 of the play that follows in chapter 1. In the summer of 2007, the museum was exhibiting a sample of what are called the Custer's Last Stand paintings.[18] Naomi had focused on two of the most dramatic paintings. Thus began the inquiry that guides this book. I wanted to learn the story behind the two paintings. Custer's Last Stand became a vehicle for re-engaging Dee Brown's project.

I interrogate the shifting places of Native Americans, Custer, and the Last Stand paintings in the contemporary American imaginary. This is an imaginary that is given in the Custer films (Hutton, 2004b; Simmon, 2003), in Last Stand paintings (Taft, 1953; Kemmick, 2002), in Last Stand cultural re-enactments, in Custer documentaries (Welch, 1994), and in Disneyland Paris performances of Wild West events that include Custer and Sitting Bull. Together, these cultural works serve to define the place of Native Americans in the New West. They give us a new imaginary, an imaginary about rodeos, wars, violence, Native Americans, and cowboys. Disturbingly, this new imaginary seems to be continuous with the old imaginary. We are back where we started. It is June 25, 1876, all over again. The Native Americans killed Custer, and the American press claimed Custer won the war.

There is more. In 2009 and 2010 Custer makes appearances in at least two new cultural sites: as a character in the movie *Night at the Museum: Battle of the Smithsonian* as an action figure riding a motorcycle, and as a toy for the same movie in a McDonald's Happy Meal.

Cultural Sighting Number 1: June 11, 2009

This week, General Custer, the infamous Indian fighter who died on that hot, dusty prairie in 1876, along with his entire detachment, reared his head again. This time, in the form of a figurine riding a motorcycle found inside McDonald's Happy Meals. The figurine is the result of a partnership between McDonald's and Twentieth Century Fox, distributor of *Night at the Museum: Battle of the Smithsonian*. The "General Custer" doll represents a figure in the movie that comes to life in the Smithsonian and has adventures alongside Ben Stiller's night watchman character. But just because a movie distributor decides to give this historical goofball a chance to make his second "last stand" doesn't mean a nationwide restaurant chain should do the same. (Abourezk, 2009)

Cultural Sighting Number 2: June 4, 2010

The public is invited to join members of the Little Big Horn Associates (LBHA) for a special bus tour of Monroe, Michigan on Friday, June 4, 2010, as they revisit General George Armstrong Custer's life and times in this historic city.

The international organization, which promotes an exchange of knowledge on the life and times of Custer and the Battle of the Little Big Horn, will hold its annual conference in Monroe on June 3–5, 2010. The conference coincides with the city's 100th anniversary of the dedication of the Custer equestrian monument that stands at the corner of Elm and Monroe Streets.[19]

Custer on Canvas becomes a way of looking for and interpreting the many presences and traces of Custer in our national imagination. Custer needs Indians, so looking for Custer means looking at Custer and his tangled, violent relationships with Native Americans. Custer, like the displaced Native American, is nowhere and everywhere across the postmodern Western landscape. Custer and the Lakota, Crow, and Cheyenne share presences and spaces in state parks and national forests. Custer's face is on the banner of newspapers. In little Montana towns, dancing redskins are athletic mascots, and Custer's name appears in ads for gas stations, hotels, and grocery stores. Western cities are named after the Lakota and the Cheyenne, and roads and subdivisions are named after Custer. Wild West Days with Custer, Buffalo Bill Cody, Sitting Bull, and Crazy Horse imitators celebrate yet one more version of the Last Stand. Historical re-enactments place Custer and Lakota and Cheyenne warriors side by side in mock battle.

Custer's continued presence in our national imagination requires the real and imaginary presence of people playing Indian to some white man's version of Custer (Deloria, 1998). So where we find Custer, we find stereotyped representations of Native Americans. And where we find stereotyped Native Americans, we find Custer. We need Native Americans if the myth of Custer is to survive, hence the need for all of those paintings, all those movies, all those re-enactments. We must perform these myths: make films, play dress-up, create paintings, have Wild West Days, stage rodeos, and hang representations of Custer's Last Stand on the walls of our museums.

※ ※ ※

There are other options. We can put a stop to these minstrel shows[20] and finally put the Wild Wild West to bed. We can draw lines in the sand. No more re-enactments of these racist cultural myths. A new generation, with new stories, new utopian visions can come forward and be heard. We must learn how to reimagine and restage the past. We need new political performances that reclaim and celebrate the inalienable rights of Native Americans to own and control their history (Denzin, 2008, p. 79).

Unless events change, we are certainly witnessing the next version of the Last Stand; tainted racist memories and failing economies will annihilate the new West (Kittridge, 2007). Increasingly, from Taos to Kalispell, Seattle to Coeur d'Alene, Cody to Denver, the Western landscape is overrun with tourists looking for and consuming versions of history that reproduce violent myths about Custer, the military, Lakota and Cheyenne and Crow (Kittridge, 2007, pp. 230–232). And for the benefit of tourists, Crow and Cheyenne re-enact battle scenes from the 1870s. Meanwhile, without fail, every June 25 at Garryowen, Montana, near the site of the battlefield monument, re-enactments of his Last Stand are staged by white performers. We may never get back to where we were, before the West was discovered by Lewis and Clark and their contemporaries.

And this is global. In Auckland and Otago, Sidney, Honolulu, London and Paris, Munich, Stockholm and São Paulo, Caracas, and Buenos Aires, even Tampere, you can find Wild West shows with cowboys, Indians, Custer, and Last Stand posters.

※ ※ ※

Cultural Sighting Number 3

The Custer Battlefield Museum presents this Special Edition of Custer's Last Fight, Anheuser-Busch Limited Edition Print, 36" x 27".

Custer's Last Fight is the most famous depiction of the Battle of the Little Bighorn and the most famously inaccurate. It has been seen by millions of people in the last 106 years. For the first time ever, Anheuser-Busch Corporation has granted special permission to the Custer Battlefield Museum to reissue on high quality paper this famous print. *All proceeds go directly to benefit the new "Peace Memorial" at Garryowen.*[21]

Interpreting Cultural Sighting Number 3

It's significant that the website that promotes the sale of prints of Cassilly Adams's *Custer's Last Stand* painting (1876) also mentions a new Lewis and Clark exhibit about the 1804–1806 "Voyage of Discovery." These two events, separated by only seventy years, figuratively and literally mark the beginning and the end of the New West in the nineteenth century. So of course they should be side by side in the same site. Can we find a new place to re-remember? Can we forget Custer? What would it mean to start over? Would Red Horse's ledger art be a starting point? Do we have to go through Lewis and Clark to get there?

Third Memory: In 1994 my wife and I bought a small cabin in the Beartooth Ranger District of the Custer National Forest. This is Custer Country.[22] Our cabin is on Rock Creek, four miles outside Red Lodge, Montana. We are sixty miles from the Buffalo Bill Historical Center in Cody, where the Custer's Last Stand paintings were exhibited in 2007. We are 69 miles over the Beartooth Mountains from Yellowstone National Park.[23] We have become cultural tourists in the New West, seasonals traveling from Champaign-Urbana, Illinois, to Billings; southeast from Billings to Hardin and the Crow Reservation and the Custer battlefield; east to the Dakotas, the Black Hills, and Wounded Knee; back west to the Prior Mountains; and then back home to Rock Creek and Red Lodge.

This book, part ethnography, part performance text, comes out of experience in two sites. I start with the Last Stand paintings themselves, their haunting, brooding, yet exuberant and violent presence in the Buffalo Bill Historical Center. I move from the paintings to the many representations of Custer and his legacies that circulate more generally in the cultural spaces of the New West.

Performing the Text

Except for the introduction and chapter 7, all chapters are intended to be performed; that is, read aloud. A "Dramatis Personæ" listing all the characters and their historical roles follows the introduction. These characters appear throughout all six plays. The act of reading aloud in a group, or co-performing, creates a shared emotional experience that brings the narrative alive in ways that silent reading cannot. The parts can be spoken going around in a circle of any number of readers or by two speakers. Each speaker names the character before reading the character's lines. In writing the monologues and dialogues that appear in each play, I was guided by Walter Benjamin's argument (1969) that a critical text consists of a series of quotations, documents, excerpts, and texts placed side by side. This narrative strategy produces a de-centered narrative, a multivoiced text with voices and speakers talking back and forth, often past one another.

The assignment of characters is done arbitrarily. A male may read a female part, and vice versa. Stage directions are suggested, such as the use of "whiteface," "redface," and "blackface" masks. The use of masks is intended to suggest that race and gender are nonessentialist identities that can be moved around with minstrel masks. Performers are encouraged to create their own sets of masks specific to the themes of this book (or a chapter) rather than generic white, red, and black.

Two recurring figures are Coyote, the trickster, and Tonto, the Indian sidekick to the Lone Ranger in the long-running "Lone Ranger" television series. Coyote is a character from Crow, Cherokee, and other Native American cultures. She/he challenges the mythologies of the dominant white culture. Sometimes disguised as a clown, Coyote makes people laugh. Coyote the clown, the trickster, functions as an essential link to the sacred. Coyote is open to life's paradoxes and contradictions and exposes cracks in official ideology (Radin, 1956; Brennan, 2003). Coyote functions in my text as an indigenous critic of white culture. Tonto is a white Indian, a minstrel figure who moves back and forth between Crow and white culture. Tonto is like Curly and White Swan, two Crow Indians who sided with Custer. Tonto, though, speaks out of both sides of his mouth. The voices of Coyote, Ms. Coyote, and Tonto are meant to be disruptive.

The speeches for each character are often presented in a poetic format. This is meant to dramatize the narrative and to emphasize the sounds of words and the rhythms of the spoken word. It is also intended to create a visual, performative space on the page. Unless otherwise indicated, quotations—words attributed to a speaker—are paraphrases of an original text that is cited. These are not the character's words but my interpretations of what they might say if they were persuaded to participate in this performance.

The caveat that appears on the copyright page of this book operates at all times:

> **This book is a product of my ethnographic imagination. Names, characters, places, events, and incidents are used fictitiously. Any resemblance to actual events, locales, or persons, living or dead, is at least partially coincidental. The dialogue contained herein is intended as a stage play and should not be quoted or considered to be the actual words of the speakers unless contained in Quote marks. The opinions of the speakers are the conjecture of the author.**

The plays should be performed around a seminar table, on a simple set or stage before an audience with costumes, sets, and props as "ornate as one imagines" (Smith, 2004, p. 6). If visual technology is available, images of the Last Stand paintings and other images indicated in the text could be projected on a screen.[24] A spotlight that moves from speaker to speaker could enhance a production. The emphasis on performance follows from the performance turn in the human disciplines. For at least a decade interpretive ethnographers have been staging reflexive, autoethnographic performances using field notes, historical documents, and autoethnographic observations to shape performance narratives—an anthropology of performance (Conquergood, 1998; Madison and Hamera, 2006; Ellis, 2009). We are in a postexperimental moment, performing culture and history as we write it.

Richardson and St. Pierre (2005) argue that the narrative genres connected to ethnographic writing have, in the past decade, "been blurred, enlarged, altered" (p. 962). These new writing practices include autoethnography, fiction stories, poetry, performance texts, polyvocal texts, readers' theater, responsive readings, visual presentations, layered accounts, writing stories, performance writing, mysteries, personal history, cultural criticism, and historical autoethnography. Custer on Canvas is in this experimental tradition.

The dividing line between performer and audience blurs; culture becomes a dramatic performance. Performance texts are situated in complex systems of discourse where traditional, everyday, and avant-garde meanings of theater, film, video, ethnography, cinema, performance, text, and audience all circulate and inform one another. Performance ethnography simultaneously creates and enacts moral texts that move from the personal to the political, the local to the historical and cultural. Following Conquergood (1998), these dialogical works create spaces for give and take, doing more than turning the other into the object of a voyeuristic, fetishistic, custodial, or paternalistic gaze.

The performance turn poses three closely interrelated problems for my project, namely how to *construct, perform,* and *critically analyze* performance texts. In this book I examine all three problems but privilege co-performance (audience-performer) texts and narratives. Co-performance stories bring audiences back into the text, creating a field of shared emotional experience. This phenomenon is created through the acts of representation and presentation. A resistance model of textual performance and interpretation is foregrounded. A good performance text must be more than cathartic; it must be political, moving people to action, reflection. The plays in the first six chapters are framed by these assumptions.

In constructing the text I am guided by Gregory Ulmer's 1989 essay, "Derrida at the Little Bighorn: A Fragment." Ulmer's essay is a montage, a layered performance text formed out of memory, the sting of the past, an intermingling of images, pictures, sightings of Custer, letters from Derrida, reflections on the Battle of Little Bighorn, a catalog of Custer jokes, family memories, personal biography, personal intersections with various versions of the Custer legacy. Ulmer graduated from Custer High School in Miles City, Montana. His father died on May 17, the same day Custer started his fateful march of 1876. Ulmer's sister Judy lived for five years in Lodge Grass, "one of the translations for the Indian name for 'Little Bighorn,' the other being 'Greasy Grass'" (Ulmer, 1989, p. 215).

Like the Last Stand paintings, I too write from the scenes of memory, including my granddaughters standing in front of Paxson's painting at the Buffalo Bill Historical Center in the summer of 2007. I also recall my father trying to sell a collection of Custer postcards under the heading of "Western Memorabilia" in a booth in his little antique mall in Amana, Iowa. And in the summer of 1951, when I was ten years old, my grandfather took me to see the movie *Little Big Horn* starring Lloyd Bridges and John Ireland. Like the Custer painters I rearrange, suppress, even invent scenes, foregoing claims to exact truth or factual accuracy, searching instead for emotional truth, for deep meaning (Stegner, 1990, p. iv; Blew, 1999, p. 7). Like the painters, I too am translating experience and memory into fictional truths, remaking the past in terms of some imaginary version of the real. In so doing I'm aligning two versions of the real, laying them alongside one another—the death of Custer and the battle itself and then the representations of the battle and Custer's death in the Custer paintings.

The nineteenth century paintings answered to a realist, military aesthetic. Many of the early Custer artists were formally trained as military painters in European academies. This meant they were trained to paint horses, saddles, military uniforms, military weaponry, and heroic figures in battlefield scenes of death and destruction. These paintings were designed to honor the state, the nation, and their political policies.

Like the paintings, my texts travel among three levels of discourse: personal experience; popular, painterly representations of Custer; and scholarly discourses on the Old and the New West. Following Benjamin and Ulmer, my intent is to disrupt history, to challenge the belief that the Custer paintings somehow evolve and build on one another, culminating in a grand truth. Such is not the case. Each painting makes its own case for being truthful, accurate, correct.

Aesthetic or painterly history unfolds as a series of interconnected presents, memories. Each painting is a montage, a series of moments quoted out of context, paintings quoting one another, back and forth, "juxtaposed fragments from widely dispersed places and times " (Ulmer, 1989, p. 112). To represent the past this way does not mean to "recognize it 'the way it really was.' It means to seize hold of a memory as it flashes up at a moment of danger" (Benjamin, 1969, p. 257), to see and rediscover the past not as a succession of events but as a series of scenes, inventions, emotions, images, and stories (Ulmer, 1989, p. 112). **Custer redux.**

In quoting from these painterly histories and discourses surrounding Custer and the Lakota and Cheyenne, I hope to expose and criticize a racist politics buried deep inside the American democratic imagination. These interrogations represent an opportunity to take up again Kittridge's (1996) and Limerick's (2001) challenges to rethink Western history and mythology by starting out at the ground level, starting all over again. In bringing the past into the autobiographical present, I insert myself into the past and create the conditions for rewriting and hence re-experiencing it. I want to invent a new version of the past, a new history. I want to create a chorus of discordant voices, memories, and images concerning Custer, the Battle of Greasy Grass, and the place of Native Americans in our collective imagination.

I read Custer metaphorically. In and across the discourses that historically define Custer and his Last Stand are deeply entrenched meanings concerning gender, nature, culture, violence, wilderness, whiteness, and Native Americans (Brown, 1971; Welch, 1994; Alexie, 2007). The presence of Native Americans in the collective white imagination is almost entirely a matter of racist myths embedded in Hollywood westerns and museum exhibits of Last Stand paintings (Spindel, 2000).

*　*　*

The following chapters build on multiple interpretations of Custer's Last Stand, starting with the day of the battle and the earliest paintings representing it. I move forward from the battle to the present. Chapter 1, "A Good Day to Die: The Battle of Many Names," addresses the contradictory interpretations surrounding the battle. I compare and contrast First Nation oral history accounts, official military records, and the accounts of pro-Custer historians, archaeologists, cultural historians, and select painterly representations of the battle. I offer a timeline for Custer's Last Stand. In interpreting the battle I navigate among the stances of white, Lakota, and Cheyenne interpreters. I end the chapter by suggesting that Last Stand narratives are stories about stories, stories written around a grand narrative that says there was a last stand. But what if that is but an illusion?

In chapter 2, "Whose Last Stand: The Early Paintings," I begin with five early paintings of the battle, those by William de la Montagne Cary (1876), Alfred R. Waud (1876), Feodor Fuchs (1876), Henry Steinegger (1878), and John Mulvany (1881). I then turn to Cassilly Adams's 1884 painting, *Custer's Last Fight*, and to Adolphus Busch's purchase of the painting in 1888 as well as its transformation into a lithograph by F. Otto Becker in 1895. These early paintings established the fundamental framework for all paintings that followed. Since there were no white eyewitnesses, these painters created what would become the canonical representation of Custer's Last Stand. These paintings were produced in the artists' studios. The artists assembled the materials they needed to paint the version of history they believed to be true. These paintings enact a culture of military heroism and the demonization of Native Americans (Taft, 1954; Maclean, 2008).

Chapter 3, "Whose Custer," skips forward to the 2007–2008 Buffalo Bill Historical Center exhibit. I ask three questions: Whose Custer is honored with these paintings? What does it mean to honor Custer? What does it mean to have pro- and anti-Custer paintings in the same space?

I begin with the 1899 Paxson pro-Custer painting, acquired by the museum for $50,000 in 1963 (Paxson, 1984, pp. 52–53). I then discuss the anti-Custer paintings of Biss (1995), Scholder (1969, 1976), and Mardon (1996). The 2007–2008 exhibit keeps the Last Stand narrative alive. The Last Stand paintings are folded into a remembered history, a history that joins the New and the Old West in a site of benign violence and nostalgia in remembering an event that happened in 1876. The anti-Custer paintings contest this narrative. In the end there is no single version of Custer, but to remember any version is to remember a sad, violent moment in American history.

Chapter 4, "Killing Custer," is a three-act play that uses Eric von Schmidt's 1976 painting,[25] "Here Fell Custer," as a backdrop for reading the representations of the battle by Lakota and Crow artists Red Horse, White Swan, and Amos Bad Heart Buffalo.[26] The play returns to the question that will not go away: Who owns this battle, anyway? I contrast the Red Horse (Lakota) and White Swan (Crow) ledger art representations of the battle with the static Last Stand imagery of the white artists. The Native artists, Red Horse especially, present the battle as a series of interconnected events, telling the story from the Lakota or Crow perspective. Custer is not a prominent figure in these drawings that focus, in part, on the effects of the battle on the Native American village.

Chapter 5, "Here Fell Custer: An Autoethnography of a Painting," offers a detailed reading of von Schmidt's "Here Fell Custer," the official National Park Service painting of the Battle of the Little Bighorn.[27] Von Schmidt's Custer is not the Custer of Biss or Scholder. His is a contemporary version of Paxson's Custer. Von Schmidt claims his painting is historically accurate and superior to those of his predecessors. He dismisses Red Horse's drawings while taking joy in telling readers that he had to paint some "Injuns" for his painting.

Chapter 6, "Custer's Last Rally,"[28] is a three-act historical drama that moves across several sites, from the Last Stand paintings exhibited in the Whitney Museum in the Buffalo Bill Historical Center to Custer's presence in William Cody's Wild West show, where he appears in a play called "Custer's Last Rally." I interrogate the relationship among the Custer paintings, the Buffalo Bill Historical Center, its Whitney Gallery of Western

Art, and Buffalo Bill's Wild West show. This chapter also examines the relationship among the Adams-Becker print, Anheuser-Busch, Cody's Wild West show, and the Custer legend.

Chapter 7, "The Last Stand," returns to the theme of memory, violence, Western art, storytelling, global cowboys and Indians, minstrel shows, museums, dark tourism, revenge narratives, the New West, and another night at the museum. I imagine a new Western art museum, one that begins to rewrite, through indigenous art, a history of the New Old West. A utopian beginning is sought: new Native American masterpieces, no more war.

Skipping ahead, Benjamin (1969) reminds us that the aura or reverence for a work of art adheres not in the art object—the painting—but in the meanings brought to it, those associated with tradition, politics, and structures of power (pp. 222–223). He also observes that with mechanical reproduction—film, lithograph, photography, recordings—the experience of art is freed from time and space. It can be freely transported from place to place, exhibited in bars, taverns, and other public places. It is brought under the gaze of a mass audience.

So it was when the Becker lithograph turned the Adams painting into an advertisement. At that moment, the meaning and importance of the Adams painting went global. Turned into a patriotic icon, it was soon tangled up in history, ideology, politics, and culture. It became the original signifier of Custer's Last Stand. Every Custer painting that followed stood in the shadow of the Becker print. That print engraved in our national imagination racist images of Native Americans and placed them forever on the margins of American history, marking them as barbarians, redskins, "injuns." It is time to roll back history and redo the original reproduction. We need a new beginning. How about starting with Red Horse?

As with *Searching for Yellowstone* (Denzin, 2008), *Performance Ethnography* (Denzin, 2003), and *Reading Race* (Denzin, 2002), this project reflects two concerns. For nearly five decades I have been working with undergraduate and graduate students at the University of Illinois, experimenting with new ways of reading, writing, and performing culture. We learned how to write and co-perform texts based on epiphanies surrounding race, gender, and the politics of identity. I owe these students a great debt; together we worked through many of the themes and issues in this book. This book is partial payment on this debt.

I continue to believe that the current generation of college students in North America has the opportunity to make a difference in race relations. It is possible to imagine and perform a multiracial society, a society in which differences are honored. If this generation is to make a difference, that difference will be defined, in part, by the opposition, resistance to, and acceptance of the representations and interpretations of the racial order that circulates in the media and social science writings. This resistance, in turn, is shaped by how we read, write, perform, and critique culture.

In challenging these myths and cultural representations, it is not enough to merely replace negative representations with positive representations. The positive-negative debate essentializes racial identity. It takes two parties to perform racial minstrelsy. Race is performative, contextual, and historical. Stereotypes of whiteness are tangled up in racial myth, in minstrel shows that replay the Wild West, leading whites to look Western and Native Americans to look Indian (Dorst, 1999).

By unraveling these myths and their meanings and origins, I point to the diversity and complexity of racial representations and racial performances in Western American popular culture. I seek to replace old stereotypes—cowboys and Indians—with new understandings. I want to show how Western historical discourse can in fact turn back on itself, revise its stance toward the past, and perform new, progressive representations of cultural difference. I advance a critical performative pedagogy that turns the ethnographic into the performative and the performative into the political. This pedagogy hopefully allows us to dream our way into a militant democratic utopian space, a space where the color line disappears and justice for all is more than a dream.

DRAMATIS PERSONÆ

These characters appear throughout the six plays in this book.

Cassilly Adams, nineteenth century artist who painted *Custer's Last Fight*
Amos Bad Heart Buffalo, Ogala Lakota artist and historian
Richard Bartlett, historian
Sherman Alexie, best-selling author of *War Dances, Flight, Reservation Blues, The Toughest Indian in the World,* and *The Lone Ranger and Tonto Fistfight in Heaven*
Stephen Ambrose, historian and author of *Crazy Horse and Custer*
F. Otto Becker, lithographer, made important copy of Cassilly Adams's *Custer's Last Fight*
Walter Benjamin, German critical theorist
Mindy Besaw, curator, Whitney Gallery of Western Art
Kate Bighead, Cheyenne woman present at Battle of Greasy Grass
Earl Biss, member of Crow nation and artist who painted *Custer in Blue and Green*
Col. William S. Brackett, who arranged for exhibits of Paxson's *Custer's Last Stand*
Douglas E. Bradley, curator of White Swan's drawings
Matthew Brady, famous Civil War–era photographer
Christine C. Brindza, acting curator, Whitney Gallery of Western Art
Dee Brown, author of *Bury My Heart at Wounded Knee*
James S. Brust, specialist in historical prints and photographs
Adolphus Busch, nineteenth century robber baron, founder of Anheuser-Busch with his father-in-law, Eberhard Anheuser
Ned Buntline, famous nineteenth century dime novelist

William de la Montagne Cary, nineteenth century artist who produced the first painting (July 19, 1876) of Custer's battle, *The Battle on Little Big Horn River—The Death Struggles of General Custer*

Winston Churchill, former prime minister of England

Edward Clements, *Boston Evening Transcript* correspondent

Louisa Cody, William Cody's wife

William F. "Buffalo Bill" Cody, performer extraordinaire

Elizabeth Cook-Lynn, Crow Creek Sioux member, author of *Anti-Indianism in Modern America*

David Cowles, author of article, "White Swan: Crow Artist at the Little Bighorn"

Jack Crawford, poet and scout

Crazy Horse, Oglala Lakota chief

Edward S. Curtis (1868–1952), photographer of the American West and of Native Americans

Elizabeth (Libbie) B. Custer, George Custer's wife

George Armstrong Custer, U.S. Army General

Philip J. Deloria, author of *Playing Indian*

Vine Deloria Jr., author of *Custer Died for Your Sins*

Norman K. Denzin, author of this book

Brian Dippie, author of *Custer's Last Stand*

John D. Dorst, author of *Looking West*

Bob Dylan, folk singer

Eliza, African-American servant of Louisa Cody

Louise Erdrich, novelist, member Turtle Mountain Band of Chippewa Indians

Richard A. Fox, Jr., archaeologist

Sigmund Freud, psychologist

Feodor Fuchs, artist, *Custer's Last Charge*, the first color lithograph of the battle (1876)

Charles Garorian, media theorist

Mr. F. F. (Fred) Gerard, interpreter; also spelled as Girard

E. S. Godfrey, general in Seventh Calvary

Grave digger at battlefield

Stuart Hall, British cultural theorist

Peter Hassrick, Western art curator and historian

Sgt. Daniel A. Kanipe, Seventh Cavalry

Ed Kemmick, journalist, *Billings (Mont.) Gazette*

Barbara Kirshenblatt-Gimblett, author of *Destination Culture*

Lakota elder

Lame White Man, Lakota warrior mistakenly killed in battle

William Least Heat-Moon, journalist, writer

Henry Wadsworth Longfellow, famous American poet

Low Dog, Oglala warrior

National Park Service ranger

Norman Maclean, author and English professor

Alan Mardon, artist, *The Battle of Greasy Grass*

Naomi Maehr, author's granddaughter

Sylvia Maehr, author's granddaughter

Charles E. McChesney, nineteenth century assistant army surgeon

Dr. Harold McCracken, Buffalo Bill Historical Center gallery director in 1963

John Medicine Crow, author of "Custer and his Crow Scouts"

Gregory F. Michno, historian, author of *Lakota Noon: The Indian Narrative of Custer's Defeat*

John Mulvany, nineteenth century artist, *Custer's Last Rally* (1881)

Lloyd Kiva New, artist, designer, instructor at the Institute of American Indian Arts

Park Superintendent

E. S. Paxson, painter, *Custer's Last Stand* (1899)

William Edgar Paxson Jr., E. S. Paxson's grandson

Charles Rankin, senior editor, University of Oklahoma Press

Red Horse, Oglala chief, painter who rendered forty-one drawings of Battle of Greasy Grass, 1881

Kevin Red Star, contemporary Crow artist

Frank Richmond, announcer for Buffalo Bill's Wild West show

Running Man, character in Eric von Schmidt painting

Charles Russell, famous Western artist

Don Russell, Western art historian

Sitting Bull, Lakota chief; also known as Tatanka-Iyotanka, he played a major part in the defeat of Custer and his men

Standing Bear, Miniconjou Lakota

Henry Steinegger, painter of *Custer's Death Struggle* (1878)

Paul Stekler, documentary filmmaker, coauthor of *Killing Custer*

Ben Stiller, movie actor

E. T. Sutton, arranged for White Swan to make the drawings

Robert Taft, Western art historian

Brig. Gen. Alfred Terry, Union general and military commander of Dakota Terrority who gave orders prior to battle

Leslie Tillett, author of *Wind on the Buffalo Grass*

Tonto, sidekick of Lone Ranger

Robert Utley, cultural historian, author of *Custer and the Great Controversy*

Herman J. Viola, curator emeritus of the Smithsonian Institution's National Museum of Natural History and author of *Little Bighorn Remembered*

Eric von Schmidt, painter of *Here Fell Custer* (1976)

Louis Warren, author of *Buffalo Bill's America*

Alfred R. Waud, painter of *Custer's Last Charge* (1876)

Capt. Thomas Weir, officer at Battle of the Little Bighorn

James Welch, novelist and coauthor of *Killing Custer*

White Swan, Crow scout, ledger artist

Walt Whitman, famous American poet

Oscar Wilde, famous writer and poet

Private Charles Windolph, Seventh Cavalry

Wooden Leg, Northern Cheyenne

Young Hawk, warrior who fought with White Swan

Howard Zinn, historian

CHAPTER ONE

A Good Day to Die: The Battle of Many Names

ACT ONE, SCENE ONE

Getting Started

Narrator

"The Battle of Many Names," or "No Remorse," is a three-act play[1] that compares and contrasts First Nation oral history accounts, official military records, and select painted representations of the Battle of the Little Bighorn. This play addresses a common fallacy with regard to the Battle of the Little Bighorn, namely, that there were no survivors. In fact, "There were plenty of survivors—Sioux and Cheyenne." (Welch, 1994, pp. 21–22)

―※―※―※―

(Stage right, the spotlight shines on Cassilly Adams's painting Custer's Last Fight.*)*

Speaker One: **Paul Stekler**

The Battle of the Little Bighorn, Custer's Last Stand, is the single most reproduced event in all of American history (1994, p. 290).

(Stage right, the spotlight shifts to a poster board listing Custer films.)

Custer Films

Custer's Last Fight (1909)	*Broken Arrow* (1950)
The Massacre (1912)	*Little Big Horn* (1951)
Custer's Last Fight (1912)	*Sitting Bull* (1954)
The Scarlet Wind (1925)	*Chief Crazy Horse* (1955)
The Flaming Frontier (1926)	*The Searchers* (1956)
Custer's Last Stand (1936)	*The Great Sioux Massacre* (1965)
The Plainsman (1937)	*Custer of the West* (1968)
They Died with Their Boots On (1941)	*Little Big Man* (1970)
Bugles in the Afternoon (1944)	*Buffalo Bill and the Indians* (1976)[2]
Fort Apache (1948)	

Speaker Two: **Ed Kemmick** *(in white face)*

Cassilly Adams's 1884 *Custer's Last Fight* has been seen by millions of people. It was turned into an advertisement for Adolphus Busch by F. Otto Becker in 1895.[3] Now prints will be sold to benefit the Tomb of the Unknown Soldier and the Peace Memorial, both on the grounds of the private Custer Battlefield Museum[4] in Garryowen, Montana (Kemmick, 2002).

Speaker One: **Coyote 1**

Whose unknown soldier?
Whose peace memorial are you talking about?
How about our men, women, and children
who were killed by the blue coats?
Who is selling whom, what?!
A beer commercial.
What is this? Political art!

Speaker Two: **Robert Taft** *(in blackface)*

The Last Stand pictures fascinate all beholders . . . [but] the scene is totally imaginary, for no white witness survived the Custer tragedy. . . . *Hence, as historical documents, pictures of Custer's Last Stand are admittedly worthless* (1953, pp. 130–131, emphasis added).

Speaker One: **Coyote 2**

Whose imaginary? Lakota and Cheyenne men, women, and children survived, told their stories, made paintings, did oral histories. Discounting the Last Stand pictures by white artists allows Taft to discount the Lakota and Cheyenne stories and drawings.

ACT ONE, SCENE TWO

Who Is Custer?

Speaker One: **Cultural Historian**

The figure of Custer cannot be separated from the battle itself. The Custer in the Last Stand paintings is a fallen but valiant military hero. The battle is presented as a massacre, a debacle. In painting after painting the event is represented as an assault on brave, heroic soldiers by nearly naked, bloodthirsty Indians carrying guns, knives, bows and arrows, and tomahawks.

Speaker Two: **Robert Taft**

The two events are folded into one another, opposite sides of the same event. As a historical group, the Custer paintings keep these negative images alive. At the same time, they marginalize First Nation representations of the battle.

Speaker One: **Robert Utley** *(in whiteface)*

"Most of the Indian testimony is so confused, and weirdly divorced from known reality that one is tempted to ignore all such evidence" (1998, p. 86).

Speaker One: **Coyote 1** *(in whiteface)*

Hold on. Those paintings by white men are presented as if they were historically accurate, objective. But it is fictional history. The painters hired actors to dress up as soldiers and Indians. And there were no white painters, journalists, photographers, or military historians present at the battle itself. So how can they say our testimony was confused and divorced from reality? Whose reality?

Speaker Two: **Coyote 2** *(in whiteface)*

The Last Stand paintings tell only one version of history. The official discourse fails to note that the battle was part of a larger campaign to kill Indians. It was called "The Great Sioux War."

Speaker One: **James S. Brust** *(in redface)*

"The Great Sioux War was intended to compel Sioux (Lakota) and Northern Cheyenne to give up their nomadic ways and live on reservations" (Brust, Pohanka, & Barnard, 2005, p. 6).

Speaker Two: **Coyote 1** *(in redface)*

Remember gold was found in them thar
Black Hills. White people wanted that gold.
My people were in their way! And Custer was out for revenge.

Bumper sticker

(Projected onto a screen in red letters on a white background)

> **Custer Died for Your Sins**   [5]—*Vine Deloria*

ACT ONE, SCENE THREE

Custer Sightings

Speaker One: **Narrator** *(as a local historian)*

If you travel through Wyoming or Montana in the summer months, you find that Custer and his battle can't be escaped. Everywhere you turn there are Custer and Last Stand sightings.

Speaker Two: **Tour Guide**

You're right. In the summer of 2007, a sample of the Last Stand paintings was exhibited in the Whitney Gallery of Western Art in the Buffalo Bill Historical Center.[6]

(This announcement may be projected onto a screen or spoken, or both.)

Exhibit Announcement

Whitney Gallery of Western Art, Buffalo Bill Historical Center

2007–2008 Mini-Exhibit: "The Battle of Many Names," June 25–26, 1876.

Fritz Scholder, *Custer and 20,000 Indians* (1975)

Earl Biss, *General Custer in Blue and Green* (1995)

Allan Mardon, *The Battle of Greasy Grass* (1996)

Olaf Wieghorst, *The Last March*

Olaf Wieghorst, *The Last March*, letter and drawing

Edgar Paxson, *Custer's Last Stand* (1899)

Speaker One: **Narrator**

In 2007, 2008, and 2010, in part because of this exhibit, Custer, his Indians, and his battle—with its many names—were all over the Greater Yellowstone region.[7] It was as if the 1876 Battle of the Little Bighorn was still going on. Tourists could buy the Anheuser-Busch/Adams-Becker ad of the battle at the private Custer Battlefield Museum in Garryowen, Montana,[8] which is virtually next door to the Little Bighorn Battlefield National Monument—the profane and the sacred, opposite sides of the same coin.

Speaker Two: **Historian (in whiteface)**

I suppose it is fitting that the Buffalo Bill Historical Center has an exhibit of the Custer paintings. After all, in 1885 Sitting Bull worked for Buffalo Bill, appearing in parades and participating in the grand review. Cody also used a poster remarkably close to the Adams-Becker painting to market his Wild West show (Reddin, 1999, pp. 79–80; Welch & Stekler, 1994, p. 282).

Speaker One: **Coyote** *(in blackface)*

But how about some of Chief Red Horse's drawings?

(Stage left, the spotlight shines on a set of Chief Red Horse's drawings from Viola (1999c).)

ACT ONE, SCENE FOUR

Whose Battle?

Speaker One: **Norman K. Denzin**

This version of the Custer story begins with the battle itself, drawing, as previously noted, on reports given by Native Americans (Tillett, 1976), pro-Custer historians (Godfrey, 1892/2004), cultural historians (Welch & Stekler, 1994), historical photographers (Brust, Pohanka, & Barnard, 2005), and archaeologists (Fox, 1997).

Speaker Two: **Coyote 1** *(in whiteface)*

Let's get this straight—whose story are you telling, anyway? Whose war? What is the point? We all know the Native Americans got a raw deal.

Speaker One: **Narrator**

That's the point! They got a raw deal but you'd never know that by looking at the recent exhibits, including the one at the Buffalo Bill Historical Center. I want to tell a different version of the last stand, like Welch and Stekler (1994). Not killing Custer but remembering those Native Americans who died, remembering that the Battle of the Little Bighorn was, in a sense, the last fight—not Wounded Knee, but a prelude to Wounded Knee.

Speaker Two: **Coyote 2** *(in mourning)*

Check out this history. It's not pretty. It's what follows Little Bighorn (Brown, 1970; Welch & Stekler, 1994).

(Stage right, the spotlight shines on a historical poster.)

> **Northern Plains Tribes timeline after June 27, 1876.**[9]
> October 1876—Lakota out of the Black Hills.
> May 1877—Sitting Bull escapes to Canada with about 300 followers.
> May 6, 1877—Crazy Horse surrenders at Fort Robinson.
> May 7, 1877—The Great Sioux Wars begin.

> September 6, 1877—Crazy Horse is killed by soldiers.
>
> July 19, 1881—Sitting Bull and 186 of his followers surrender.
>
> 1883—Sitting Bull is allowed to go to Standing Rock reservation.
>
> 1885—Sitting Bull tours with Buffalo Bill's Wild West show.
>
> 1887—The Lakota reservation is divided into six small reservations.
>
> 1890—Ghost Dance Revival.
>
> December 15, 1890—Sitting Bull is killed by Native American police.
>
> December 29, 1890—Minneconjou massacred at Wounded Knee by Custer's old outfit.
>
> December 29, 1890—Three dead soldiers: Custer, Crazy Horse, Sitting Bull. Whose justice?

Speaker One: **Narrator with a point of view**

This is a sad story, with a sad ending. Just because they outlived Custer, how can you say Sitting Bull and Crazy Horse got the last word?

Speaker Two: **Coyote 1**

You call outliving Custer having the last word! After Little Bighorn, it is all over for the Lakota and Cheyenne. This is the back story to all those white men paintings—the story that says, "We will get even." And they did! This is the sad irony. In struggling to paint the story just right, the painters were telling a story that had ended, even before the battle was over. But that was the point, because in the Custer paintings, Custer did win, and he never really has died!

Speaker One: **Robert Taft**

The Last Stand painters used realism and meticulous attention to detail to honor Custer and his battle. By laboring over their paintings for years at a time, they reinforced two beliefs: great events like the Last Stand demand major commitments of time, money, and talent, and *only great artists can make great paintings* about such events.

Speaker Two: **Narrator as critic**

All of these paintings circulate in the present. They keep the myth alive. They offer viewers a visual experience grounded in violence and warfare. There is no remorse over the deaths of Sitting Bull and Crazy Horse. No! According to official white history, they got what they deserved. No white artist rushed out to honor their murders.

Speaker One: **Robert Taft** *(in whiteface)*

To repeat, no white witnesses survived the Battle of the Little Bighorn.

Speaker Two: **Coyote 2**

Whiteman, the myth of no survivors is a lie.

Speaker One: **Chorus of Custer Historians** *(in whiteface)*

Controversy continues to swirl around Custer, the man and the legend, including what he did and did not do, how he died. Who killed Custer? (Deloria, 2004; Dippie, 1974, p. 59; Gray, 1991; Hassrick, 1983, p. 170; Hutchins, 1999; Hutton, 2004a; Langellier, 1999; Scott, 1999; Welch, 1994; Viola, 1999a, 1999b, 1999c).

Speaker Two: **Coyote 1** *(in redface)*

How did he die?

Speaker One: **Coyote 2** *(in whiteface)*

He committed suicide!

Speaker Two: **Coyote 1** *(in redface)*

He disobeyed orders.

Bumper Sticker

(Projected onto a screen in red letters on a white background)

> **Custer Died for Your Sins** —Vine Deloria

Speaker One: **Coyote 1** *(in whiteface)*

> He was arrogant!

Speaker Two: **Coyote 2** *(in redface)*

> He abandoned Reno and his men.

Speaker One: **Coyote 1** *(in redface)*

> There was no last charge! There was no last stand!

Speaker Two: **Coyote 2** *(in whiteface)*

> How about a fatal retreat?

Speaker One: **Coyote 1** *(in whiteface)*

> Are you kidding? Let's be kind and call it bad luck.

Speaker Two: **Coyote 2** *(in redface)*

> Who killed Custer? Who cares?

Speaker One: **Military Historian**

> Custer killed Custer.

Speaker Two: **Coyote 1**

> The American military killed Custer.

Speaker One: **Coyote 2** *(in redface)*

> Maybe he got what he deserved!

Speaker Two: **Coyote 1** *(in whiteface)*

> Why is it all about Custer? Why not about Chief Sitting Bull and Chief Crazy Horse, or the women, the children, our old people? I know this is a dumb question. It's always about the white man and his story. You know Native Americans died, too. Furthermore, in a very short period of time, Wounded Knee ended everything.

Speaker One: **Norman K. Denzin**

> Let's summarize. Where have we come so far? The Last Stand paintings tell only one side of the story. They make a hero out of Custer

when the record is less than clear-cut on this count. The paintings discount First Nation versions of the battle. This is an irony. Without the presence of Native Americans, there would have been no battle. And the battle really signaled the end of Native Americans in the 19th century West.

Speaker Two: **Winston Churchill**

History is written by the victors.

Speaker One: **Oscar Wilde**

History is a big lie.

Speaker Two: **Custer, the anthropologist**

Let's jump ahead on history. It's June 28, 1876. The big battle is over. I know I've been dead a couple of days. But let me tell you about the Indians' character. Contrary to the novelists like Cooper, the Indian is not a noble red man. The Indian is a savage, in every sense of the word . . . one whose cruel and ferocious nature far exceeds that of any wild beast of the desert. . . . He kills, robs, steals, lies. . . . He cannot be civilized (1874/1962, pp. 13–14, 21).

ACT TWO, SCENE ONE

The Battle of Greasy Grass: Semiofficial Timeline

Speaker One: **Narrator as military historian**

The facts are few. It is a short story. It is over in a week, or three hours, or less then 35 minutes, depending on where you start.[10] Or, it is still being fought. Let's start with a timeline.

⁎ ⁎ ⁎

Abbreviated Semiofficial Timeline for Custer's Last Stand

(Text excerpted from the timeline in Appendix A can be read as well as projected onto a screen.)

Speaker Two: **James Welch**

June 17, 1876: Crazy Horse has a dream about how to fight the Blue Coats, and they win a battle that day—the Battle on the Rosebud. After this battle the chiefs move west to the Valley of the Greasy Grass.

Speaker One: **Paul Stekler**

June 24, 1876: Custer's Seventh Cavalry moves toward the large, three-mile-long Indian encampment in the Valley of the Greasy Grass along the Bighorn River. Sitting Bull had reservations about Crazy Horse's dream that the Blue Coats could be easily tricked. By this time Sitting Bull's traveling village had nearly two thousand fighting men (Welch, 1994, p. 127).

Speaker Two: **Stephen Ambrose**

June 25, 1876: Custer discovers the large Indian village and at roughly 12:15 divides the Seventh Cavalry into four groups.[11] The first fighting begins around 3 p.m. and lasts until around 5:25 with no survivors from the battalion led by Custer. Some reported that the fight involving Custer lasted less than one-half hour (Miller, 1957, p. 158). It is estimated that the warriors outnumbered the Seventh Cavalry approximately 3 to 1, or roughly 1,800 against 600; and in Custer's actual fight, 1,800 against 268 (Ambrose, 1975, p. 444).

Speaker One: **Gregory Michno**

June 25, 1876: The deaths toll is 36 Native Americans and 268 American troops.[12] There may not have been a last stand, per se; rather, the troops were overwhelmed by a single charge (Michno, 1997, p. 215).

Speaker Two: **Custer, the General**

June 25, 1876: It is hard for me to tell the story. I had the reputation as the most famous Indian fighter in the history of the army. Five of the Seventh Cavalry's companies were annihilated. My two brothers were killed. I lost a nephew and a brother-in-law. I don't know what happened. We went on the attack. Reno and Banteen took their men in one direction; I took my men along the ridge, above the river and the village. But the Indians outflanked Reno and they retreated. They were joined by Banteen's column. I was cut off from Reno and Banteen. Everywhere I turned there were Indians. I couldn't get my men across the river. We were cut off. I tried to get to the bluffs, to high ground, dig in, and wait for help. But it was too late. I saw Crazy Horse and Gall and maybe a thousand warriors. I tried to get to the top of the hill. I turned around with my men, over 200 of them, and there was Crazy Horse. We had nowhere to go. They came at us from every direction. Our guns were of little value. Everything flashed in my mind at once. The savages won! Was it an ambush? No, but we were out-numbered.

Speaker One: **Stephen Ambrose**

June 25, 1876: What Crazy Horse, Gall, and their men saw was a long slope with fewer than 200 soldiers with their backs to the top of the hill. They were horseless, bloody, dirty, exhausted, fighting for their lives; many were wounded or dying (Ambrose 1975, p. 442).

Speaker Two: **Coyote**

June 26, 1876: The morning after, Native Americans continued to fight other members of Custer's troops.

Speaker One: **James Welch**

June 27, 1876: Relief troops reach the battle site. The Indian dead have been removed from the field. The bodies of the troops were naked, scalped, and mutilated, except for Custer (Welch, 1994, pp. 175–177).

Speaker Two: **Stephen Ambrose**

June 28–29, 1876: The dead Seventh Cavalry members are buried on the battlefield, with few identifying markers.

Speaker One: **Coyote**

June 28, 1876: There were three battle sites in the Little Bighorn Valley: the Reno-Benteen site, Weir Point, and Custer Hill.

ACT TWO, SCENE TWO

Aftermath

Speaker One: **Elizabeth Custer**

July 7, 1876: George was a brilliant soldier. I'm so proud of him. He was a great leader of men. He helped bring civilization to the West. He died for his country. Those savages finally got what was due them when they killed Crazy Horse and Sitting Bull. The rest of them were lucky to have a reservation to go to. They are like the dumb Negroes who act like monkeys (Custer, 1895/1994, p. 320).

Speaker Two: **Sherman Alexie**

June 28, 2007: Hey George, hey Libbie. Say what you want, but don't call me a dumb Indian monkey!

Speaker One: **Stephen Ambrose**

June 26, 1975: The warriors had the smell of victory in their nostrils.

Speaker Two: **Coyote 1**

Wow, dumb Negroes, monkeys, savages. No wonder they got so upset. Civilization was destroyed by the savages.

Speaker One: **James Welch**

July 5, 1876: General Terry's report of the battle is telegraphed all across the country.

Speaker Two: **Coyote 2**

July 6, 1876: National newspapers carry the first accounts of the battle.

Speaker One: **Stephen Ambrose**

July 22, 1876: All Native Americans in Lakota country are treated as prisoners of war.

Speaker One: **Coyote 1**

So this is what all the fuss is about! This is the last stand! You could say no one lost; a fleeting victory for Native Americans, a momentary loss for the U.S. military. And Custer is still alive!

Speaker Two: **Sherman Alexie**

Boy, that Crazy Horse had one cool dream.

ACT TWO, SCENE THREE

The Battle of Greasy Grass: The First Nation Narrative

Speaker One: **Kate Bighead**

OK, audience. Let's do another version of the Battle of Greasy Grass. We were terrified. The Blue Coats were everywhere. They were shooting at us, killing our horses, killing little children, setting fire to our tipis. Our warriors were brave, they were afraid for their families and their village. Our brave warriors saved us and defeated the Blue Coats.

Speaker Two: **Coyote 1**

Some of the women were frightened, but then they got angry and went onto the battlefield and avenged the deaths of their brave men.

Speaker One: **Kate Bighead**

We felt a joy from the victory, but we mourned the death of the young warriors.

Speaker Two: **Sherman Alexie**

I got it: *Custer died for HIS sins, not OUR sins.*

Speaker One: **Cheyenne Elder** *(to young men in village)*

June 25, 1876, 9:30 a.m.: Soldiers are here! Young men, go out and fight them! You have only one life! (Welch, 1994, p. 110).

Speaker Two: **Kate Bighead**

Let me give you details and a timeline.
June 25, 1876, 11:45 a.m.
"Shortly after noon, the peace was broken.
Shooting and shouting could be heard.
War ponies were brought into the camp.
The warriors mounted them and galloped away.
But the battle seemed to come in phases,
moving . . . from ridge to ridge, coulee to coulee,
across the battlefield, one phase ending at the top of the hill,
later to be called 'Last Stand on Custer Hill'"
(Gray, 1991, pp. 268–269).

Speaker One: **Young Cheyenne Woman**

> June 25, 1876, 12:30 to 2:30 p.m.
> One group of soldiers was running on foot,
> chased by Indians on horses. Warriors were arriving
> from each of the six camps, most with bows and arrows.
> Bands of Indians moved toward the waiting soldiers
> who were hiding along a second ridge. The soldiers were terrified.

Speaker Two: **Coyote 2** *(in whiteface)*

> June 25, 1876, 12:30 to 2:30 p.m.
> So few Blue Coats. Did they think we would
> give up and run away?

Speaker One: **Young Cheyenne Man**

> June 25, 1876, 12:30 to 2:30 p.m.
> A great number of older
> men and young boys gathered on the surrounding hills
> to watch the last traces of the fighting.
> The Indians thought all the soldiers were dead and
> rushed toward the ridge to complete the battle.
> Seven soldiers were still alive. They killed
> themselves before the warriors reached them.

Speaker Two: **Old Lakota Warrior**

> June 25, 1876, 3:30 to 5:30 p.m.
> It was all over very quickly.
> Indians began collecting guns and ammunition.
> Women and old men rounded up the horses.
> The women brought in wooden sledges pulled by ponies to carry the
> dead and wounded away.
> The women who lost their men cried
> and cut the bodies of the dead soldiers
> in a ritual of revenge and mourning.
> Many women and children were yelling,
> laughing, and singing (Welch, 1994, p. 180).
> They sang these words:
> "Our brave women and warriors went onto
> the battlefield and avenged the

deaths of our brave men.
We fought today to save
the sacred Black Hills."[13]

Speaker One: **Old Cheyenne Woman**

June 25, 1876, 5 p.m.
Hi-es-tzie (Custer) was accorded
special treatment. Instead of cutting off an entire arm or leg,
they cut off only one joint of one finger.
They then pierced his eardrums with an awl,
saying his hearing needed improvement.
It seems he had not heard the promises he
himself had made.

Speaker Two: **Coyote 1** *(in blackface)*

June 26, 1876, 8 a.m.
I guess he hadn't heard the warning of the
Cheyenne chiefs; they had told him that the
Everywhere Spirit would kill him
if he broke the peace (Bighead, 1992/2004, pp. 52–57).

Speaker One: **Amos Bad Heart Buffalo**

June 27, 1876, 11:30 a.m.
The Indian nation did not wish to fight. Always,
the whites start shooting first and the Indians
start last (Tillett, 1976, p. 65).

Speaker Two: **Crazy Horse**

June 25, 1876, 6:30 p.m.
Long Hair's troops panicked
when we attacked. They hid behind their dead horses
(Welch, 1994, p. 169).

Speaker One: **Richard Fox** *(in redface)*

The battalion disintegrated. There was little or no
organization or resistance.

Speaker Two: **James Welch**

> This is not a pretty picture of the famed Seventh Cavalry and brave George Armstrong Custer (1994, p. 170).

Speaker One: **Coyote 2**

> What did you expect?
> There was no last stand on Custer's Hill.

Speaker Two: **Edward S. Curtis** *(in whiteface)*

> According to some, Custer refused to come to the help of Reno and his troops. He left them to die (Hutchins, 1999, pp. 158–160).

Speaker One: **Sitting Bull (Tatanka-Iyotanka)**

> June 25, 1876, 7:30 p.m.
> The noise was deafening: war cries, soldiers
> screaming, gunfire, horses dying (von Schmidt, 1976, p. 3).
> The dust was so thick I almost choked. There was
> much confusion. Custer was not a hero.
> There were no white heroes.

Speaker Two: **Coyote 1** *(in whiteface)*

> June 25, 1876, 8:30 p.m.
> We left.
> We were sad,
> we were happy.
> We were proud.
> We wanted no more fighting.

Speaker One: **Reporter for the New York Herald** *(1877)*

> July 3, 1876
> How did Custer die?

Speaker Two: **Sitting Bull (Tatanka-Iyotanka)**

> July 4, 1876
> These details were told to me.
> Custer's hair had been cut short.
> It was not long and flowing
> like in all those paintings.

It is said that Long Hair stood like a sheaf of corn
with all ears fallen around him.
He killed a man when he fell.
He laughed.

Speaker One: **Reporter** *(in whiteface)*

July 3, 1876
You mean he cried out?

Speaker Two: **Sitting Bull (Tatanka-Iyotanka)**

June 25, 1875, 9 p.m.
No, he laughed; he had fired his last shot
(Ambrose, 1975, p. 443; Tillett, 1976, p. 71).

Speaker One: **Sherman Alexie**

Dumb ass!

Speaker Two: **Vine Deloria Jr.** *(telling Custer jokes)*

July 4, 1969
"George Custer is falling mortally wounded to the ground. He sees the multitude of warriors charging up the hill. Custer: 'Where are those %8#@& Indians coming from? Well, it's better than going back to North Dakota'" (Deloria, 1969, p. 149).

Speaker One: **Sherman Alexie**

February 26, 2010. OK, let's do a quick recap. What do we have so far with this story of the Last Stand? Looks like at the end of the first inning it's Indians 1, White Men 0. Man, it's a shut-out! Custer got creamed by the South Dakota Indians.

Speaker Two: **Coyote 2**

It was like three all-stars were on the same field at the same time: Sitting Bull, Crazy Horse, and Custer.

ACT TWO, SCENE FOUR

Greasy Grass one year later: The White Man's narrative, version 1.01

Speaker One: **Narrator**

So this is another version of the Battle of Greasy Grass. A sweet event, a victory by the Lakota and Cheyenne over the Blue Coats.

Speaker Two: **Coyote 1**

YES, YES, YES!

Speaker One: **First Seventh Cavalry Grave Digger** *(in whiteface)*

Bones, bones, only bones. Where do we dig the graves?

Speaker Two: **Coyote 2**

Bunch of cry babies!

Speaker One: **Second Seventh Cavalry Grave Digger** *(in whiteface)*

Even a year later you could still see some of the markers where the soldiers had been buried. But there are no markers for dead Indians.

Speaker Two: **Mother of Lame White Man**

You are wrong. There was a marker for my son, Lame White Man. He was killed by his Lakota allies who mistook him for a Crow scout. There are some white stones where he fell.

Speaker One: **Sherman Alexie**

They say it was not our battlefield! Who do they think won?

Speaker Two: **First Seventh Cavalry Grave Digger** *(in whiteface)*

There are no markers where Indians died. I guess you could say it was not their battlefield, but that seems kind of funny (Welch, 1994, pp. 104–105).[14]

Speaker One: **Coyote 1** *(in redface)*

Why do you think this is funny?
There were really two battlefields.
What we saw and what they saw.

Speaker Two: **Second Seventh Cavalry Grave Digger** (*in whiteface*)

    The Indians had no right to bury their dead here.

Speaker One: **Coyote 2**

    Hey, white man. We have the right to do anything we want! We were here before you were!

(*Stage left, the spotlight returns to the set of Chief Red Horse's drawings highlighted at the end of Act One, Scene Two*).

―*―*―*―

Bumper sticker

(*Projected onto a screen in red letters on a white background*)

> **Custer Died for HIS Sins**—*Vine Deloria*

―*―*―*―

ACT TWO, SCENE FIVE

The Battle of Greasy Grass, White Man's version 1.02, or The Morning After

Speaker One: **Coyote 1**

    OK, let's get back to the white man version of what was a glorious event for us.

Speaker Two: **Custer** (*to Capt. Benteen upon seeing the northern half of the Indian village*)

    Benteen.
    Come on.
    Big Village.
    Be quick! (Scott, Fox, Connor, & Harmon, 1989, p. 17)

Speaker One: **Sherman Alexie**

Yah, Custer didn't have a clue.

Speaker Two: **General E. S. Godfrey I** *(in whiteface)*[15]

The sky was filled with dust.
We could see stationary groups of horsemen.
From the manner in which they sat astride their horses
we knew they were Indians. We heard occasional shots.
While watching this group the conclusion was reached
that Custer had been repulsed. The firing ceased,
and the groups dispersed (Godfrey, 2004, p. 293).

Speaker One: **General E. S. Godfrey II** *(in whiteface)*

All the accounts by the hostiles say there was no organized close-quarter fighting (Godfrey, 2004, p. 305).

Speaker Two: **Robert M. Utley**

The Indian hordes melted away into the night (1962/1998, p. 26).

Speaker One: **Coyote 2** *(in whiteface)*

Oh, who were they talking to? Hordes? Hostiles?

Speaker Two: **General E. S. Godfrey III**

It is difficult to imagine what the bodies looked like . . .
all of them, except a few, were stripped of their clothing . . .
nearly all were scalped or mutilated . . .
There was one notable exception,
that of General Custer,
whose face and expression were natural . . .
his body had been laid out.
He had been shot in the left temple
and the left breast.
There were no powder marks
or signs of mutilation (Welch, 1994, p. 175).

Speaker One: **Coyote 1** *(in redface)*

That is not what the Old Cheyenne woman said. She said they cut off one joint of one finger.

Speaker Two: **Mr. Gerard, the interpreter**[16] *(in red face)*

> I preceded the troops there.
> I found the naked bodies of two soldiers,
> one across the other and
> "Custer's naked body in a sitting posture
> between and leaning against them, his
> upper right arm along and on the topmost body, his right forearm
> and hand supporting his head in an inclining posture,
> like one resting or asleep" (Welch, 1994, pp. 175, 177).

Speaker One: **Coyote 2**

> This sounds pretty fake to me, almost made up to make Custer look heroic! How could his dead body have been in an inclining posture a day later?

Speaker Two: **James Welch**

> This is not a very romantic portrait. The Indians were doubtless responsible for Custer's posture.

Speaker One: **Captain Weir**

> The White Bodies:
> The mutilated bodies were so white!
> They were horrible to look at.
> The faces were grimy with dust, blood, dirt, and gunpowder.

Speaker Two: **James Welch**

> Tom Custer's heart was missing. He lay facedown, arrows bristling in his back, his entrails leaking out. He was recognized by the burial party only by his tattoos: the American flag, the goddess of liberty, and his initials, T. W. C. (Welch, 1994, pp. 175, 176).

Speaker One: **Mr. Gerard, the interpreter**

> On the hill were forty-two dead bodies and forty-two dead horses. It was terribly hot. The stench of bloody, bloated dead bodies was overpowering (Scott, Fox, Connor, & Harmon, 1989, p. 21).

Speaker Two: **General "One Star" Alfred Terry** *(in whiteface)*

On June 27, Custer and his troops had been dead forty-eight hours. Over the next two days we hastily buried the bodies, as best we could. Each man was buried at or close to the spot where he fell. The graves were marked with crude wooden stakes (Snow & Fitzpatrick, 1989, p. 245).

Speaker One: **Robert M. Utley** *(in whiteface)*

George Armstrong Custer died a spectacular death at the Battle of the Little Big Horn on June 25, 1876 (Utley, 2004, p. 239).

Speaker Two: **Coyote 1** *(in whiteface)*

Oh, yah! That's not the story my people tell!

Speaker One: **First Seventh Cavalry Grave Digger** *(in whiteface)*

You shoulda seen the hill a year later. Made me cry! Look at John Fouch's July 7, 1877, photograph. That tells part of the story. There were only bones, piles of bones, animal bones, horse heads (Brust, Pohanka, & Barnard, 2005, pp. 131–135).

Speaker Two: **Second Grave Digger**

Even though the Lakota and Cheyenne women removed the dead bodies of their warriors, there should have been an attempt to at least show their presence on the battlefield. I understand they started doing this just a few years ago. It's about time.

Bumper Sticker

(Projected onto a screen in red letters on a white background)

> **Custer Died for Your Sins**—*Vine Deloria*

ACT THREE, SCENE ONE

News Travels Fast

Speaker One: **General E. S. Godfrey**

"At noon July 3, the *Far West* steamboat—loaded with the wounded—made her memorable voyage down the Yellowstone and Missouri rivers, reaching Bismarck at 11:30 p.m. July 5 and then giving to the thirty-nine widows at Fort Lincoln, and to the world, the astounding news of Custer's Last Battle" (Godfrey, 2004, p. 315).

Speaker Two: **Sherman Alexie**

Bad news travels fast!

Speaker One: **Coyote 1**

You can't keep a good story down!

Speaker Two: **James Welch**

Word of the Custer disaster ruined the Great Philadelphia Exposition.

Speaker One: **Coyote 2**

What a doggone shame! Those thoughtless Indians spoiling a white man's party. Imagine that. Indeed.

Speaker Two: **Local Journalist**

The *Bismarck Tribune* carried the first account. Its correspondent Mark Kellogg, who called the Indians "the red devils," was killed, along with Custer (Welch, 1994, p. 189).

※ ※ ※

(These headlines are projected on the screen.)

**MASSACRED
Gen. Custer and 261 Men,
The Victims**

**No Officer or Man of 5
Companies Left to
Tell the Tale**

3 Days Desperate Fighting

Squaws Mutilate and Rob the Dead

—The *Bismarck Tribune*, July 6, 1876
(Welch, 1994, p. 191).

※ ※ ※

Speaker Two: **Dee Brown**

"When the white men in the East heard of the Long Hair's defeat, they called it a massacre and went crazy with anger. They wanted to punish all the Indians in the West" (Brown, 1970, p. 282).

Speaker One: **Reporter** *(writing on July 6, 1876)*

All of the bodies
except Custer's were terribly mutilated . . .
the heads of some
were severed from the body . . .
the Indian fighting force numbered
nearly 4,000 (Welch, 1994, p. 192).

Speaker Two: **Coyote 2**

The number was actually closer to 1,000 (Welch, 1994, p 193).

Speaker One: **James Welch**

There is a great deal of distortion and anger in the *Tribune* story. The mutilation is described not as a ritual of mourning, but rather in bloodthirsty detail. There is no effort to present the battle through the eyes of the Indians, including their fierce defense of their village. Instead the Indians are dehumanized while Custer and his soldiers are glorified, brave men fighting to the death (1994, pp. 192–193).

Speaker Two: **Art Historian**

This is why the July 19, 1876, crude drawing of the battle by M. Cary in the *New York Graphic and Illustrated Evening Newspaper* is so important (see chapter 2). It created the original imagery, the framework for all subsequent representations of the event. Hordes of heartless red devils with hatchets and bows and arrows attack brave soldiers from all directions. In the midst of this violence stands Custer. Triumphant, even in defeat, he is waving his sword, one foot resting on a dead horse (Russell, 1968, p. 16).

Speaker One: **Coyote 1** *(in redface)*

See what I mean.
THEY ATTACKED OUR VILLAGE!
We fought back to protect ourselves.
How did they become the victims?
It's easy to believe in a conspiracy theory here.
The press jumped all over this story
so they could protect Custer's image and justify the
"Great Sioux War."

—✶—✶—✶—

Bumper Sticker

(Projected onto a screen in red letters on a white background)

> **Custer Died for Your Sins**—*Vine Deloria*

—✶—✶—✶—

ACT THREE, SCENE TWO

The Battles of Greasy Grass: Whose Version?

Speaker One: **Narrator**

It would appear that we have an instance of the "Rashomon effect."[17] Two sets of participants, that is, Native Americans and U.S. military, have produced substantially different accounts of the same event. This involves more than the subjectivity of perception or the effects of memory on recollection. It involves the politics of representation, how an event is located and given meaning in popular memory. In fact, there were many battles: the one experienced by the women, children, and older men in the Lakota and Cheyenne nations; the one experienced by Sitting Bull and Crazy Horse and their warriors; and the battle experienced by the Blue Coats, the men of the Seventh Cavalry, including Custer's battle, his brother Tom's battle, Reno's battle, the battle as reported in the press, the widows' versions of the battle, and so forth.

Speaker Two: **Narrator (as semiotic analyst)**

In the case of the Battle of Greasy Grass, a series of oppositions are at work:

> Indians—Blue Coats
> Victory—massacre
> Protect villages against hostiles—Destroy bloodthirsty hostiles
> Rituals of mourning—Mutilation of bodies
> Honor the dead—Desecrate the dead
> Leave battlefield—Honor battlefield
> Remove dead—Bury dead

Speaker One: **Narrator (as historian)**

Each representation of the battle, whether by a journalist, a white painter, a dime novelist, an archaeologist, a historian, a photographer, or a Plains Indian, represents a different version of the event.

Speaker Two: **Coyote 1 (as tour director)**

Hundreds of thousands of people trek to the battlefield in south central Montana every summer, busloads of tourists from around the world.

58 Chapter One

Staged re-enactments are held in nearby Hardin, Montana, featuring Crow Indians playing Sitting Bull and other Lakota—revisionist role-playing, as their Crow ancestors were scouts for the Seventh Cavalry that day (Stekler, 1994, p. 290).

Speaker One: **Coyote 2 (as historian)**

Don't forget the blond plumber
from Michigan playing
Custer (Stekler, 1994, p. 290).

Speaker Two: **Coyote 1**

It wasn't just Indians versus the soldiers.
There were Native Americans on both
sides of the battle—Wounded Knee too!
It was not all black and white.

Speaker One: **Narrator (as tourist to fellow tourist)**

Scene: Yellowstone Basin Inn, Gardiner, Montana
Date: July 22, 2008

Nice lookin' Harley!

Speaker Two: **Fellow Tourist**

Yeah, she rides like a dream. Wife and I just rode in from the Custer Battlefield.

Speaker One: **Narrator**

Oh, yeah. We're headed that way.

Speaker Two: **Fellow Tourist**

It's amazing. Custer never had a chance.
It's a sad place. I've been there four
times now. Take my kids, too.
In a way, it was a magnificent victory, too.

Speaker One: **Paul Stekler**

Of course, the fact that Little Bighorn was one of the final acts in the dispossession of the last free tribes on the northern plains is never a part of the picture, nor is it a story told at these annual re-enactments (1994, p. 291).

Speaker Two: **Chorus** *(in whiteface, reciting Walt Whitman poem (1876) on Custer's death)*

Thou of the tawny flowing hair in battle,
I erewhile saw, with erect head, pressing ever in front, bearing a bright sword in thy hand,
Now ending well in death the splendid fever of thy deeds.

Speaker One: **Narrator** *(cynically)*

What are you gonna do when America's national poet goes around writing poetry like this! I mean, really! And this was even before he saw that painting by M. Cary published a week later (July 19, 1876).

Speaker Two: **Coyote 2**

I don't want to harp. But all of those Last Stand paintings by those white men look the same. They all pretty much tell the same story, don't they?

Coda: Who Killed Custer?

The Battle of Many Names—Custer's Last Stand, the Battle of Greasy Grass, the Battle of the Little Bighorn, Custer's Last Fight—is more than a battle over names. It is a battle over history, a battle over who controls history and its representations. The Last Stand narratives represent a battle over who has the right to write, paint, and narrate history. It is a battle about who listens, who hears, who watches, who reads. And, who has the power to discount what is heard, read, or seen? Who is right? Whose history is it, anyway?

Howard Zinn (2003) reminds us that history ought not be written as the official memory of states and governments (pp. 9–11). History should be written from the perspective of the downtrodden, the poor, marginalized people of color, Native Americans, the weak, the disenfranchised. Accepting official memory/history conceals fierce conflicts of interest between conquerors and conquered, between masters and slaves, Indians and whites, a world of victims and executioners (Zinn,

2003, p. 10). In such a world, it is "the job of thinking people not to be on the side of the executioners" (Zinn, 2003, p. 10) in the case of Custer, the American military.

The Custer Last Stand narratives are about the endless production of official history. They represent a preoccupation with power, memory, loss, race, masculinity, heroes, Manifest Destiny. They are about war, genocide, the annihilation of a people and their way of life. War, Zinn reminds us, is always against the innocent; there is no flag big enough to cover the shame of killing innocent people. Custer's Last Stand is all about killing innocent people in the name of fame and glory. But the battle is also about a people who show their ability to resist together, to join together so as to win together. The First Nation version of the Last Stand is one of the past's "fugitive moments of compassion" (Zinn, 2003, p. 11), a moment when the oppressed successfully stood arm to arm in opposition to the oppressor.

The Last Stand Native Americans refused to accept white domination. But their voices are left out of the record books, their view of the Last Stand as a glorious moment of achievement is suppressed. This absence makes it possible to sustain two contemporary fictions: While Native Americans are downtrodden, oppressed, and in need of protection, they are also uncivilized, barbaric, and bloodthirsty. The first fiction seems obvious, today, but that is only after Native Americans took on "civilization" and became acculturated. The process of becoming "white" is the process of accepting domination. The Last Stand Native Americans did not accept this definition. Those undefeated voices are indeed left out of the record books, or are present only as savages. So the contemporary story of the defeated, exploited Native American is the problem. It would be unethical to use this coda to retell that narrative, to reinscribe that narrative on our consciousness without question. The multiplicity of all the accounts I have reviewed tells us we will never know the truth about Custer.

On the surface, these multiple views seem to fight each other, but actually they complement one another. They tell us a story about "storying" itself, tales about winners and losers, and this is certainly not the story we should keep telling and retelling. That is, while this play has performed multiple views that on the surface seem to fight each other, underneath they are all part of the same grand narrative. So the Custer narratives are stories about "storying," and my narrative has been an attempt to problematize the concept of the Custer "script" itself. My script, my play, is a subversive response to the script we have all been handed through pictures, movies, stories, and historical re-enactments. I've taken snippets of the existing scripts and recontextualized them to create a bricolage, to damn the grand narrative of Custer's Last Stand. In rescripting the grand narrative, I am attempting to de-script, to perform de-scription, to undo the Last Stand.

There is no last stand. There is no stand. There is no last. There is nowhere to stand. And, dear reader, my dramatic format leaves you with nowhere to stand (except to know that what you knew before was certainly not the whole picture). The story was the "real" last stand; this play is an ambush that that story walked right into.[18]

I have charted several different versions of the Last Stand as a battle. In the next chapter I address the first round of Last Stand paintings (1876–1881), including Cassilly Adams's 1884 painting, its purchase by Adolphus Busch in 1888, and its transformations into a lithograph in 1895 by F. Otto Becker.

CHAPTER TWO

Whose Last Stand?
The Early Paintings

ACT ONE, SCENE ONE

The Early Paintings

Narrator

"Whose Last Stand?" is a two-act play that moves from five early paintings (1876–1881) of the Battle of the Little Bighorn (1876) to Cassilly Adams's 1884 painting, Adolphus Busch's purchase of the painting in 1888, and its transformations into a lithograph[1] by F. Otto Becker in 1895–1896.[2] It asks how an artist creates a Last Stand painting when there is no record of the original event. Whose Last Stand is it, then? Whose meanings prevail when the original event is highly politicized? Here's a timeline for our little play.[3]

※ ※ ※

(This timeline may be projected on a screen, as well as spoken.)

Paintings of
Battle of Many Names, Battle of the Little Big Horn, Battle of Greasy Grass, Custer's Last Stand[4]
June 26, 1876

July 19, 1876   William M. Cary, *The Battle on Little Big Horn River—The Death Struggles of General Custer*, full-page depiction appears in *New York Daily Graphic* (Dippie, 1974, p. 64).

1876   Alfred R. Waud, *Custer's Last Fight*, illustration in Frederick Whittaker, *A Complete Life of Gen. George A. Custer.* New York: Sheldon & Co., p. 606 (Dippie, 1974, p. 64).

1876   Feodor Fuchs, *Custer's Last Charge*, the first color lithograph of the battle

1878   H. Steinegger, *Custer's Death Struggle*

1879   E.S. Paxson announces desire to paint his version of the Battle of the Little Bighorn.

1881   Chief Red Horse's forty-one color drawings

         John Mulvany, *Custer's Last Rally*

         J.W. Buel, *Death of General Custer*

1883   Barnsley, del., *Custer's Last Fight on the Little Big Horn*

1884   John Elder, *Custer's Last Charge*

1884   William M. Cary, *Battle of the Little Big Horn: Death of Custer*, illustration for poem by Frederick Whittaker in Charles J. Barnes and Marshall Hawkes (Eds.) *National Fifth Reader*. New York: American Book Co.

1884   Cassilly Adams paints the first version of the painting known as *Custer's Last Fight*. It measured 16 feet 5 inches by 9 feet 6 inches and was painted on a wagon canvas for a traveling exhibit. There were two end panels; one depicted Custer as a young child, and a second showed Custer dead on the battlefield (Kemmick, 2002; Taft, 1953, p. 143).

1888   E. Pierpont, *Cyclorama of Gen. Custer's Last Fight*

1888   Adolphus Busch has an idea of an advertising campaign based on the Battle of the Little Big Horn. He acquires

	Adams's Custer painting, which hung on the wall of a St. Louis tavern owned by John C. Furber (Taft, 1953, p. 335).
1889	Busch employs the Milwaukee Lithographing Co. to make prints of Adams's painting. The lithograph is copyrighted in 1896.
1889	Rufus Zogbaum, *The Last Stand*
1890	Paxson completes research for his painting.
1890	F. Remington, *Custer's Last Stand*
1891	Williams, *Custer's Last Battle*
1895	F. Otto Becker, an employee of the Milwaukee Lithographing Co., is hired by Busch to make a master painting of *Custer's Last Fight*, from which the famous advertising lithograph would be created. Busch pays for the painting but never takes possession of it, and it remains in Becker's hands. Becker's lithograph differs from Adams's painting in terms of detail and emphasis (Taft, 1953, pp. 144–146).
1895	Cassilly Adams's *Custer's Last Fight* is presented to the Seventh Cavalry at Fort Riley by Anheuser-Busch.
1896	Gen. E. S. Godfrey, a member of the Custer burial party, writes E. S. Paxson, saying he hopes the artist corrects the errors in Adams's painting.

※ ※ ※

Speaker One: **Western Art Historian No. 1** *(in whiteface)*

So let's get to the paintings! While most histories start with Cassilly Adams's *Custer's Last Fight* (1884/1885), you need to go back to five earlier paintings: Cary's 1876 *The Battle on the Little Big Horn River—The Death Struggle of General Custer*; Waud's 1876 *Custer's Last Fight*; Fuchs's 1876 *Custer's Last Charge*; Steinegger's 1878 *General Custer's Death Struggle*; and Mulvany's gigantic 1881 20-by-11-foot *Custer's Last Rally*.

Speaker Two: **Western Art Historian No. 2** *(in whiteface)*

Granted, and don't forget Chief Red Horse's forty-one color drawings which were done in 1881. But let's start with Cary. I think we can say, as Taft (1953, p. 142) said of Mulvany, that Cary's drawing served as the template for subsequent artists, including Waud, Steinegger, Mulvany, Adams, and Paxson. But not Chief Red Horse.

66 Chapter Two

Speaker One: **Coyote 1**

This seems fair. But hey, before you have paintings, you have to have painters. I assume these painters were all men. So who were these guys, anyway?

Speaker Two: **Coyote 2**

Well, it's hard to generalize. Let the painters speak for themselves.

ACT ONE, SCENE TWO

The Painters Tell a Little About Themselves

Speaker One: **Cassilly Adams** (1843–1921)

I was born in Ohio. I'm a descendent of John Adams and studied at the Boston Academy of Arts. I also served in the Civil War. I opened a studio in St. Louis in 1878. That's where I did my famous painting. At age 62 I described myself as: artist; 5 feet 11 inches tall; 159 pounds; blue eyes, gray hair, light complexion; blue dot tattooed on left forearm (Russell, 1968, p. 31).

I was very pleased when I read these lines from Norman Maclean: "Cassilly Adams's painting called *Custer's Last Fight* . . . has become America's best known work of art" (Maclean, 2008, p. 58).

Speaker Two: **F. Otto Becker** (1854–1945)

I was born in Germany and studied at the Royal Academy of Arts in Dresden. They taught me how to paint battlefield scenes.

Speaker One: **William de la Montagne Cary** (1840–1922)

I like my middle name—it's French. My parents were rather wealthy. I loved to paint and I was an established illustrator by the age of 20. A friend and I took a trip out west in 1861. We had a guide and a cook. We lived with the Indians for a while and later joined a wagon train. I went back west in 1874. My works appeared in *Harper's Weekly* and *Scribner's Weekly* (Samuels, 1976, p. 84).

Speaker Two: **Feodor Fuchs** (1856–?)

I worked in Philadelphia as a lithographer and made a pretty good living painting portraits of Civil War personalities.

Speaker One: **John Mulvany** *(1844–1906)*

I was born in Ireland and I emigrated to New York City when I was 12. I served in the Union Army and later I studied as a military painter with Wagner, Piloty, and DeKeyser in Dusseldorf, Munich, and Antwerp. I visited the Custer battlefield in 1876. They say my work influenced Remington and Russell. I committed suicide in 1906 (Samuels, 1976, p. 339).

Speaker Two: **E. S. Paxson** *(1852–1919)*

I grew up working as an apprentice sign painter and decorator in my father's shop. I went to Montana in 1877. I had a variety of jobs; I worked as a cowboy on a ranch, as a stage driver, and as a scout in the Nez Perce war. I also served in the Montana National Guard for ten years. In 1879 I began painting in oils and working as a commercial artist, painting signs for saloons and theater sets. I decided to paint Custer's Last Stand in 1879. It took over twenty years (1899) to finish. In 1881 I moved my business to Butte, Montana (Samuels, 1976, p. 363).

Speaker One: **Henry Steinegger** *(1831–?)*

I was trained as a lithographer. I was born in Switzerland, and worked in San Francisco for the Pacific Art Company. I based my Last Stand painting on the earlier paintings of Cary and Waud.

Speaker Two: **Alfred R. Waud** *(1828–1878)*

I was born in London and studied at the Royal Academy before coming to the U.S. They say I was an important Civil War and Western illustrator. A lot of my work appeared in *Harper's Weekly* (Samuels, 1976, pp. 513–514).

Speaker One: **Coyote**

Let's try to summarize. The Last Stand painters were trained in a nineteenth century realist aesthetic, emphasizing detail, motion, action, nature. Like the Civil War photographers, they were taught to carefully represent important historical events and battles. Some were trained as commercial illustrators. Most came from middle- to upper-class families. Some had Civil War experience, and later traveled in the West. Only Mulvany and Paxson seem to have actually visited the Custer battlefield. The early painters were influenced by Cary, whose 1876 painting was an imaginary representation based in newspaper accounts.

Speaker Two: **Art Historian** *(in redface)*

> Just for the record. With few exceptions—Mulvany and Paxson—and later Remington (1861–1909) and Russell (1864–1926), the Custer painters were not nationally recognized (Taft, 1953, p. 215). They did not achieve the stature of the famous Western landscape artists such as Moran (1829–1901) and Bierstadt (1830–1902), who painted sites such as the Grand Canyon or Yellowstone. Nor were the Custer painters aligned with the ethnographic project of Catlin (1796–1872) or Audubon's (1785–1833) efforts to naturalistically record bird life. They were not really frontier artists, either (Hassrick, 2007, 1983).

Speaker Two: **Peter Hassrick**

> Still, in order to get any attention, these paintings had to meet two conditions: They needed to be defined as historically accurate and authentic, and they needed to reinforce public attitudes about Custer, the battle, Indians, and the winning of the West (Hassrick, 2007, p. 9).

Speaker One: **Coyote**

> But hey, the paintings created the conditions for the myth. They defined what was authentic and accurate, and they showed Custer as the tragic winner. They created the terms for defining what was a good painting.

Speaker One: **Tonto** *(in whiteface)*

> My point exactly, and remember, these Custer dudes were not encouraged or trained to paint Indians. Folks didn't think Indians were important enough to be painted. Except for Catlin, there was no call to produce an accurate pictorial record of who we were (Taft, 1953, pp. 212–225). We were painted only when we were part of a story the artist was telling, like Custer's Last Stand. Ironically, many artist-painters descended on us after 1890, when we were all on reservations (Taft, 1953, p. 215).

ACT ONE, SCENE THREE

How Do You Make a Painting?

Speaker One: **Western Art Historian No. 1** (*in redface*)

OK—now how do you produce a Custer Last Stand painting?

Speaker Two: **Cassilly Adams**

You have to paint it as an event, a live battle, not as something that has already happened. I mean, there were only dead, mutilated, naked bodies on Custer's Hill. You can't make a painting out of that.

Speaker One: **Chief Red Horse**

I disagree. In my paintings, the battlefield is alive. There are naked men, joyous Indians, horses flying through the air.

Speaker Two: **Western Art Historian No. 2** (*in blackface*)

This is how you create a Last Stand painting. First you need Custer, then you need a battlefield, maybe the American flag, then you need Indians, headdresses, soldiers, horses, guns, spears, bows and arrows, dead people, smoke, dust. That's about all.

Speaker One: **Western Art Historian No. 3** (*in whiteface*)

You have to be a storytelling action painter. You had better attempt to tell the story from the point of view of the soldiers, as they were being attacked.[5]

Speaker Two: **Coyote**

Gotcha! And it is all here in Cary's print. The battlefield is filled with smoke, struggling bodies in the throes of death, faces marked by pain, suffering, and anguish, blood on the ground. Guns are firing, arrows are flying. Indians are everywhere, some half naked, some dead or near death, lying next to dead soldiers and dead horses.

Speaker One: **Brian W. Dippie** (*in whiteface*)

Battlefield, Indians, blood, guns. Now you need Custer, heroic Custer. Dress him in army blues. Have him wearing knee-high leather boots. Put a sash around his waist. He must stand erect, waving a saber, about to deliver a "devastating blow to a nearby Indian" (1974, p. 64;

1994; 1996). His long curly hair should be covered by a hat set at a rakish angle (1974, p. 64). His left foot might rest on the back of a dead horse. Have him gripping a pistol in his left hand. He should be surrounded by Indians and dead soldiers. Be sure he faces stage left; his back might be turned away from the attacking Indians.

Speaker Two: **Coyote**

Are any facts important here? Custer did not have long hair. He'd had a haircut before the battle, and in fact, he was growing prematurely bald (Welch, 1994, p. 177). There were no dead horses on the hill. Nearly all the bodies, including Custer's, were stripped of clothing, and many were scalped or mutilated (Welch, 1994, p. 177). These paintings are entirely imaginary. They are made up to make Custer and his men look like heroes.

ACT ONE, SCENE FOUR

Let's Take a Look

(Stage right, a spotlight shines on the paintings of Cary, Waud, Fuchs, and Steinegger.)

Speaker One: **Western Art Historian No. 1** *(in blackface)*

Let's look at Cary, Waud, Fuchs, and Steinegger.

Speaker Two: **Coyote 1**

Go back a minute to Cary (1876). It all begins with his melodrama, *The Battle of Little Big Horn River—The Death Struggle of General Custer.* This is the original against which all copies are measured. Remember, it occupied a full page in the *New York Daily Graphic* on July 19, 1876. He painted it in less than two weeks after the news of the battle was first received in the East (Dippie, 1974, p. 64).

Speaker One: **Tonto**

Amazing. He worked really fast. He got great national publicity. No wonder so many painters climbed on the Custer bandwagon.

Speaker One: **Coyote 2**

His Custer stands erect. He has long, flowing hair. His hat is at a devil-may-care slant. He is dressed in army blues. He has his foot on the haunches of a dead horse. He waves a saber in one hand, in the other he grips a pistol, about to kill an attacking Indian. The painting is a mass of bodies in motion.

Speaker One: **Western Art Historian No. 1** *(in blackface)*

Waud's 1876 "Custer's Last Fight" extends Cary. This melodrama appeared in a biography of Custer rushed into print a few months after the battle. Here Custer is ice-calm, unflappable. He is standing tall, facing stage right, a slightly quizzical look on his face. He is holding a pistol in his right hand, a rifle in his left, dressed in buckskin, a flowing scarf around his neck; a wide-brimmed hat covers his hair. Surrounded by charging Indians, Custer and his men form a pyramid in the center of the painting. Three men are still firing their rifles; three more are dying (Dippie, 1974, p. 64; Russell, 1968, p. 18). A whooping warrior on horseback carrying a stolen American flag races past Custer.[6]

Speaker Two: **Western Art Historian No. 2** *(in redface)*

Fuchs goes beyond Waud. His *Custer's Last Charge* (1876) appeared as a print published by the Milwaukee lithographic firm of Seifert, Gugler & Co. in a collection of other Last Stand paintings (Samuels, 1976, p. 181). Waud places saber-waving Custer, his troopers, and near-naked Indians looking like Zulu warriors on an open plain, in full gallop, racing left to right. The battlefield is littered with dead bodies and dead horses. Custer, wearing a white hat and a red scarf around his neck, is in the center of the painting. His blond hair flows in the wind. A river is in the background. In the foreground, a cowardly Indian, clutching a rifle and blanket, seems to be running away from the battle. It is hard to imagine how Custer could have lost this battle (von Schmidt, 1976, p. 1).[7]

Speaker One: **Western Art Historian No. 1** *(in whiteface)*

Now Steinegger. He drew his lithograph for the Pacific Art Company of San Francisco. His *General Custer's Death Struggle* steals from Cary and Waud. He takes from Cary a saber-waving Custer in full dress, facing stage left, his foot on a dead horse. From Waud he took the whooping, flag-waving warrior, and a second Custer. This Custer stands on flat ground and is clad in buckskin, firing his pistol at attacking Indians. The result: "two Custers strike heroic poses, and the viewer is left to choose between them" (Dippie, 1974, p. 64). Whose Custer do we have, a frontiersman or a military officer?

Speaker Two: **Coyote**

After moving west, Custer began to assume the guise of a frontiersman, setting aside his cavalier image for a new persona as a man who knows Indians. He started wearing buckskin clothing (Langellier, 1999, p. 194). Maybe this is why Steinegger painted two Custers.

Speaker Two: **Brian W. Dippie** *(in redface)*

"The repercussions of the 1876 Cary and Waud artwork registered far beyond their original audiences, leaving an indelible impression on many later 'last stands'" (Dippie, 1974, p. 64).

Speaker One: **Western Art Historian No. 1** *(in whiteface)*

I get it. I get it! They all look the same. So what did Mulvany do, and how about Red Horse?

Speaker Two: **Western Art Historian No. 2** *(in whiteface)*

We'll get to Red Horse in a minute.

Speaker One: **Coyote**

Don't forget: *Custer Died for Your Sins* (Deloria, 1969, p. 148).

ACT ONE, SCENE FIVE

Coyote Causes Trouble

(Stage right, a spotlight shines on the Last Stand paintings of Adams, Cary, Waud, Fuchs, Steinegger, and Mulvany. The paintings are held by six actors who stand side by side. A bell rings and the actors change places. The spotlight moves from painting to painting, faster and faster. The paintings seem to blur onto a single montage.)

Narrator

> A seventh actor, Coyote 1 in whiteface, walks on stage, holding a huge painting. The spotlight shines on the new painting. It is made up of the six paintings which have been cut into pieces and then glued back together. Tiny little Custers seem to float in space across the large canvas. Coyote walks in front of the six actors and places the new painting on a large easel. The six actors line up in a row behind the new painting. Coyote moves to center stage, singing.

Speaker One: **Coyote 1** *(in whiteface)*

> Custer died for your sins!
> Custer died for his sins!
> Custer died for our sins!
> Custer died for the white man's sins!

ACT ONE, SCENE SIX

Segue to Red Horse

(Stage right, a spotlight shines on two paintings by Red Horse.)

Speaker One: **Eric von Schmidt** *(in redface)*

> "Five years after the battle, Red Horse made forty-two[8] careful drawings with colored pencils on sheets of manila paper. Superficially, they represent the drawing of a talented child, but they are charged with a special power—lean, emotionless, quantitative" (1976, p. 1).

Speaker Two: **Coyote 2** *(in blackface)*

> Oh, really, and how is that so? And childlike. Come on! What do you mean, they make no attempt at interpretation? They are panoramic, they offer a colorful, flowing chronology of the battle. They start with the encampment, then the approach and attack by the troops, the counter-attack by the Indians, the battle and the battlefield with dead bodies and dead horses. In the final set of panels, the warriors are riding off with trophies, including horses, saddles, clothing, and guns (Viola, 1999c, pp. 82–83).

74 Chapter Two

Speaker One: **Sitting Bull**

I warned my people not to take the guns and horses from the dead soldiers. Many did not heed and it will prove a curse to this nation. Indians who set their hearts upon the goods of the white man will be at his mercy and will starve at his hands (Viola, 1999c, p. 100).

Speaker Two: **Western Art Historian No. 2** *(in redface)*

So much for the Indian drawings! Let's get back to the real artwork.

Speaker One: **Christine C. Brindza**

Hold on. Representations from Native Americans show a distinctive angle of the event previously ignored. A painted deer hide of the event, Lakota, circa 1895, depicts warriors on foot and horseback. The soldiers are dressed in blue and yellow uniforms. Custer has yellow hair and is wearing buckskins. Representations like this are thought to be truer records. This is so because they have been created by those who actually witnessed the battle and survived (Brindza, 2010, p. 6).

ACT TWO, SCENE ONE

Back to Real Custer Art: The Irishman's Masterpiece

(Stage right, a spotlight shines on Mulvany's painting.)

Speaker One: **Western Art Historian No. 1** *(in whiteface)*

John Mulvany's 1879 *Custer's Last Rally* was lithographed in color, and upon completion immediately exhibited in Kansas City, Boston, New York City, and Chicago. It was owned by H. J. Heinz, the ketchup magnate (Samuels, 1976, p. 339).

Speaker Two: **John Mulvany**

I visited the battlefield in 1879 and made sketches. I visited the Lakota on the reservation. I studied military dress, got portraits and descriptions of Custer and his officers. I wanted to rid my painting of any conventionality. "Whatever nature is to be represented it should be nature itself, and not somebody's guess" (Taft, 1953, p. 135).

Speaker One: **Edward S. Curtis**

How long did you work on it?

Speaker Two: **John Mulvany**

Two years. I also studied Indian headdresses, the gay caparisoning of their ponies, the dress of the braves and chiefs, everything that could bear on the work (Taft, 1953, p. 135).

Speaker One: **Western Art Historian No. 1** *(in whiteface)*

Mulvany's Custer is the center figure. He is facing stage right. He is hatless and has short hair. He wears a lapelled uniform coat. He aims a revolver and "holds the inevitable saber" (Russell, 1968, p. 28). His face is flushed with the heat of battle. His demeanor expresses the certainty of a man facing death. Despair and fear are pushed aside by courage. You could say he shows hatred for his bloodthirsty foe, but pity and love for his gallant men (Taft, 1953, p. 136).

Speaker Two: **Coyote**

Don't get too noble here! Custer and his men are not exactly rushing out to do battle. I mean, they are huddled together, firing at Lakota braves who are out of the frame. It's pitiful. Who could feel sorry? Mulvany wants the viewer to have pity. Come on! He has Captain Cook kneeling on the ground, blood spurting from his hand. Cook is surrounded by wounded men, trying to hide behind dead horses. Pure melodrama.

Speaker One: **Tonto**

In the foreground are two Cheyenne warriors, both dead. The face of one is covered with paint, the ears and nose are pierced, and a gaudy bonnet of eagle feathers adorns the head. Gruesome. And sad.

Speaker One: **Western Art Historian No. 1** *(in whiteface)*

The Indians' features are horribly savage, even in death. The artist has been true to nature in his treatment of the redskin; even the breech cloth and headdress are faithfully painted (Taft, 1953, pp. 135–136).

Speaker Two: **Coyote**

Who is being a savage here?

76 Chapter Two

Speaker One: **Walt Whitman**

There is little of the barbarism vs. civilization that is present in the Cary, Waud, and Fuchs paintings (Lane, 1973, p. 90). This is a "grim, dismal melee . . . the dense cloud of dust almost concealing the overwhelming cloud of savages" (Clements, 1881, p. 6, quoted in Taft, 1953, pp. 137–138; Taft, 1953, plate 55).

Speaker Two: **Tonto**

I'd say the writers are being barbaric! Calling Indians "horribly savage" is barbaric.

Speaker One: **Edward Clements**, *Boston Evening Transcript*

The fighting here is painfully real, not like the conventional battle scenes of European art. This is great American art! It stands head and shoulders above the earlier work of Cary, Waud, Fuchs, and Steinegger. They pale by comparison (Taft, 1953, pp. 136–138).

Speaker Two: **Tonto**

Hey! Maybe it got all this attention because it was huge—20 by 11 feet is big!

Speaker One: **Western Art Historian No. 1** *(in whiteface)*

It takes a great artist to create this kind of picture. He brilliantly captures the war dance bravado of the Indians and the tragic heroism of the devoted three hundred (Clements, 1881, p. 6, quoted in Taft, 1953, p. 137).

Speaker Two: **Coyote** *(in redface)*

Aren't you getting carried away? So now you make the painter out to be a hero, too! Hold on, white man. Not so fast. You have to spend more time than this on Red Horse's drawings. By your logic, he was also a genius.

Speaker One: **Western Art Historian No. 2** *(in redface)*

OK, OK, we'll come back to them. Hold your horses.

Speaker Two: **Walt Whitman** *(in blackface)*

"I went today and spent over an hour in front of John Mulvany's vast canvas. There are no tricks . . . altogether a Western autochthonic phase of America, the frontiers . . . heroic . . . nothing in the books like it, nothing in Homer, nothing in Shakespeare . . . all our own . . . a great lot of muscular, tan-faced men . . . death ahold of them, yet every man undaunted . . . forty or fifty figures, perhaps more . . . with three times that number or more in the background, through the smoke, like a hurricane of demons . . . Custer (his hair cut short) . . . aiming a huge cavalry pistol . . . the clouds of war-bonneted Lakota . . . the whole scene, inexpressible, dreadful . . . a certain Greek continence pervades it . . . but almost a total absence of the stock traits of European war pictures. . . . The work is realistic and Western . . . it has an ethic purpose below all, as all great art must have. I told Mr. Mulvany he should take it to Paris and show them that we can do great art in America. Above all, this is a deliberate artistic expression for our land and our people" (Whitman, 1881/1982, pp. 910–911).[9]

Speaker Two: **Coyote 1** (*in whiteface*)

You call this great art! What is great? By whose standards? It's nothing compared to Red Horse's drawings. Now those are real original American art.

Speaker One: **Coyote 2**

I don't get Whitman. He wants to call Mulvany's painting great American art, art that Europeans should admire. I want to get this just right. The back story here is the failed attempt by three hundred cavalry to slaughter three thousand Indians. Custer betrayed his men, and they died because of his stupidity. How do you turn that into a story, a painting, a something as great or greater than Homer or Shakespeare? Neat trick, if you can pull it off. Neat trick!

Speaker Two: **Howard Zinn**

The painting celebrates violence and death. Custer's Last Stand—the battle and the paintings—is emblematic of America's military history. We engage artists to produce tragic representations of the men who give their lives in the fraudulent wars staged by our leaders.

Speaker One: **Western Art Historian No. 1** (*in blackface*)

They say Mulvany had a long career, but in later life depended on portrait work for a living. They say that in the end, liquor got the best of him and he killed himself by jumping into New York's East River in May, 1906. The newspapers reported that he had sunk to a ragged derelict, uncertain of a place to sleep or a day's food (Taft, 1053, p. 141).

ACT TWO, SCENE TWO

Adams and His Originals

(Stage right, a spotlight shines on Adams's 1886 painting.)

Speaker One: **Western Art Historian No. 1** *(in whiteface)*

We've already said that Cassilly Adams's *Custer's Last Fight* is the best known of all the Last Stand paintings. The original was destroyed in a fire in 1946, so we are really dealing with a reproduction of a reproduction. The original borrows from Cary, Waud, Fuchs, and Mulvany. It contains all the standard elements in a Custer painting: saber-waving Custer, hordes of attacking Indians, mayhem, death, dead horses, dead soldiers, mutilation, smoke, fear hanging in the air (Dippie, 1974, p. 57; Lane, 1973, pp. 68–69; Russell, 1968, pp. 34–35; Taft, 1953, pp. 144–146).

Speaker Two: **Coyote 1** *(in whiteface)*

Before we go too far, let me get this straight. Adams finishes his painting between 1884 and 1886. He paints his masterpiece in his studio at the corner of Fifth and Olive streets in St. Louis. The "Indian figures were posed by Lakota Indians in war paint and also by cavalrymen in the costumes of the period" (Taft, 1953, pp. 142–143).[10] (Adams may have visited the battlefield.) Adolphus Busch gets the painting in 1888 and holds it until 1895, when Becker enters the picture.

Speaker One: **Cassilly Adams**

Actually, the original, the one dated April 26, 1886, was 12 feet high and 32 feet long. It had two side panels. I wanted to frame Custer's life, from childhood to death. The picture on the right, called "Coming Events Cast Their Shadows Before," illustrates an episode from Custer's childhood. His father is showing him how to fire a gun. The picture on the left, "Revered Even by His Savage Foes," shows the reverence the Indians must have had for him. All the bodies, except Custer's, are naked, scalped, and mutilated (Russell, 1968, p. 33).

Speaker Two: **Coyote 2**

So why is everybody wearing clothes in your big painting? If everybody was naked and scalped, why show just the opposite?

Speaker One: **Cassilly Adams**

I had to show it that way. Like I said before, if you showed the end of the battle, with mutilated naked bodies, there would be no heroism—it would have been a desultory story. I really did the Lakota and Cheyenne a favor showing it the way I did. People would have been really mad if I had shown Indians scalping our noble soldiers.

Speaker Two: **Charles Garorian**

This is a little like it was during the recent U.S. War in Iraq, in which the news media were forbidden from showing body bags coming home from the war.

Speaker Two: **Coyote 1**

The second original, the one that Adolphus Busch acquires in 1888 and has lithographed in 1896, measures 9 feet 6 inches by 16 feet 5 inches, and the side panels have been eliminated (Russell 1968, p. 31; Taft, 1953, p. 143). This is the second Adams painting of the event, and the one that is duplicated in the history books (Taft, 1953, plate 56).

Speaker One: **Western Art Historian No. 1** (*in whiteface*)

There is another version, the one Becker makes from the main lines of Adams's second original, the smaller painting (Russell, 1968, p. 35).

Speaker Two: **Cassilly Adams**

For purposes of discussion, let's call them painting A (April 1886), painting B (small version of A), and painting C (Becker's lithograph). There is another version of the original: the one Becker restored in 1938, measuring 24 by 40 inches, also acquired by Anheuser-Busch; call this painting D.

Speaker One: **Western Art Historian No. 2** *(in redface)*

What's the story they tell? Somebody said it was like a morality play.

Speaker Two: **Western Art Historian No. 1** *(in redface)*

The originals—A, B, and D—and the lithograph C are somewhat different. The lithograph, based on the second, 9-foot 6-inch by 16-foot 5-inch original, shows the valley of the Little Big Horn. This was not present in the first rendition, which has a steep hill rising abruptly behind Custer. In painting B, Custer is lunging forward with his saber; in painting C, he swings his saber back over his head. In C, a fallen soldier about to be attacked is hatless; in B he wears a hat. In B, two Indians, one with a headdress, stand close to one another. They are missing in C. Painting B, unlike C, uses a small stage; there are few side events. All action points toward Custer, who is in the center of the frame.

Speaker One: **Coyote 1**

Speaking as a Lakota for the moment, there are other differences between the two productions, that is, between B and C. I agree the scale is much smaller in B—there are far fewer Indians. In C, Lakota and Cheyenne are everywhere, and along the bottom of the painting, he has given us names.

Speaker Two: **Coyote 2**

When the painters give our warriors names, they humanize them. If the warriors are nameless, it is easier to view them as faceless demons.

Speaker One: **Historian** *(in whiteface)*

It's the same old painting all over again. Oh, some details are rearranged. Adams's Custer in B is clad in buckskin. He stands at the base of a steep hill, in front of a dead horse. His arm is out-thrust. His saber is "piercing an Indian standing erect, with tomahawk in his raised hand" (Russell, 1968, p. 35). Only a few soldiers are still alive. A figure in the center of the painting, his back turned to the viewer, is an observer, fighting for neither side. Nearly-naked Indians wearing headdresses and war paint appear as sticklike figures posed in aggressive fighting stances. In the pamphlet accompanying painting C, Adams named various figures in the painting, including Rain in the Face, Custer, and other members of the troop.

Speaker Two: **Coyote 1** *(in redface)*

Why Rain in the Face? Well, Rain in the Face was one of our heroes. He was a kind of outlaw. He vowed to eat Tom Custer's heart someday. "At the Battle of Little Bighorn Tom Custer's heart was missing" (Welch, 1994, p. 178). Rain in the Face got a lot of bad press and on more than one occasion, claimed that he killed Custer.

Speaker One: **James Welch**

In keeping with the dominant narrative, Adams deliberately painted a negative picture of Native Americans.

Speaker Two: **Historian** *(in redface)*

So these are the Adams paintings. What did Becker do with them? I know he was hired to produce a painting that was turned into a lithograph that was turned into an advertisement. We know Adams through the Becker lithograph; the reproduction is truly better known than the original (Taft, 1953, p. 146).

Speaker One: **Walter Benjamin**

In the age of mechanical reproduction, the work of art is transformed into a lithographic print. There is no longer an original, only endless reproductions of the lithograph print. This makes the work available for mass distribution and mass consumption. Stereotypes now circulate widely through the culture, in ways that were previously impossible.

ACT TWO, SCENE THREE

Becker Reworks Adams

Speaker One: **F. Otto Becker** *(in whiteface)*

Using the Cassilly Adams painting as a model, I painted my *Custer's Last Stand* in 1895. I still have the original. But I was forced to cut it into nine pieces so a team of artists could work on it at the same time. This is how the Milwaukee Lithographing Company made the color plates. From those plates, they ran off thousands of prints that were sold and distributed in bars and saloons all over America, courtesy of

Mr. Busch and his beer company. In 1936 my son Roland had the sections mounted on a piece of masonite, and I painted over the seams . . . the painting was restored to its original condition and purchased by Anheuser-Busch, Inc. in 1939 (Russell, 1968, p. 34).

Speaker Two: **Coyote 1** *(in whiteface)*

I'll get fancy here. So there is the original 1895 Becker, a simulacra of the original 1884 Adams painting. Then there are the prints from Becker's 1896 lithograph, and prints from the 1939 restored original! Maybe too many originals—this really is Walter Benjamin's work of art in the age of mechanical reproduction (1968b).

Speaker Two: **Historian** *(in blackface)*

By 1943 more than 150,000 copies of the print had been distributed by Anheuser-Busch. In 1942, they were being mailed to servicemen and others, here and overseas, at the rate of two thousand per month (Taft, 1943, p. 146).

Speaker One: **Sherman Alexie**

Instead of talking about drunken Indians, how about drunken white soldiers? It seems Anheuser-Busch had the contract to supply the American troops with beer during World War II, and the ad went along with the beer. It all fit together; our troops were once again fighting the dark, nameless, bloodthirsty other.

Speaker Two: **Coyote 2**

This is truly ironic.

Speaker One: **Coyote 1** *(in blackface)*

This lurid melodramatic lithograph
with its flowing-maned,
red-scarved, saber-swinging
Custer was an invention of the artist.

Speaker Two: **Western Art Historian No. 1** *(in whiteface)*

Let's get to the painting, PLEASE! Becker's Custer, like Adams's Custer, is a lonely figure in buckskin at the center of the painting. A red scarf around his neck, he holds a pistol by the barrel in his left hand. He is surrounded by dead or dying soldiers. He faces stage right, waving his saber at attacking Indians. Indians on foot and on horseback are charging from all sides.

Speaker One: **Western Art Historian No. 2** *(in redface)*

Becker, like all the other nineteenth century Custer painters, puts a large event on a small stage. He surrounds this event with a number of vignettes or scenes: in the lower right panel, Indians are scalping soldiers; in the lower left panel, Indians have overrun Custer's men; closer to the center of the painting, an Indian points a gun directly at Custer; a dead warrior lies next to a buckskin-clad figure in the middle left foreground.

Speaker Two: **Western Art Historian No. 1** *(in whiteface)*

This guy in buckskin is familiar. He is, as he was for Adams, dominant, but mysterious. He is not an Indian, but he is not fighting the Indians. Is he natural man? Is he the observer, like James Fenimore Cooper's hero, Natty Bumpo? (Lane, 1973, p. 68). What is he observing? The death of whom, the death of what?

Speaker One: **Coyote 1** *(in redface)*

Hey, stupid. The man in buckskin records the event for white people! He witnesses the heroism of Custer and his men, and registers the barbarism of the Indians. His presence suggests that the soldiers are the real victors, not the losers.

Speaker Two: **Western Art Historian No. 2** *(in redface)*

This makes sense. Read along the bottom of the painting. A series of names, from left to right, is associated with the figures in the painting.

※—※—※

(Stage right, the spotlight shifts to a poster board listing names in painting.)

> Rain in the Face, Lakota warrior who killed Custer
> Cheyenne warrior
> Audrey Reed, Custer's nephew
> half breed
> Capt. T. W. Custer
> General Custer
> half breed
> Lt. A. E. Smith
> Lt. Cook
> Capt. G. W. Yates
> Lieut. W. Van W. Reily
> Courier from Sitting Bull
> Squaw killing wounded
> O. Becker
> Milwaukee Litho and Engraving Co.
>
> "Entered according to Act of Congress by Adolphus Busch, March 30, 1896, in the Office of the Librarian of Congress at Washington, D.C."

—*—*—*—

Speaker One: **Coyote** *(in blackface)*

Half breeds and squaws!

Speaker Two: **Western Art Historian No. 1** *(in whiteface)*

These must be the same names that were in the Adams pamphlet.

Speaker One: **Western Art Historian No. 2** *(in redface)*

Don't forget the following wording, which is centered at the bottom of the painting and print.

—*—*—*—

(The spotlight shines on this document.)

> Custer's Last Fight
> Taken from the artist's sketches
> The original painting by CASSILLY ADAMS
> has been presented to
> The Seventh Regiment U.S. Cavalry
> By ANHEUSER BUSCH BREWING ASSOCIATION
> ST. LOUIS, MO. U.S.A. 11

※ ※ ※

ACT TWO, SCENE FOUR

What Becker Did to Adams

Speaker One: **Historian** *(to F. Otto Becker, in blackface)*

What did you take from the Adams painting?

Speaker Two: **F. Otto Becker** *(in whiteface)*

You could say I started all over. There are similarities; some of the same features are in both paintings. But I made many changes and additions. Mine is a new painting. The viewpoint is totally different. I worked from the 1882 Haynes photograph of the battlefield and the valley of the Little Bighorn River. There is no river in the Adams painting. I have Indians coming at Custer from all sides. Adams didn't. I show the Indian villages along the river, and the tipis. He didn't. My Custer is swinging a saber back over his shoulder; his Custer is lunging forward at an Indian. I think my painting is more complex, more nuanced, closer to historical reality.

Speaker One: **Historian** *(in blackface)*

On the other hand, Adams's art is more stark; it has a bareness that gives it a different dramatic feel. But then you have more Indians, more soldiers. You show more detail in terms of facial expressions, costume, color, the number of different activities that are going on, the actual violence, including the detailed scalping in center foreground. You show three or four scalped heads. Adams had one scalped head. It's gruesome. You have three naked soldiers. He had one.

Speaker Two: **Cassilly Adams**

Otto did a better job. His painting has motion, life, action. Mine was more of a tableaux, a static representation of the event. Otto has everything in motion! And his scale is much better than mine. It was a real touch to put the Indian village in the background, along with the river. But I mean, you can see movement in his painting! I think he must have studied Mulvany's painting, too.

Speaker One: **F. Otto Becker** *(in whiteface)*

I gave Custer a red tie. Mrs. Custer suggested this. She said he wore a flowing red merino cravat when he was with the Third cavalry (Dippie, 1974, p. 57; Lane, 1973, p. 69; Russell, 1968, p. 35; Taft, 1953, pp. 146–148; Tate, 1953, p. 336; von Schmidt, 1976, p. 1).

Speaker Two: **Historian** *(to F. Otto Becker, in blackface)*

What else did you do?

Speaker One: **F. Otto Becker** *(in whiteface)*

I had to correct factual errors. Adams has Rain in the Face firing his pistol and killing Custer. I have another Indian, not Rain in the Face, firing his pistol.

Speaker Two: **Coyote** *(in whiteface)*

What is a fact here? Whose facts? What did Becker think he was doing? He invented his version of the story, and got others to go along with him. Pure and simple.

Speaker One: **Robert Taft** *(in blackface)*

But in a sense, the two works tell the same story, a "powerful, if melodramatic and horrendous tale . . . but it is no more terribly melodramatic or horrendous than the event itself. Troopers are being brained, scalped, stripped; white men, Indians, and horses are dying by the dozens . . . a careful survey of the lithograph (and the Adams painting) is enough to give a sensitive soul a nightmare for a week" (Taft, 1953, p. 146).

Speaker Two: **James Welch**

A nightmare for a week! Sensitive souls! Troopers being scalped. Everybody knows these were ritual acts.

Speaker One: **Coyote** (*in redface*)

For my people, it was a glorious victory. We got even with Custer. Our braves were brave. We rode like the wind. Our women, children, and elderly were strong. We protected our village. We told the blue coats that they could not just come in and attack us any time they wanted. And now they want everybody to feel sorry for them.

Act Two, Scene Five
Custer Redux

Speaker One: **Coyote 1**

So where are we? We've looked at six Custer Last Stand paintings including Becker's lithographic transformations of Adams's famous *Custer's Last Fight*.

Speaker Two: **Coyote 2**

And what do we find? A clear progression can be seen in the paintings, to wit; Custer goes from long hair to short hair; he changes from formal military attire to buckskin dress; the battlefield expands from small to large; the number of Indians increases; Indians are named; Indian violence becomes more graphic, more intense; the point of view is on the soldiers confronting the Indians; the use of a double or Custer look-alike figure is present in three of the six paintings.

Speaker One: **Walter Benjamin**

The doubling of the Custer figure is interesting; he is both frontiersman and military officer, a figure on the frontier between civilization and the Wild West, and a man bringing law and order to the West. As a military officer, he embodies law and order. The violence attached to the Indians underscores the need for the military to be present on the borderland between civilization and the frontier.

Speaker Two: **Don Russell**

It took ten short years, from 1876 to 1886, for the iconography of Custer's Last Stand to be firmly established. And no fewer than 967 paintings of the battle have been made since (Lane, 1973, p. 68).

Speaker Two: **Coyote 1**

It's all political, art and politics, art and history. It's all made up!

Coda

The canonical works of art associated with the first generation of Custer paintings were lithographic reproductions. This feature freed the experience of the painting from time and place and brought it, as Benjamin predicted, under the gaze and control of a mass audience. In such situations, because there is no actual original to be viewed in a sacred site, the meaning of the paintings is increasingly political, and hence contextual. Viewers looked at the Cassilly Adams reproduction, for example, in taverns and bars. Furthermore, they interpreted the painting through the news reports of the battle, which said it was a massacre! The violent historical events that preceded the battle were ignored. The attacks on Native Americans by the American military and the attempts to remove them from their native lands were not incorporated in the massacre framework. Thus, the paintings stood outside historical time, even as they were firmly anchored in a specific site and moment: June 26, 1876.

The absence of an original account of the Last Stand takes on additional meaning in the case of the Custer paintings. The painters built on the constructions of the painters that came before them. Each was committed to a realist aesthetic, that is, to an accurate re-representation of an imaginary event that had become real. This was historical painting depicting actual events in a manner "dependent as much upon fact as on the imagination of the artist and a staged re-creation of a scene" (Molon, 2010, p. 17).

The artists followed the time-honored tradition of hiring models. They paid Native Americans to dress in authentic garb. They collected weapons, flags, uniforms, used photographs. A few even made visits to the battlefield. They reconstructed the battle in their studios. In these studios, Custer painters like Paxson surrounded themselves with the very artifacts they placed in their paintings.

In imagining the battle, each painter staged a version of Native Americans and soldiers in mortal, hand-to-hand combat. This was not the battle experienced by Native Americans; it was an imaginary original, a social construction of a historical imaginary. The artist's studio became the site for this historical reconstruction, a theatrical site where "history was perpetually restaged and reconsidered" (Molon, 2010, p. 22). In this restaging, the Indians lost even though Custer died, and the painter controlled history and its representations.

So for the first generation of Last Stand painters, the studio became the site for painting a version of history that invited revenge, instilled hatred, perpetuated stereotyping, and validated genocide. It would remain for new generations of pro- and anti-Custer artists (Biss, Scholder, Red Star, von Schmidt, Mardon) to move the event and its representations in the same and different directions at the same time. These are topics explored in the next chapter.

CHAPTER THREE

Whose Custer?

ACT ONE, SCENE ONE
Let the Artists Speak

Speaker One: **Narrator**

Pro- and anti-Custer Last Stand paintings hang side by side in the Whitney Museum of Western Art in The Buffalo Bill Historical Center.[1] "Whose Custer?" is a three-act play that works back and forth between five of these paintings: Paxson's huge 1899 *Custer's Last Stand*, Earl Biss's 1995 *Custer*, Fritz Scholder's 1969 *Custer and 20,000 Indians*[2] and 1976 *American Landscape*,[3] and Allan Mardon's 1996 *Battle of Greasy Grass*. The play asks three questions:

Whose Custer are we honoring with these paintings?

What does it mean to honor Custer?

What does it mean to have pro- and anti-Custer paintings in the same space at the same time?

Speaker Two: **Allan Mardon** *(to audience)*

"In the past, we white [artists] have portrayed Indian life from our point of view, forgetting our greed, forgetting the incredible atrocities we committed against Native Americans. . . . I know I will have made some mistakes . . . but I'm doing my best to archive their history without bringing white prejudice to my approach."[4]

Speaker One: **William Edgar Paxson** *(to audience)*

Edgar Paxson worked from photographs for likenesses of some of the Indians in *Custer's Last Stand*. He interviewed Chiefs Two Moon and Gall and Custer's scout Curley on the Custer battlefield (Paxson Jr., 1984, p. 93).

Speaker Two: **Charles Russell** *(to audience)*

I can't paint an Indian head with Ed Paxson. Nor can I mix his paint (Charles Russell, quoted in Paxson, 1984, p. 92, 116; also see Noyes, 1917, p. 26).

Speaker One: **Coyote 1** *(to Charlie Russell)*

You whites are really good at constructing yourselves as nonprejudiced. You think your so-called authentic, accurate paintings of Indians aren't examples of stereotype and prejudice. Don't you understand? You are still turning us into the exotic other.

Speaker Two: **Tonto** *(to E. S. Paxson)*

We've learned to dress up and look like real Indians. So you can do your accurate paintings.

Speaker One: **E. S. Paxson** *(to Tonto)*

Listen, I was friends with Rain in the Face, Gall, and Sitting Bull. I visited the battlefield many times (Brindza, 2010, p. 7).

ACT ONE, SCENE TWO

Enter E. S. Paxson, Frontier Artist

Speaker One: **Narrator** *(as historian)*

Let's restart this little play by skipping backward to 1899 when E. S. Paxson (1852–1919) completes his huge, six-foot by nine-foot painting.[5] Mr. Paxson worked on his painting for twenty years. Call it Becker or Mulvany redux. He started it before Adams and Becker, but was clearly influenced by them, as well as by Cary, Waud, and Fuchs,

Steinegger and Mulvany, probably Remington, too. It was exhibited in New York, Washington, Philadelphia, and Chicago. It contains at least two hundred separate figures, including the portraits of thirty-six members of Custer's command (Dippie, 1976, p. 50, 61; Lane, 1973, pp. 74–75; Russell, 1968, pp. 36–37; Taft, 1946, pp. 27–28, 48; also see Appendix A).

(Stage right, a spotlight shines on Paxson's Custer's Last Stand.)

Speaker Two: Col. **William S. Brackett**

"On December 11, 1899, I signed a contract with Paxson to exhibit his painting at my cost in North America and Europe. I agreed to pay him $250, plus $25 a month for the first four months, then $30 for the next four months, and $35 for the remaining four months. We agreed that it would be exhibited by itself, surrounded by Indian curios and photographs. In a second room there would be a display of other paintings by Paxson offered for sale" (Paxson, 1984, p. 47).

(Stage right, a spotlight shines on a 1905 photo of Paxson's Butte Studio, 30 East Woolman, from Paxson, 1984, p. 59.)

Speaker One: **E. S. Paxson** *(in whiteface)*

My goal, "so far as possible was to depict with absolute faithfulness of detail that disastrous battle" (Dippie, 1976, p. 50). Starting in 1877, I visited the battlefield countless times. I exchanged letters with E. S. Godfrey. He gave me a graphic description of the battlefield as it appeared three days after the slaughter. I followed the details outlined in Gen. Godfrey's letter to me of January 16, 1896 (Paxson, 1984, p. 52).

(Stage right, a spotlight shines on a photo of the Custer battlefield from Paxson, 1984, p. 42.)

Speaker Two: **E. S. Paxson** *(in whiteface)*

I filled notebooks with sketches and data. I started the actual painting in early 1890 and completed it almost ten years later, in December 1899. It has gone by various titles: *Custer's Last Stand, Custer's Last Fight, Custer's Last Battle on the Little Big Horn* (Dippie, 1976, p. 50). I prefer to call it *Custer's Last Stand*. It was reproduced many times in black-and-white and in color, and in 1963 as an 18-by-27-inch lithograph (Russell, 1968, p. 36).

Speaker One: **Coyote 1** *(in redface)*

OK, white man. Did you really get Indians to pose for your painting?

Speaker Two: **E. S. Paxson** *(in whiteface)*

Look, I paid them. Yeah, many notables sat for my masterpiece: Sitting Bull, Gall, Two Moon, Rain in the Face, Nag-s-sha (Russell, 1968, p. 36).

Speaker One: **William Edgar Paxson Jr.** *(in redface)*

Great-grandpa told me all about his painting and how he did it. He never used interpreters when talking to the Indians. Several times he went over the battlefield with them. He shared a blanket with Two Moon. Curly, Custer's famous scout, gave great-grandpa his story of the battle. Grandpa interviewed ninety-six officers and men who were close to the battle. He worked from photographs of many of the soldiers. He had a large collection of Lakota and Cheyenne war shirts, war bonnets, clubs, and lances, even an old Winchester with Lakota markings on it (W. E. Paxson Jr., 1984, pp. 46–47).

(Display photograph of E. S. Paxson's studio from page 46, Paxson, W. E., E. S. Paxson, Frontier Artist (1st ed.). 1984, Boulder, Colo.: Pruett Pub. Co.)

Speaker Two: **Narrator**

In this photo, Paxson poses in front of his Custer painting, painter and painting merge into one another, each authorizes the other's presence.

ACT ONE, SCENE THREE

Being Accurate

Speaker One: **Coyote 1** *(in whiteface)*

So he was "I am Mr. Historically Accurate Painter." Is that right?

Speaker Two: **William Edgar Paxson Jr.** *(in redface)*

He sure tried. Before he even started the actual painting, he made pencil sketches of every figure in the finished painting on eight-by-twelve-inch sheets of paper. Then he did a scaled-down (eighteen-by-thirty-six-inch) drawing of the entire work. In 1895 he started painting on a canvas measuring six feet by nine feet. Slowly, each major participant in the battle appeared as a recognizable portrait, but in dramatic action. They were all here: Custer, his brother Tom, Lt. Calhoun, Capt. Yates, half-breed scout Mitch Boyer, Crazy Horse, Rain in the Face, Two Moon, Crown King, and Gall. When it was done, it weighed over one thousand pounds, including frame! (Paxson Jr., 1984, p. 47).

Speaker One: **Coyote 1** *(still in whiteface)*

Aren't these the same people that Adams named in his painting?

Speaker Two: **Coyote 2**

Yup, pretty much.

Speaker One: **Coyote 1** *(in whiteface)*

It is a fraud! It was all made up. When General Godfrey and his men came to the battlefield a day later, there were only naked, unrecognizable, mutilated bodies. There was little clothing, an occasional bloody undershirt, drawers, or socks. How white they looked! The dead. Dead white bodies everywhere (W. E. Paxson, Jr., 1984, p. 45, quoting from E. S. Godfrey's January 16, 1896, letter to E. Paxson).[6]

Speaker Two: **E. S. Godfrey** *(in whiteface)*

Hey, Coyote. I helped my friend E. S. Paxson get it right. The Cassilly Adams painting had it all wrong—the color and location of Custer's horse, Custer's firearms, his hat, his buckskin suit, his blouse, the location of the other officers on the battlefield, their clothing, the presence of sabers, accessories, clothing, and dead Indians and ponies on the field. E. S. Paxson got it right!

Speaker One: **E. S. Paxson**

I tried really hard to get it right!

Speaker Two: **E. S. Godfrey**

When I saw the painting in his studio I noticed that Custer's personal flag of yellow silk was not in the painting. I said something about this to Edgar. Eight years later, I viewed the painting for a second time and there was the flag, fluttering in the smoke and dust of the battle (Paxson Jr., 1984, pp. 44–46).

Speaker One: **Tonto**

What does being accurate mean to a white man?

Speaker Two: **Coyote 1**

Accuracy means making the dead look like you want them to look. You know, give Custer the yellow silk flag.

Speaker One: **Coyote 2**

In this case it also means honoring the dead by telling the story with as much accuracy as possible. This commitment to paint Indians (and soldiers) in ways that even the great Charlie Russell admires ignores the fact that the Native American is being portrayed from the white point of view. There is a deadly political downside to this form of painstakingly accurate realism.

Speaker Two: **Art Curator**

Paxson did "historical research and then reconstructed it imaginatively in a complex arrangement of figures to summarize a great moment in history" (Dr. Sarah Boeheme, curator of the Buffalo Bill Historical Center, quoted in Everett, 2002).

Speaker One: **Tonto**

I get it now. In the wrong hands historical accuracy honors dead Indians, representing them as strange, exotic Noble Savages. No stereotypes here, this is how they really look.

Speaker Two: **Philip J. Deloria**

> History does not stand still. It gets expanded and reinterpreted constantly. What was historically accurate in Paxson's day is different from today. Different points of view tell different histories.

Speaker One: **Richard A. Fox Jr.**

> Archaeological work, in fact, undercuts many elements in the official Custer story, including locations of the troops during the battle, as well as who died where, and when.

Speaker Two: **White Settler**

> Well, yes! And our government had to kill them. We had to be protected. They were murderous people.

Speaker One: **Coyote 1**

> This is slanderous. We had to be protected from your army! Your soldiers murdered our mothers, fathers, children, parents, and grandparents.

Speaker Two: **White Settler**

> This is ancient history. Let's get back to this great painting. The attention to detail was amazing.

Speaker One: **Christine C. Brindza**

> The final version . . . is a densely packed canvas that shows action and drama much derived from the artist's imagination (2010, p. 7).

ACT ONE, SCENE FOUR

Reading the Painting

Speaker One: **E. S. Paxson** (*in whiteface*)

> Well, I did want it to be correct! I positioned the officers and cavalry according to where Gen. Godfrey said they fell. I tell the story from the point of view of the soldiers. I locate the battle on the ridge of the hill. Smoke and dust fill the air, so there is nothing beyond the battlefield itself. Indians are closing in from all sides.

Speaker Two: **Cynic**

But Godfrey waited twenty years to give you the details. Do you think there might have been some memory slippage? (Godfrey, 1892/1994).

Speaker One: **E. S. Paxson**

I trust the general.

Speaker Two: **William Edgar Paxson Jr.**

There are several things going on at the same time in the painting, a series of interconnected dramas. Each panel or section tells a different story, although they all center on Custer.

Speaker One: **E. S. Paxson**

I wanted to do two things. While there are over two hundred people in the painting, each major participant had to "appear in the canvas as a recognizable portrait, but in dramatic action" (Paxson, 1984, p. 47). The key people were Custer, Capt. Tom Custer, Adj. Cooke, Lt. Porter, Capt. Yates, Sgt. Ryan, half-breed scout Mitch Boyer, Crazy Horse, Rain in the Face, Hump, Two Moon, Crow King, and Gall (Paxson, 1984, p. 47).

―※―※―※―

(*Stage right, a spotlight shines on a poster listing the main panels in Paxson's Custer's Last Stand.*)

Across the top: Indians attacking on horses

Center left and center: Solders firing on Indians

In the center: Custer on Hill, Adj. Cooke, Tom Custer protecting Custer

Top center: Rain in the Face attacks Tom Custer from rear

Left center: Two Moon and Gall lead attack from left

Center right: Mitch Boyer fires gun at Crazy Horse

Lower right: Crow King leads attack from lower right

―※―※―※―

Speaker Two: **E. S. Paxson**

Custer is in the center of my painting, a red scarf around his neck. He holds a pearl-handled revolver in his right hand. His hair is short, not the flowing hair he has in the Adams painting. His gauntleted left hand clutches a wound on his left side. Adjutant W. W. Cooke is behind Custer. He is kneeling on his left knee. He fires his revolver with his right hand, while making an effort to support Custer with his left hand (Paxson, 1984, p. 52). A little farther up Custer Hill is Custer's brother, Capt. Tom Custer, in a buckskin shirt that is open in front. He fires one revolver while cocking the other over his shoulder. A mounted Rain in the Face is about to strike down Tom from behind. Custer's personal battle flag of yellow waves in the air, and farther to the right is the Seventh Cavalry's purple satin banner. In the distant right, Custer's brother-in-law, Lt. James Calhoun, mounted on a light gray horse, is about to be shot (Paxson, 1984, p. 52). Custer's "'half-breed' scout, Mitch Boyer, is at right-center, clad in buckskin with a feather in his hat. He is firing his gun at Crazy Horse,[7] who raises a three-pronged war club" (Paxson, 1984, p. 54). Below Crazy Horse is the Lakota chief Crow King. Two Moon is on the far left side of the painting. In the left upper foreground is the Lakota chief Gall. He is wearing a war bonnet and carrying a lance (Paxson Jr., 1984, pp. 52–53).

Speaker One: **Critic**

All of this seething action creates the effect of a moving tableau, even though action seems frozen in time. Each figure is poised in action, about to fire a gun, fall to the ground dead, look skyward as if in prayer, shout a battle cry, hold a flag, race into the battle waving a club on horseback. Oddly, the recognizable figures do not seem to be engaged in direct contact with one another, even though they are poised on the battlefield in recognizable action. What does this say for historical accuracy?

Speaker Two: **Tonto**

Let's not get carried away with accuracy, white man. Paxson's painting records death, dying, and violence in ways that humanize the whites—we see their pain, the terror in their eyes. But not so for the Indians. He turns the Indians into caricatures of themselves. None of them are foregrounded in the painting, even though their presence on the perimeter and sides of the battlefield define the action that the whites are responding to.

Speaker One: **Coyote 1**

Another white man's story. But stories like this keep the whites fighting the Indians. It's paintings like this that keep the Custer legacy alive, and honor Custer and his men as tragic fallen heroes.

Speaker Two: **Dee Brown**

It is a ghastly gruesome painting, like Mulvany's! Granted, there are no bloody scalps lying on the ground, like we get in Adams, but we see plenty of blood and gore, and the haunting look of death on the soldiers' faces. Unfortunately, the Indians look almost wooden. Their painted faces are frozen in fixed, unfeeling gazes.

Speaker One: **Coyote 1**

It goes deeper. For the soldiers, there is a sense of pathos, fear, resignation, helplessness, but not for the Indians. And there are only these dead bodies—that is the focus. When you get close to the painting you realize Paxson has arranged the bodies on an upward incline—they fell uphill.

Speaker Two: **Narrator** *(in whiteface)*

The painting dwarfs everything that came before Adams, including Waud, Fuchs, Steinegger, and Mulvany. Adams pales in comparison. Paxson's masterpiece is a flurry of action, dense in detail, figures falling over one another, the brown earth covered by dying bodies, men firing guns at faceless enemies. The dying trumpeter blows his horn, his head falls back against a dead horse. Lakota and Cheyenne riding white horses attack from three sides. Somber and claustrophobic in tone, the painting suffocates, cuts off air, strangling the men of the Seventh Cavalry in clouds of dust. The battlefield reverberates with the sounds of death, ear-splitting screams of pain and terror.

Speaker One: **Coyote 2** *(in redface)*

How about the Lakota and Cheyenne warriors? How about their pain, their screams? Your Indians look cartoonish. At least Adams gave them faces. Granted, your Indians have headdresses, feathers, and painted faces, but they are caricatures. They are violently attacking helpless, wounded white men! You are presenting them as unfeeling agents of death, automatons on white horses. When you paint my people this way, you dehumanize them. You make it easy for white people to hate my people. You make it easy to make Custer a hero and his soldiers victims. And you call this great art?

Speaker Two: **White Art Critic**

It's too busy, there is too much going on. There is an extravagance of detail. This is the fatal flaw of all documentary western art—it is too realistic (Paxson Jr., 1984, p. 53).

Speaker One: **Coyote 1** *(in redface)*

Too realistic! Too much detail! Whose realism? Whose detail? Not Lakota and Cheyenne realism, or detail. You white guys use so-called realism to paint sad stories that make your guys look like heroes, and our people like subhuman barbarians.

Speaker Two: **Dr. Harold McCracken**[8] *(in whiteface)*

"In my opinion, this is one of the most important pictures in Western history. It is the best pictorial representation of all the pictures which have been created to immortalize that dramatic event. From a purely artistic standpoint the painting is the finest by an artist who has long been recognized as one of the West's best historical painters" (Paxson Jr., 1984, p. 52).

Speaker One: **Coyote 1** *(in blackface)*

Who gets the last word? It can only go downhill from here!
Come on, most important picture in Western history? Whose history?

Speaker Two: **Coyote 2** *(in whiteface)*

Hold on, he has some more of those damned paintings to talk about.

Speaker One: **Coyote 1**

Let's summarize where we are. Let's go back to the three questions this play asks, although we can't answer the third question until we get through Act Two.

Whose Custer are we honoring with these paintings?

What does it mean to honor Custer?

What does it mean to have pro- and anti-Custer paintings in the same space at the same time?

Clearly with Paxson we are honoring the standard Anglo narrative about Custer-the-fallen-hero. We are also honoring the realist aesthetic, history as melodrama, history as Manifest Destiny. We know, looking at this painting, that the Indians' days are numbered, their victory on Custer Hill short lived. In honoring this version of Custer, the painting validates this historical narrative.

ACT TWO, SCENE ONE

Biss's Gentle Counter-Narrative

Speaker One: **Historian**

Earl Biss's[9] *General Custer in Blue and Green* (1996)[10] was part of the 2007–2008 Buffalo Bill Historical Center "Battle of Many Names" exhibit.[11] Biss's painting was based on a photograph of Custer in full dress uniform taken by Matthew Brady on May 23, 1865, eleven years before the Battle of the Little Bighorn. Biss's Custer is a virtual replica of Brady's photograph—same pose, same turn of the head, arms crossed the same way, same formal dress, same far-off look staring at something in the distance.

(Stage right, a spotlight shines on Brady's photograph of Custer and Biss's painting of Custer.)

Speaker Two: **Observer**

In the Buffalo Bill Historical Center exhibit, Biss's painting is exhibited on the wall directly opposite Allan Mardon's *Battle of Greasy Grass*. As the visitor turns to the left from this viewing space, about 75 feet away, Paxson's huge painting can be seen. A Native American's Custer stands between two versions of Custer and the battle, and, in this sense, it comments on both versions.

Speaker One: **Art Critic**

Like Brady's photo, Biss's is a half-length portrait. Blond-haired Custer's head is turned slightly to the left, concealing his left eye and eyebrow. Only his right eye is visible, beneath a furrowed brow, indicating, perhaps, deep thought. He is tight lipped. There is little facial expression of emotion. He has a blondish-brown goatee with a slender sideburn extending from his goatee to just beneath his ear. His uniform jacket and wide-brimmed hat are deep blue. The blue of the jacket and hat are accented by two rows of gold buttons. A knotted, light blue scarf extends under his jacket collar. Gold stars adorn his shoulder lapels. His arms are crossed. His hands are in white elbow-length gloves. Two of the three colors of the flag—white and blue—define his somber presence.

Speaker Two: **Observer**

Would you call this painting an instance of photographic realism, or is it some strand of impressionism?

Speaker One: **Art Critic**

This is photographic realism. It is Biss's Custer, but it is a painted version of Matthew Brady's photograph. They are not the same Custer. The man in the Brady photograph is road-weary, tired, his jacket is ill-fitting, too big for his slender frame.

Speaker Two: **Matthew Brady**

Earl and I are both representing a man who stands outside time and place, a fully confident, maybe arrogant, soldier. Our Custer is a 26-year-old man who is deeply self-confident, proud of his military position, perhaps not one who learns from experience. You might say the photograph and the painting celebrate the idea of Custer the man, more than the man himself.

Speaker One: **Narrator** *(as observer)*

The location of Biss's Custer between the other two Last Stand paintings is significant. Mardon's Custer is kneeling, red scarf around his head, firing his pistol. Paxson's Custer is a tragic, valiant figure in the center of the battle. Biss's Custer stands outside the battle. Biss's Custer transcends the battle. Paxson's and Mardon's Custer dies on the battlefield.

Speaker Two: **Coyote 1**

I get it! Biss's Custer is a contradictory figure. On the one hand, the painting immortalizes the man. His Custer transcends the Last Stand. This is the Custer mainstream history wants to remember. But Earl undercuts this imagery. And his Custer is painted by a Crow Indian, A NATIVE AMERICAN. What does this say? I mean, Crow scouts worked for Custer and now Earl goes and paints the man who killed the Lakota and the Cheyenne.

Speaker One: **Tonto**

If Custer died for our sins, then it is only fitting that a Native American paint his portrait. We made him famous. He owes us a lot, and Earl is just returning the favor. I think Earl would agree with Sherman Alexie.

Speaker Two: **Sherman Alexie**

Hey, "Custer is a crazy egomaniac who thinks he is going to be President of the United States. Custer is one of the two or three dumb asses in American history" (Alexie, 2007, p. 69). This is the Custer that I see in Earl's painting.

Speaker One: **Military Historian 1**

Remember, Custer's reputation was severely tarnished after the Last Stand debacle. General Philip H. Sheridan concluded that George A. Custer had made several important mistakes at the Little Bighorn. He argued that after their 70-mile journey, Custer's men were too tired to fight effectively. Custer had also made a mistake in developing a plan of attack on the false assumption that the Lakota and Cheyenne would attempt to escape rather than fight the soldiers. Sheridan also criticized Custer's decision to divide his men into three groups: "Had the Seventh Cavalry been held together, it would have been able to handle the Indians on the Little Bighorn."[12]

Speaker Two: **Military Historian 2**

Custer's final mistake was to attack what was probably the largest group of Native Americans ever assembled on the North American continent. President Ulysses Grant agreed with this assessment and when interviewed by the *New York Herald,* he said, "I regard Custer's Massacre as a sacrifice of troops, brought on by Custer himself, that was wholly unnecessary."[13]

Speaker One: **Tonto**

>Despite this criticism, George Custer was given a hero's burial at West Point.

Speaker Two: **Coyote 1**

>So why are we still celebrating him?

Speaker One: **Coyote 2**

>Who is celebrating him?

Speaker Two: **Vine Deloria Jr.**

>Custer Died for His Sins.

Speaker One: **Earl Biss**

>This is what my painting represents. An arrogant soldier who died for his arrogance, a dumb ass!

Speaker Two: **Allan Mardon**

>Custer was a weasel. I call the Custer in my 2007 oil painting George "Armstrong." He can't look you in the eye.

Speaker One: **Coyote 1**

>Let's get on with it. Can we talk about Allan Mardon's masterpiece?

ACT TWO, SCENE TWO

Fritz Scholder's Two Counter-Narratives

Speaker One: **Coyote 1**

>Before we talk about Mardon, let's look at two paintings by Luiseno artist Fritz Scholder (1937–2005). His work is called abstract expressionism. Scholder rejected the tradition of studio art, the realist tradition embraced by Paxson and others. Studio art produces representations, including precise line drawings, based on the use of models, photographs, and natural artifacts. This tradition lies behind the concept of the "Noble Indian." Scholder would have nothing to do with that aesthetic.

(Stage right, a spotlight shines on copies of two Fritz Scholder paintings: "Custer and 20,000 Indians"[14] *(1969), and "American Landscape"*[15]*(1976).*

Speaker Two: **Christine C. Brindza**

Scholder was famous for stating that he would no longer paint Indians. In *Custer and 20,000 Indians* he interrogates one of the lasting images of Custer, that of the valiant warrior waving his sword in the air, one foot on the haunches of a dead horse.[16] In the painting, Custer's foot rests on a white rock. There are no other images, just Custer surrounded by a "field of black with scarlet slashes in the background [which] represent a mass of Native American warriors. Custer appears to be combating them single-handedly, enhancing the perception of [his] martyrdom" (Brindza, 2010, p. 9).

Speaker One: **Tonto**

Pretty stark, but you get the point—this ridiculous narrative about Custer and his men dying for a lost cause. Scholder cuts through myth, turning Custer into a kind of superhero—one man—David against Goliath, or is Custer Goliath?

Speaker Two: **Coyote 1**

This is the power of the Custer narrative—poor Custer is turned into David attacked by the merciless Indians—Goliath. Scholder mocks that story. The Indians see Custer and his army as the all-powerful Goliath. This is the image that Custer and 20,000 Indians deconstructs.

Speaker One: **Christine C. Brindza**

Let's look at "American Landscape," the second Scholder painting in the exhibit. Scholder created this painting in 1976, the centennial anniversary of the Battle of the Little Bighorn.

Speaker Two: **Historian**

Don't forget, the Americans formally declared their independence from Great Britain on July 4, 1776. So Fritz's painting marks two historical moments.

Speaker One: **Coyote 1**

The Battle of Greasy Grass on June 25–26, 1876, was one hundred years after the American Declaration of Independence. Scholder's 1976 painting continues the centennial anniversary theme. The irony here, of course, is that the Lakota and Cheyenne lost their freedom after battle.

Speaker Two: **Christine C. Brindza**

He bases his painting on Paxson's *Custer's Last Stand*. It is a counterpoint to that painting. Scholder's interpretation in an *American Landscape* reverses and distorts Paxson's painting. The painting is in black-and-white. Scholder literally recreates, then overturns the central imagery in Paxson's work. Pistol-firing Custer is in the center, shooting at Indians. He is surrounded by cartoonlike soldiers with bulging white arms. Grotesque horses with deadly white heads lunge forward into battle. Dead men as dark silhouette images are sprawled on the ground. This American landscape is a nightmare.

Speaker One: **Coyote 2**

He mocks Custer. He demolishes the Custer-is-a-great-man theory.

Speaker Two: **Tonto**

You could say Scholder shoots an arrow through the white American psyche. He holds a mirror up to the centennial celebration of the Last Stand, treating it as a form of genocide. He shatters Paxson's myth and calls for new vistas, a new beginning. But first he suggests that we must get beyond the nightmares of a culture that persists in celebrating Custer and his violence (Brindza, 2010, p. 9).

Speaker Two: **Coyote 1**

Indeed!

ACT THREE, SCENE ONE
Mardon's Counter-Narrative

(Stage right, a spotlight shines on Allan Mardon's "Battle of Greasy Grass.") [17]

Speaker One: **Narrator**

Mardon's 11-by-6-foot oil on linen mural-size painting is modeled after Indian ledger art, including Red Horse's forty-one drawings of "Battle of the Little Bighorn."[18]

108 Chapter Three

Speaker Two: **Allan Mardon**[19]

I do narrative art, I paint stories, paintings that tell a story. I studied Indian ledger art, wall hangings, murals, any painting that tells a story—I was influenced by it. I like Indian ledger art because the artists used crayons to make their colorful drawings. That is how I got my idea about the colored horses in my painting. I was aware of the Red Horse drawings. But they did not influence me directly.

Speaker One: **Red Horse**

Like my drawings, Allan's painting tells the story of Custer's Last Stand, but from the Native American point of view. Both of our stories unfold hour by hour. This temporal feature sets our stories apart from Paxson's, which represents the Last Stand as an event, frozen in time. Allan and I are painting a series of interconnected events, several last stands that evolved over the course of two days. Our paintings tell how Custer got all boxed in, nowhere to go.

Speaker Two: **Allan Mardon**

I'm on the side of the Indians. As I said, I think Custer was a weasel. I didn't like all this glorifying of Custer. A lot of the other Last Stand paintings are just wrong. There were no sabers in this battle, for example. Paxson has Custer using the wrong type of gun. I called my painting the *Battle of Greasy Grass*. This is how the Indians talked about the grass along the Little Bighorn River. My painting covers twenty-four hours—3:00 p.m. on Sunday, June 25 to 3:00 p.m. on Monday, June 26, 1876. All the other paintings are just focused on one point in time; that is, the battle. I wanted to show not what happened, but rather how the battle happened.

(Stage right, a spotlight shines on a facsimile of the general reference map from Michno, 1997, pp. vi–vii.)

Speaker One: **Gregory F. Michno**

As you can see from my map, several key sites exist: the Indian camp in the valley along the river, the timber along the river, Greasy Grass Ridge, Last Stand Hill, Nye-Cartwright Ridge, Medicine Tail Coulee, Weir Point, Reno-Benteen Site. Mardon's painting moves through these sites, starting with Reno's troops attacking the Indian camp along Greasy Grass River.

Speaker One: **Naomi Maehr**

So how do I make sense of this painting, Grandpa?

Speaker Two: **Whitney Gallery Curator**

Good question, Naomi. Let me help your grandfather with this one. See this book? It goes through Mr. Mardon's painting, scene by scene, hour by hour.

(Stage right, a spotlight shines on a bound loose-leaf book with a scene from Allan Mardon's "Battle of Greasy Grass" on the front. The back cover says, "Please do not remove from the gallery.")

Speaker One: **Naomi Maehr**

Grandpa, why did you take this book from the Museum?

Speaker Two: **Whitney Gallery Curator**

We put this book together so patrons could better appreciate and understand Mr. Mardon's epic painting. Don't be mad at your grandfather. We have plenty of copies of this book. They disappear all the time.

Speaker One: **Naomi Maehr**

So where do I start?

Speaker Two: **Whitney Gallery Curator**

Naomi, let's let Mr. Mardon tell the story of his painting.

ACT THREE, SCENE TWO

Mr. Mardon's Story

Speaker One: **Allan Mardon**

Naomi, my canvas can be divided into major sections, or quadrants, each corresponding to the phases of the battle. The title of the painting—*Battle of Greasy Grass*—is in the far upper right-hand corner, alongside the words "Sunday, June 25th 1876." The painting is divided from top to lower bottom by the blue-colored Greasy Grass River. Cemetery Ridge, Deep Ravine, and Custer Hill are in the upper left-hand quadrant. Calhoun Hill, Deep Coulee, Nye-Cartwright Ridge, Medicine Tail Coulee, and Weir Point are in the upper center panels. Weir Point, Sharpshooter Ridge, Reno Hill, and Water Carrier Ridge define the upper right-hand panel. But these are just geographical and temporal markers. The real story is in the action that takes place in these spaces, over the course of the two days of the battle.

Speaker Two: **Narrator**

So Mardon's map combines space and time in a complex narrative.

Speaker One: **Allan Mardon**

Yes. The story starts in the center lower quadrant in the "Indian camp of seven circles" (Hunkpapa, Oglala, Minneconjou, Sans Arc, Brule, Cheyenne, Blackfeet). It is high noon. People are swimming in the river, some are digging for wild turnips. The story will unfold from this point, with the battle starting at 3:10 in the afternoon when Reno's soldiers cross the river from the north and attack the village. Several young warriors run into the camp, reporting that soldiers are coming. The attacks that follow move the narrative from right to left, and back again across the main panels of the painting. The key times are Sunday afternoon, June 25: 2:40, 3:00, 3:25, 3:27, 3:45, 4:00, 4:10, 4:20, 4:30, 5:00, 5:20, 5:35, 7:00; Monday afternoon, June 26: 3:00.

Speaker One: **Whitney Gallery Curator**

Before we go into each of the frames within the painting, let's stand back and look at what Mr. Mardon is doing. This is a bold, complex painting, framed on four sides by Indians (tiny metal figures) on horses of seven different colors. Those colors could be said to represent the seven Indian nations in the village.[20] Note that Custer is a tiny figure in the painting, considerably smaller then Gall, Crazy Horse, or Sitting Bull.

Speaker Two: **Allan Mardon**

I had to figure out how to make the Indian horses look different from the soldiers' horses. That is how I got the idea for different colors of

Indian horses. And then the soldiers had different colored horses for each troop—brown, black, gray, and so on. So my painting has black, blue, gray, green, orange, red, white, and yellow horses.

Speaker One: **Coyote 1**

This is a Last Stand painting without a last stand. Actually, three last stands are found in the painting. There are some dead bodies, but they just lie there. It is not gruesome. Custer's Last Stand is not the focal point of the painting. Mardon's point is that it was a battle that occurred over a large area, over two days' time, with separate events, skirmishes, and struggles taking place.

Speaker Two: **Allan Mardon**

I deliberately gave my painting a red-orange tint to suggest the idea of blood. But I did not want to reproduce what was in the other Custer paintings—scalps, arrows, bloodshed. Those paintings turned the Indians into barbarians. The real barbarians where the white soldiers carrying out a mission of death on behalf of the American government.

Speaker One: **Naomi Maehr**

Mr. Mardon, please help me understand your painting.

ACT THREE, SCENE THREE

Mr. Mardon's Three or Four Last Stands

Speaker Two: **Allan Mardon**

As I said, the story starts at 3:00 p.m. at the lower right-hand side of the painting, when Reno's troops charge down Reno Hill, cross the river, and attack the Indian camps. The Indians start a fire, create a smoke screen, and drive Reno's men back across the river. Meanwhile, Custer and his troops move from the top of Reno Hill toward Weir Point, arriving at Medicine Tail Coulee with companies C, E, F, I, and L at 3:45 p.m. At the same time in the Indian village, Gall learns that his family has been killed by Arikara scouts working for Custer.

Speaker One: **Coyote 1**

So in the first forty-five minutes of the painting, quite a bit has happened. A lot of movement back and forth happens among Indians and soldiers.

Speaker Two: **Allan Mardon**

Exactly—it's not all happening at once, but it feels like that. Remember, I took two years to produce this painting, so it has lots of detail! At 4:00 p.m., Reno's troops are becoming disoriented. Bloody Knife, one of Custer's favorite scouts, is shot. The Blue Coats run back toward Reno Hill. At 4:10, at the upper left-hand section of the painting, at Medicine Coulee, Companies E (on gray horses) and F go down to the river to get information for Custer. The Indians see the gray horses. Meanwhile, also at 4:10, Company I is on the Nye-Cartwright Ridge. They are supposed to be a backup unit for Custer. At 4:20, near Water Carrier's Ravine, Captain Benteen and his troops are also on their way to help Custer. Reno calls them back to Reno Hill, where a makeshift hospital is formed. At 4:40 volunteers walk down to the river to get water for the wounded. Many are killed. At 4:30, on Cemetery Ridge, above and to the right of Calhoun Hill, Custer and his men are looking for women and children. Custer panics; he sees the camp of "seven circles" and knows his men are scattered all over the battlefield.

Speaker One: **Curator**

The First Last Stand: At 4:30, Gall and his men cross the river and ride toward Calhoun Hill, near Custer Hill. Fierce fighting ensues. The Indians call this the "First Last Stand."

Speaker Two: **Allan Mardon**

The Third Last Stand: At 5:00 p.m., Companies C, E, F, and L are in hand-to-hand combat on Nye-Cartwright Ridge. By 5:20 on Custer Hill, shown at the upper left center of the painting, Custer and his men know they will die. Twenty of his men make a run for the river and are killed. The Indians call this the "Third Last Stand."

Speaker One: **Curator**

Mardon's Custer is on one knee, wearing a black shirt, red scarf around his neck, tan trousers, black knee-high boots, and wide-brimmed hat, with brown hair and a dark mustache. He is firing a pistol. Dying soldiers surround him. Custer is one among many. While not the center of the large painting, he is in the center of the battle on Custer Hill.

Speaker Two: **Allan Mardon**: *The Second Last Stand*

The time is 5:20 p.m. We are back on Custer Hill. Captain Keogh is killed. Custer is about to die. Indians surround the soldiers and cut them off from all escape. Some soldiers are killed with gunfire, others with hatchets and clubs. The Indians call this the "Second Last Stand."

Speaker One: **Coyote 1**

Help me. The time is 5:20 p.m. and I'm looking back at Reno Hill. I think I see Crazy Horse—wasn't he just over on Custer Hill? Now he is riding with Sitting Bull. So he is in the painting twice.

Speaker Two: **Allan Mardon**

Yes, he is painted twice. There is more to my story. At 5:35 p.m., we are at Weir Point. Reno and Benteen can see Indians on the top of Custer Hill. The Indians are using guidons—company flags on poles—as coup sticks to carry their battle trophies. Reno's troops retreat to Reno Hill. At 7:00 p.m. on Reno Hill, Indians are using weapons captured in the battle. Most of the warriors return to camp to care for the wounded and to perform death dances.

Speaker One: **Coyote 1**

Skip ahead to Sunday at 3:00 p.m. Sitting Bull, on his black horse, tells the young warriors, "Let the soldiers go!"

Speaker Two: **Narrator**

We could call this the "Fourth Last Stand." The "Last Last Stand."

Speaker One: **Allan Mardon**

Fair enough. Sitting Bull is in my painting four different times in four different places: in the camp of "seven circles" praying; leading the women, children, and elderly men to safety; riding with Crazy Horse to the left of Reno Hill; and calling an end to the fighting on Sunday afternoon.

Speaker Two: **Curator**

>Naomi, there are three other figures in Mr. Mardon's painting that we should consider. On the bank of the river, to the right of the Indian camp, below Weir Point, is Isaiah Dorman. He wears a white shirt, blue pants, and a large tan hat. He is the only black man in this battle, and he dies. He was a translator and scout for Custer. The second figure is Kate Bighead. A Cheyenne, she is an eyewitness of the battle. She is directly across the river from the Indian camp, below Custer Hill. Her back is turned to the viewer. She is wearing buckskin garments with colorful bead trimming. She tells her story of the battle to Dr. Thomas Marquis in 1922 (Bighead, 1992/2004). The third figure is Mark Kellogg, a reporter for the *Bismarck Tribune*, who was killed in the battle. He is dressed in a somber dark red shirt and dark trousers and wears a black hat. He is located near Deep Ravine, on the bank of the river, across from the camp. Papers are scattered around his body on the grass.

Speaker One: **Naomi Maehr**

>Why are they in the painting?

Speaker Two: **Curator**

>You'd have to ask Mr. Mardon. For me, they give the painting historical depth. Kate Bighead is not in any of the other Custer paintings. Mark Kellogg traveled with Custer and was filing news reports. Isaiah Dorman—the "black white man"—deserves to be in the painting, a black man dying for his country, even if he did fight against the Indians!

Speaker One: **Naomi Maehr**

>In the upper left-hand corner of the painting, I see a large compass made of up three overlapping circles. It is bisected by two arrows—one is marked Indian North and the other is marked Magnetic North.

Speaker Two: **Allan Mardon**

>Naomi, I want to show that the soldiers and the Indians had different ways of judging time, space, and direction. The soldiers used the magnetism of the North and South Poles. The Indians used the positions of the stars. The North of the soldiers did not point in the same direction as the North of the Indians. This may explain why the soldiers' accounts of the battle were different from the accounts told by the Indians. At a very fundamental level, the soldiers and the Indians did not under-

stand one another. Even though they were in the same place—the spaces of the battle—their understandings of time and space were not the same. So it's possible for people to come together but not understand one another.

Speaker One: **Narrator**

Let's go back to Mr. Mardon's three last stands. They take place at 4:30, 5:00, and 5:20 p.m. They represent the battle from the point of view of the Indians. And actually, as noted above, you could say there was a fourth Last Stand: when Sitting Bull, on Sunday afternoon, calls an end to the fighting.

Speaker Two: **Coyote 1**

Mr. Mardon's painting tells a story—a story of victory, the triumph of the Indians over Custer and his men. His colorful painting celebrates ledger art, colored horses flying through the air, as in a Joan Miro or Paul Klee painting.[21] His painting shows the Indians outsmarting Custer, Reno, and their men. His painting celebrates Native American life.

Speaker One: **Narrator**

How would you compare it to Earl Biss's or Fritz Scholder's works?

Speaker Two: **Coyote 1**

All three painters bring Custer down to earth—he is one among many soldiers who die. Scholder's two paintings, alongside Mardon's, evoke a counter-narrative which challenges the Paxson–great man–studio art version of the battle/massacre. For them, the battle is a series of interconnected events in which no single man dominates, except possibly Sitting Bull.

ACT THREE, SCENE FOUR

In Whose Honor? Whose Custer?

Speaker One: **Narrator** *(to audience)*

Let's go back to the beginning of this little play. What do we make of the pro- and anti-Custer Last Stand paintings that hang side by side in the Whitney Museum of Western Art? Remember, in taking up the

Custer paintings by Paxson, Biss, Scholder, and Mardon, the play asks these questions:

Whose Custer are we honoring with these paintings?

What does it mean to honor Custer?

What does it mean to have pro- and anti-Custer paintings in the same space at the same time?

Speaker Two: **Coyote 1**

Be subversive. There is no single version of Custer. At least three versions of Custer are honored in these paintings: Custer as mythic, tragic hero; Custer as self-important military officer; Custer as just another dead soldier.

Speaker One: **Tonto**

You can't separate Custer from the battle. Biss gives us Custer the soldier, in formal uniform. He stands outside battle. Paxson gives us Custer as the victim of a disastrous battle. Paxson embeds his Custer in the minutiae of military history, as if that attention to detail validated the battle and its representation. Scholder gives us a bloated Custer, a Goliath with his back turned to his enemy. Mardon makes Custer part of the battle and reduces him to one player among many. The painting does not center on Custer.

Speaker Two: **Curator**

We are not honoring Custer so much as we are asking people to remember a sad moment in the history of the American West. In placing these paintings in the same space, we are saying that this is a violent history, a history of death.

Speaker One: **Sherman Alexie**

We are also suggesting to get rid of this nonsense about heroes, great men, bravery, and honor. How about a new discourse on how to live together in harmony, without war or battles or conflict?

Speaker One: **Coyote 1**

Until then: *Custer died for his sins!*

CHAPTER FOUR

Killing Custer

ACT ONE, SCENE ONE

Point-Counterpoint

Speaker One: **Norman K. Denzin**

"Killing Custer" is a three-act play that uses Eric von Schmidt's 1976 painting, *Here Fell Custer,* as a backdrop[1] for reading the representations of the battle by three Native American artists: Red Horse's forty-one drawings (1881; Viola, 1998, 1999c); six of White Swan's (1897) drawings (Bradley, 1991; Cowles, 1982) and selections from Amos Bad Heart Buffalo's drawings[2] depicting every phase of the battle (Blish, 1967; Fox, 1997; Tillett, 1976). The play returns to the question that will not go away: Who owns this battle, anyway?

Speaker Two: **Narrator**

June 26, 1976

National Park Service Centennial Celebration of Custer's Last Stand to commemorate the Centennial of the Battle of the Little Bighorn, the National Park Service selected Eric von Schmidt's *Here Fell Custer* as the official painting depicting Custer's Last Stand. The painting is displayed on the wayside exhibit at Last Stand Hill near where Custer fell, as well as in the National Park Service brochure.

118   Chapter Four

(Stage right, a spotlight shines on Eric von Schmidt's 1976 painting Here Fell Custer.*)*

Speaker One: **Vine Deloria Jr.**

Custer died for his sins.

Speaker Two: **Coyote 1**

You can say that again. But von Schmidt's painting is not exactly Fritz Scholder's 1976 *American Landscape*,[3] which was also painted to commemorate the centennial. Looks like another white man's telling of this story to me!

Speaker One: **Lakota Elder**

A people without history is like wind on the buffalo grass (Tillett, 1976, p. xii).

Speaker Two: **Allan Mardon**

We need to fill museums and art galleries with Native American paintings of the Battle of the Little Bighorn, like those by White Swan, Red Horse, Fritz Scholder, Earl Biss, Kevin Red Star,[4] John Nieto.[5]

Speaker One: **Eric von Schmidt**

I disagree. I'm not so sure about the Red Horse drawings. They give no detail concerning dress or weapons. They offer no special insight into the battle. They are a record of the event, but they make no attempt to interpret it (1976, p. 1).

Speaker Two: **Tonto**

Hey white man, what do you mean, interpret?

Speaker One: **Eric von Schmidt**

I mean—what it meant for the soldiers. They have a special power, but the viewer's vantage point is that of an attacking Indian. Red Horse was one of the attacking Indians—no wonder he shows their point of view. But how did the soldiers feel? Red Horse has none of that. That is what I wanted to paint and that is what my painting shows, what the soldiers saw and felt (von Schmidt, 1976, p. 2.).

Speaker Two: **Coyote**

> So there is interpretation.
> You just don't like the interpretation.
> And how about all those other
> Custer Last Stand paintings—
> Cary, Adams, Fuchs, Steinegger, Mulvany, Paxson—
> they all tell the story from
> the soldiers' point of view.

Speaker One: **Narrator** *(to audience)*

> Hold on. Let's shift focus. Here is a beginning. It's out of harm's way. A painted deer hide of the Battle of the Little Bighorn done by a Lakota artist (c.1895) is exhibited in the Plains Indian Museum collection in the Buffalo Bill Historical Center.

Speaker Two: **Coyote 1**

> Ah, another Native American painting. This is good. "In the painting warriors are on foot and on horseback. Soldiers are dressed in blue and yellow uniforms. Custer, with yellow hair and wearing buckskin, stands armed with two revolvers at center left" (Brindza, 2010, p. 6).

Speaker One: **Coyote 2**

> So there is some detail,
> but heaven, help me!
> Not another Custer!

Speaker Two: **Norman K. Denzin**

> Hold on. This single deer hide is counterpoint to the pro- and anti-Custer Last Stand paintings discussed in the previous play, "Whose Custer?"

Speaker One: **Lloyd Kiva New**

> "Remember, drawings and paintings done by Indians of scenes from the Battle of the Little Bighorn . . . give a preprogrammed 20th century audience the opportunity to see some fascinating and exquisitely executed Indian art in connection with one of the classic turnabout events in the history of Indian/white relations. Today is a very good time to rethink the entire matter of Indians in America" (New, 1976, pp. viii–ix).

Speaker Two: **Coyote 1**

> Maybe we don't know how to look at and interpret these paintings. Eric von Schmidt says they offer no special insight into the battle.

Speaker One: **Coyote 2**

> Why listen to Eric von Schmidt? Is it because his father also did a Last Stand painting?

Speaker Two: **Coyote 1**

> Yes, it was for *Esquire* in 1950.

Speaker One: **Leslie Tillett** *(to audience)*

> Forget the white men. The Little Bighorn Plains Indian artists were recording indigenous history; Custer was engaged in genocide.

Speaker Two: **Coyote 1**

> Exactly. Don't forget—Custer first attacked the Indian villages. He wanted to kill our women and children, so that the warriors would have to fight in the open to defend them (Tillett, 1976, p. xii).

Speaker One: **Leslie Tillett**

> "Who can forget? The Battle of the Little Bighorn is the most important single event in Plains Indian history, a date by which they measure all other events, including the Ghost Dance Movement, Wounded Knee massacre, and the beginning of the American Indian Movement a century later in 1972" (Tillett, 1976, p. x).

Speaker Two: **Chief Red Horse**

> It was also a time of victory, of community
> solidarity. Our people stopped the
> spread of the white man across our lands.
> We defeated the U. S. Army
> and brought down their national hero—Custer.
> We felt joy and pride and love. We were
> unified. But we desired peace.[6] (Tillett, 1976, p. xii).

Speaker One: **Douglas E. Bradley**

The Chief is right. The battle was America's greatest defeat at the hands of hostile Indians, a defining event in the conquest of the West (1991, p. 14).

Speaker Two: **James Welch**

"Most of the Indians escaped unharmed. The warriors took the soldiers' clothes, boots, guns, and horses. They dismembered the vanquished. They believed that an enemy without arms or legs or a head could do them no harm in the world beyond. For centuries, wars have been fought in this way" (Welch, 1994, pp. 147–148).

Speaker One: **Coyote 1**

Yeah, but these ritual acts fueled racist,
anti-Redskin beliefs, supplied the national media
with grotesque images and gave ammunition
to the national movement to "exterminate" the Indians,
spare no cost! And they gave white artists license
to paint us as barbarians.
If you were a critic of recent American politics
You'd say there are September 11 parallels.
All Indians were targeted,
not just the ones involved in
The Battle of Greasy Grass.
Like Muslims in the U. S. after September 11.

Speaker Two: **Coyote 2**

Listen to one of America's national poets talk about the battle. This sounds pretty racist to me.

Speaker One: **Coyote 1**

Well—it is Mr. Longfellow. What would you expect?

Speaker Two: **Henry Wadsworth Longfellow**

"By their fires the Lakota chiefs
Muttered their woes and griefs

And the menace of their wrath.
"Revenge," cried Rain in the Face,
"Revenge upon all the race
of the White Chief with yellow hair!"
... And Rain in the Face, in his flight,
Uplifted high in the air
A ghastly trophy, bore
The brave heart, that beat no more,
Of the White Chief with yellow hair"
(Longfellow, 1878; Miller, 1957, p. 209).

Speaker One: **Coyote 2**

I guess there is no question about how white America's national poet saw the battle! He was like Walt Whitman in this regard. They were both caught up in the Manifest Destiny kill-the-Indians movement.

Speaker Two: **Kevin Red Star**

Hey, my painting *Rain in the Face* celebrates this fearless Hunkpapa Lakota leader. That Easterner Longfellow understood nothing.

Speaker One: **Leslie Tillett**

These acts Longfellow writes about also found their way into a lot of other bad books, bad poetry, and bad paintings (Tillett, 1976, p. xiii).

Speaker Two: **Coyote 2**

Yes. But did any of this get reflected in the Native paintings?

Speaker One: **Coyote 1**

Yes and no. The violence is here in the drawings by Red Horse and others, certainly. But what you have, as Allan Mardon told us in the last chapter, is two completely different ways of representing and interpreting the battle.

Speaker Two: **Tonto**

Take another look at Red Star's *Rain in the Face*.
That is a proud, strong face.

(Project Red Star painting, which can be found at http://www.kevinredstar.com)

Speaker One: **Peter Hassrick** *(in an aside to the audience)*

While you are at it, listen to what an archaeologist says about the Native American drawings. In his discussion of Indian drawings of Custer's last battle, archaeologist Richard Fox (1997, pp. 166–171) briefly analyzes three other Indian artists: Standing Bear, White Bull, Spotted Wolf-Yellow Nose. Their paintings have received less attention, but they display, as we shall soon see, the same categories of warrior-soldier behavior as exhibited in the Red Horse, White Swan, and Amos Bad Heart Buffalo drawings, namely: Indian-soldier battle scenes; scenes of Indians and cavalry dead; Indians in pursuit of cavalry horses; individual Indian prowess against soldiers; Indians taking the upper hand among the disorganized cavalry; the end of the battle and its aftermath; leaving the battlefield (Fox, 1997, p. 179).

Speaker Two: **Coyote 1**

Why point this out now?

Speaker One: **Coyote 2**

To set the context. There are many Native American paintings of Greasy Grass. I don't want folks to think we are talking about every Last Stand painting made by Native Americans!

ACT ONE, SCENE TWO

Chief Red Horse Gets the First and the Last Word

(Stage left, a spotlight shines on a set of Chief Red Horse's drawings from Viola (1999c, pp. 88–89, 92–93, 94–95). The viewer is directed to Red Horse drawings in chapter 1 and to http://sirismm.si.edu/naa/2367a/08568000.jpg)

Speaker One: **Herman J. Viola**

"In 1881 Red Horse, a Miniconjou chief, drew forty-one pictographs chronicling the events of June 25, 1876 at the Battle of the Little Bighorn. He did this at the Cheyenne River Agency in Dakota territory for Army surgeon Charles E. McChesney. They were done with colored pencils and ink on 24-by-26-inch sheets of brown manila paper. They are housed at the Smithsonian Institution, in the National Anthropological Archives" (Viola, 1991c, pp. 82–83). The entire set was reproduced in full color for the first time in Viola (1999c, pp. 86–103).

Speaker Two: **Red Horse** *(to Charles E. McChesney, assistant army surgeon)*

Here is my oral history. Five springs ago,
I, with many Lakotas . . . moved to the Little Bighorn River
and pitched our lodges. I was a Lakota chief in the council lodge.
The day of the attack I and four women were digging wild turnips.
We saw a cloud of dust, soldiers were attacking the camp.
The day was hot. They crossed the Little Bighorn River
and attacked the lodges of the Hunkpapas.
They set fire to the lodges.
The Lakota charged the soldiers and drove
them back across the river.
Several soldiers drowned.

Speaker One: **Charles E. McChesney**

Go on. This is all very dramatic and exciting.

Speaker Two: **Narrator**

It overflows with drama. Unlike all the works discussed thus far, these drawings are made by a person who was present at the battle. This ought to give them some weight. They are not representations based on myth, make-believe, or fantasy. They are counter-narratives that tell a story of resistance, a story of the Last Stand that does not need Custer.

Speaker One: **Museum Curator**

That is correct. The drawings, or sheets, are numbered from 0 to 41. The Smithsonian groups them into eight clusters, each describing a different part of the battle: approaching the village, Indian village, Indians charging soldiers, Custer's column fighting, dead cavalry horses—Custer's, Dead Lakota killed by Custer's column, dead cavalry—Custer's column, and Indians leaving the battleground.[7]

Speaker One: **Red Horse**

> I tried to draw the battle as it happened for my people. It started in our village and ended with our people, victorious, leaving the battlefield. The battle starts in the heat of the day and ends late afternoon the next day.

(Stage left, a light shines on a drawing of a Lakota village: see photos at the Old Picture website at http://www.old-picture.com/old-west/Village-Indian-Lakota.htm; also the EyeWitness to History website at http://www.eyewitnesstohistory.com/custer.htm)

Speaker Two: **Red Horse**

> There was an officer who rode a horse with four
> white feet. This man was very brave.
> I don't know if this was General Custer or not.

Speaker One: **Narrator**

> It was not Custer, but Captain Thomas French.

Speaker Two: **Red Horse**

> Maybe it was not Custer. But this man saved the lives of many soldiers.

Speaker One: **Lakota Mother**

> Maybe he saved the lives of soldiers.
> But they were out to kill us. They charged
> our camp around midday.
> (Pause)
> A party of soldiers took all the
> women and children as prisoners.
> The children were screaming.

Speaker Two: **Coyote 1**

> Back to the drawings. They move across the page,
> no background landscape, no blue sky,
> no clouds, no mountains or trees. This is
> how we tell our stories, without any unnecessary
> background.

126   Chapter Four

Speaker One: **Herman Viola**

Correct. This is ledger art, sheet after sheet of movement, mayhem, excitement, carnage, death, hand-to-hand struggle, vivid and graphic detail, proud warriors leaving the battlefield with captured horses.

Speaker Two: **Red Horse**

The Lakota charged the soldiers and drove
them back in confusion.
The Lakota did not take a single soldier prisoner.
The different soldiers, those with Custer, made five brave stands.
(Pause)
The Lakota surrounded the soldiers.
I could see officers riding in front of the soldiers
and hear them shouting.

Speaker Two: **Allan Mardon**

Left to the imagination is the suffocating dust . . .
the sounds of the battle, gunshots, shouts,
screams of pain, dying men, dead horses (Viola, 1999c, p. 82).

Speaker One: **Coyote 1**

And the body count in the drawings?
Sixty-one dead Indians (Viola, 1999c, p. 83).

Speaker Two: **Red Horse**

The Lakota killed all these different soldiers in the ravine.
The Lakota chiefs said, "Lakota men,
go watch the soldiers on the hill."
The Lakota men took the clothing off the dead
and dressed themselves in it.

Speaker One: **Kate Bighead**

I was with the women. We also stripped the soldiers of their clothing.

Speaker Two: **Red Horse**

The banks of the Little Bighorn River were high,
and the Lakota killed many of the soldiers while
crossing the river. The soldiers on the hill dug up

the ground, creating piles of dirt to hide behind.
The fight continued until the walking soldiers came.
(Pause)
There are many little incidents I cannot remember. I do not like to talk about the fight. If I ever hear my people talking about it, I always walk away (Viola, 1999c, p. 85).

Speaker One: **Kate Bighead**

I shudder whenever I hear this story, whenever I look at Red Horse's drawings. We were proud and terrified at the same time.

Speaker Two: **Red Horse**

I do not remember anything about the battle.
Nothing!

Speaker One: **Coyote 1**

So should we read these drawings?

Speaker Two: **Narrator**

Well, this kind of drawing, the pictographic narrative, has a long history in Native American culture. Typically these narratives were about battles, and often the painter signed the drawings, sometimes painting himself into the representation. These drawings typically contained only information that was relevant to the event being recorded, nothing extraneous. They are purely event-driven.

Speaker One: **Red Horse**

Coyote, this kind of drawing is partially autobiographical. I was there. I am drawing what I saw and experienced.

Speaker Two: **Curator**

If you look closely, you can see that Red Horse, using the pictographic form, carefully records heroic deeds on the battlefield.

Speaker One: **Red Horse**

My story—you can call it the visual narrative—is organized around the ideas of war, conquest, loss, death, honor on the field of battle.

Speaker Two: **Narrator**

> This is a logic that moves from the personal, to the tribal, to the nation-state. This is, after all, a record of a battle, one nation battling another nation.

Speaker One: **Curator**

> So it is. But look at it carefully. Hung on a wall, Red Horse's drawings look like a child's drawings, or a work of surrealist art, a Chagall, Miro, or a Paul Klee montage. Viewed this way, there are traces of Marc Chagall's *I and my Village* (1935). There are floating heads, upside-down people, some falling from the sky.

Speaker Two: **Coyote** (*in a serious voice*)

> A playful reading of the pictographs is misleading.
> There is violence in these drawings.
> This is a record of military violence, guns, battles,
> dead bodies, dead Indians.
> White men are shooting at Lakota and Cheyenne
> warriors. Warriors are shooting white men.
> Two Native American nations facing destruction
> are being chased by the American military.

Speaker One: **Curator**

> The author of these drawings, the cartographer, the painter, is himself part of the story. He may or may not be present in the battles, but his presence as a narrator touches every drawing in the set.

Speaker Two: **Herman Viola**

> I agree. At a deeper level the drawings are all about cultural and political genocide, the death of a way of life. Never again will the Lakota and Cheyenne nations be victorious over the American military.

Speaker One: **Curator**

> I agree completely. Red Horse's aesthetic involves a military grid, tales of violence, ancient sacred rituals of manhood and conquest, men killing men. For those white Americans who followed Custer, Little Bighorn would become a sacred site of conquest, honor.

Plate 1. Black and white photographic print of General George A. Custer, full figure in military uniform, standing three-quarter profile to camera, arms folded at chest. A draped table stands to the left. A square object lies on the floor behind his right foot. Matthew Brady photo, c.1865. Courtesy of Buffalo Bill Historical Center, Cody, Wyoming; Vincent Mercaldo Collection, p.71, 1925.3.

Plate 2. Wood engraving after drawing, William de la Montagne Cary, *The Battle on the Little Big Horn River—The Death Struggle of General Custer,* in the *Daily Graphic and Illustrated Evening Newspaper,* New York, July 19, 1876. Courtesy of Buffalo Bill Historical Center, Cody, Wyoming; Don Russell Collection, Gift of Mrs. John Bissell, MS62.1.0.3.27.

Plate 3. Chromolithograph, John Mulvany; "Custer's Last Rally, 1881. LRC of print: John/Mulvany/1881. LRC of bottom in pencil: Compliments/John Mulvany. Printed LLC under print: John Mulvany, Pinxt. Bottom center: Copyrighted, LRC: National Photogravure Co. Printed bottom center under print: Custer's Last Rally./Battle of the Little Big Horn./June 25, 1876. Courtesy of Buffalo Bill Historical Center, Cody, Wyoming; Museum Purchase, 149.69.

Plate 4. Cassilly Adams, artist, Otto Becker (1854–1945), lithographer. *Custer's Last Fight,* 1896. Inscribed: The Original has been Presented to the Seventh Regiment U.S. Cavalry/By Anheuser-Busch St. Louis, Missouri, U.S.A./World's Largest Brewery/Home of Budweiser and/other Anheuser-Busch Fine Beers. Courtesy of Buffalo Bill Historical Center, Cody, Wyoming; Gift of The Coe Foundation, 1.69.420B.

Plate 5. Painted deer hide of the Battle of the Little Bighorn, c.1895. Courtesy of Buffalo Bill Historical Center, Cody, Wyoming; Gift of Robert G. Charles, NA.702.4.

Plate 6. Oil painting, Edgar Samuel Paxson, *Custer's Last Stand*, 1899. Courtesy of Buffalo Bill Historical Center, Cody, Wyoming; Museum purchase, 19.69.

Plate 7. Painting, Allan Mardon, *The Battle of Greasy Grass*, 1996. Courtesy of Buffalo Bill Historical Center, Cody, Wyoming; Museum Purchase with funds from the William E. Weiss Memorial Fund, Mr. and Mrs. Gordon H. Barrows, and the Franklin A. West Memorial Fund, 6.01.

Plate 8. Painting, Earl Biss, *General Custer in Blue and Green*, 1996. Courtesy of Buffalo Bill Historical Center, Cody, Wyoming; Gift of Mr. and Mrs. Charles B. Israel of Aspen, Colorado, 18.00. Permission to reproduce, Lou Lou Goss.

Plate 9. Painting, Fritz Scholder, *Custer and 20,000 Indians,* 1969. Courtesy of Buffalo Bill Historical Center, Cody, Wyoming; Gift of Janis and Wiley T. Buchannan III, 7.08. Permission to reproduce image, Lisa Scholder.

Plate 10. Painting, Fritz Scholder, *American Landscape*, 1976. Courtesy of Buffalo Bill Historical Center, Cody, Wyoming; Gift of Jack and Carol O'Grady, 10.00.4. Permission to reproduce image, Lisa Scholder.

Plate 11. Photograph, unknown artist, "Little Bighorn National Monument," 1994. Courtesy of Buffalo Bill Historical Center.

Plate 12. Drawing, White Swan, "White Swan Kills a Sleeping Sioux," 1897. White Swan uses a name glyph to sign his work. Courtesy of Philmont Museum-Seton Memorial Library (IMG: 3732 JPG).

Plate 13. Drawing, White Swan, "White Swan with Spy Glass Watching Sioux Teepees," 1897. Courtesy of Philmont Museum-Seton Memorial Library (IMG: 3716 JPG).

Plate 14. Drawing, Red Horse, "Red Horse drawing of Indians fighting Custer's troops at Battle of Little Bighorn," 1881. Local Number: OPPS NEG 470COD BW; Courtesy of the National Anthropological Archives, Smithsonian Institution (see http://collections.si.edu/search/results.jsp?q=Red+Horse)

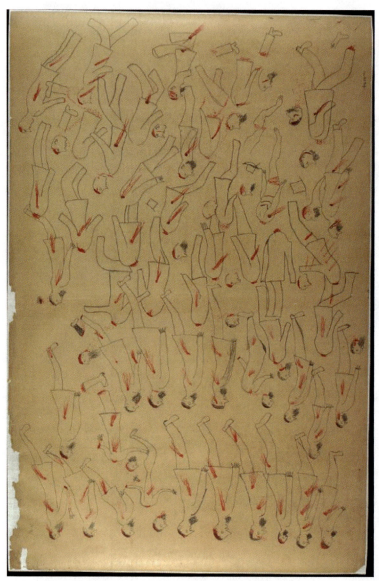

Plate 15. Drawing, Red Horse, "Red Horse drawing of dead cavalry," 1881. Local number: OPPS NEG 47001 B/W; Courtesy of the National Anthropological Archives, Smithsonian Institution.

Plate 16. Drawing, Red Horse, "Red Horse drawing of Indians leaving the Battle of Little Big Horn," 1881. Local Number: OPPS NEG 47001F B/W. Courtesy of the National Anthropological Archives, Smithsonian Institution.

Plate 17. Painting, Eric von Schmidt, *Here Fell Custer*, 1977. Courtesy of Catlin von Schmidt, Montana Historical Society and Bob Reece, President, Friends of the Little Bighorn Battlefield.

Speaker Two: **Dee Brown**

Red Horse undercuts this aesthetic. His drawings record an event that helped the post–Civil War American war machine drive Native Americans out of the West so that it would be safe for White America.

Speaker Two: **Tonto**

So how do you read them?

Speaker One: **Narrator**

Well, Red Horse laid out the drawings when he said he tried to tell the story from the point of view of his people. The Smithsonian organized them into eight clusters. They need to be experienced in their fullness, one section at a time.

But for our purposes here, let's focus on the main moments, or sequences—the village before the attack, the charge of the military, the counterattack by the warriors, dead Lakota, dead cavalry.

ACT ONE, SCENE THREE

The Village, Attack/Counterattack

Speaker One: **Narrator**

Start with the first set of scenes, those of the village along the river. They are drawings of row after row of evenly spaced, overlapping triangular-shaped tipis with lodge poles protruding at their tops. A tribal medicine tipi is located in the bottom row of panel two. A large, yellow-colored tipi is in the top row.

Speaker Two: **Coyote 1**

A lot of tipis. I guess Red Horse is trying to show each of the six separate camps.

Speaker One: **Red Horse**

Each of the six separate camps had its open side toward the east, to greet the morning sun. Our tribal medicine lodge contained our sacred Buffalo Head and other sacred objects.

Speaker Two: **Coyote 1**

The next set of scenes shows rows of soldiers on blue and orange horses charging the village. The soldiers have cropped beards, are wearing small hats. Attached to the horse saddles are scabbards for holding a sword, or large blade or rifle.

Speaker One: **Narrator**

Turn the page. The theme is counterattack. The Indians are fighting with the soldiers who have charged the village. The fighting is going on in front of the village.

Speaker Two: **Coyote 1**

I get it! This is hand-to-hand combat—
there are four riderless horses, three dead soldiers
lie on the ground.
A soldier on horseback is being chased
by an Indian on a black horse.
The Indian is carrying a long spear.

Speaker One: **Narrator**

In the next set of panels, Lakota wearing loin cloths and elaborate headdresses are on horses chasing Blue Coats, also on horses.

It gets more confusing, and more violent. Body parts—a torso, a leg and foot, a head—are flying; a naked body lies on the ground underneath a horse.

A fallen soldier is about to be trampled by a horse, a riderless horse is running off the page chased by an Indian wearing a full head bonnet.

A Lakota on a yellow horse fires at a Blue Coat who has turned around and is firing back. A Native American with a large war shield has just shot a Blue Coat.

Speaker Two: **Low Dog, Oglala**

They came on us like a thunderbolt.
We retreated and got all our men together.
Then we charged them.
I yelled to my men,
"This is a good day to die—follow me!"
And they did. And we formed a mass,

and whipped our horses,
and we rushed them (Viola, 1999c, p. 91).

Speaker One: **Coyote 1**

Let's hear it,
on the count of *three*:
It's a good day to die. Custer is going to die for his sins.

ACT TWO, SCENE ONE

Custer's Men Fight Indians and Die

Speaker One: **Narrator**

It's midafternoon. The battle is in full swing on multiple fronts.

Speaker Two: **Standing Bear**

Our warriors were everywhere,
like shadows. It was dark.
There was dust and smoke.
The noise was loud,
but it seemed quiet in there,
inside the battle,
and the voices seemed
to be on top of a cloud.
It was like a bad dream (Viola, 1999c, p. 92).

Speaker One: **Red Horse**

I wanted to show what the battlefield looked
like. I drew military bugles and soldiers' hats
and placed them near the bodies of naked soldiers.
I drew wounded soldiers slumped across horsebacks.
Body parts, legs, heads, hands, arms, are strewn everywhere.
The bodies of slain soldiers are sprawled on the ground,
arrows stick out of their backs, some are naked.
There are no dead Indians.
The Indians are winning the battle at every turn.

Speaker Two: **Coyote 1**

> It gets better. Headless men
> are walking around,
> some hold their heads
> in their hands.
>
> Heads, arms, legs, and feet
> are floating in midair.
>
> A headless soldier steps
> on someone else's head.
>
> Another soldier gazes back at his body,
> as his head is sliced off his neck.
>
> Blood flows over the chest and across
> the thighs of a naked man whose
> penis has been cut off.

Speaker One: **Private Charles Windolph**

> It was a horrible sight.
> There were mostly naked bodies
> scattered over a half-mile square field.
> We tried to see how many
> we could recognize.
> Very few.

Speaker One: **Narrator**

> Red Horse pulls no punches here. These drawings honor the warriors and how they defended their village, the women, children, and the old people. But Indians did die.

Speaker Two: **Coyote 1**

> Remember, the day started with a garden scene. They were digging for wild turnips, swimming in the river.

Speaker One: **Coyote 2**

> Yes, Lakota and Cheyenne did die. Red Horse told us this in his oral history.

Speaker Two: **Wooden Leg**

Each warrior who died was disposed of by his women relatives and his young male friends (Viola, 1997c, p. 96).

Speaker One: **Narrator**

Red Horse painted thirteen Lakota Indians in war dress. All have been shot, and show gunshot wounds to the head, back, shoulders, chest, stomach, legs, and neck. Blood flows from their wounds. Weapons are falling to the ground. There is no expression of grief, pain, or fear on their faces.

Speaker Two: **Sgt. Daniel A. Kanipe**

The dead horses were scattered all over the battlefield (Viola, 1999c, p. 99).

Speaker One: **Tonto**

And they were stripped of their saddles.
Many of the horses had been shot,
with wounds that were still bleeding.

ACT TWO, SCENE TWO

Indian Victory at Greasy Grass

Speaker One: **Narrator**

We are nearing the end of Red Horse's story. The last set of scenes are about the Indians leaving the battlefield.
    Custer is nowhere to be seen.
    All we see are dead horses and dead white men out of uniform.

Speaker Two: **Sitting Bull**

"I warned my people.
Do not touch the spoils of the battle.

But they did not listen to me.
This will be a curse to our nation.
If you take the white man's goods
he will own your heart
and you will forever be at his mercy.

You will starve at his hands" (Viola, 1999c, p. 100).

Speaker One: **Coyote 1**

> If Red Horse's sketches are to be believed,
> I guess they did not listen to their leader.
>
> Red Horse shows braves with colorful warrior
> shields leading and riding cavalry horses off the battlefield.
>
> Saddles have been taken off some of the horses.
> A look of glee spreads across the faces of the men,
> as they take control of the white man's horses.
>
> This is the look of victory.

Speaker Two: **Narrator**

> Red Horse's story of the battle ends with cavalier, cocky warriors, some wearing military hats, riding unsaddled cavalry horses over a battlefield littered with decapitated soldier bodies.

Speaker One: **Coyote 1**

> All the themes are back on the page,
> heads and legs floating in space,
> arrows penetrating buttocks.
>
> The pages are filled with vivid colors, red, yellow,
> shades of blue and black. Perfectly drawn horses
> trot along under the control of their new masters.

Speaker Two: **Tonto**

> It is not a good day for the boys of Custer.
> And where is Custer?
> It seems this is a Last Stand painting
> without Custer!

Speaker One: **Coyote 1**

> Agreed. At one level it is a painful drawing. A fully dressed, headless torso lies across the legs of a dead man. A horse's hoof tramples the chest of a fallen soldier.
>
> And across the page warriors move with focus and purpose toward the village they have saved. Working men coming home from battle.
>
> THEY WON.

Speaker Two: **Tonto**

> And Custer? Where is Custer?

Speaker One: **Coyote 1**

> Red Horse seems to be saying this battle is about our side, not the army's side. He can tell this story without the Last Stand narrative.

Speaker Two: **Red Horse**

> The victory we had that day was short lived.
> And while everybody celebrates Custer,
> nobody celebrates our chiefs.

Speaker One: **Custer**

> We just plain blew it!
> You gotta hand it to the Indians,
> damned barbarians,
> heathens.

Speaker Two: **Narrator**

> You can't give Custer the last word. It is a melancholy set of paintings. Together, they constitute a sad commentary on the Battle of the Little Bighorn aka Battle of Greasy Grass.

Speaker One: **Red Horse**

> Why did this fight happen?
> We wanted peace.
>
> On that day, and the day after and the day after that,
> it was hard to understand how disastrous
> it would be for our people (Welch, 1994).
>
> What does victory mean, anyway?

ACT TWO, SCENE THREE

A Last Stand Without Custer

Speaker One: **Narrator**

> Custer is not the key
> to Red Horse's story.
> For Red Horse, this is not
> a Last Stand narrative,
> not about Custer.
>
> It is about memory, remembering,
> making a painful
> past present,
>
> bringing it forward
> in a way that
> honors those Lakota and Cheyenne
> who fought in that battle.

Speaker Two: **Coyote 1**

> So it is not about a Last Stand. Red Horse takes that narrative away from white culture.
>
> Red Horse's painting opens the space for a new genre, or new tradition, that is art that honors Native Americans who fought in that battle.

Speaker One: **Coyote 2**

> I get it. So Kevin Red Star can honor Rain in the Face.
>
> Fritz Scholder can turn Custer into a cartoonlike figure, foot planted on a huge boulder.
> Earl Biss can make Custer look like a vain, insolent officer.
>
> John Nieto[8] can paint his "Custer Suite," situating a red-haired Custer, head turned to the right, surrounded by head portraits of four Native American warriors, one with a miniature American flag stenciled on his shirt.
>
> Pure irony.

Speaker Two: **Curator**

> What is happening here is pretty clear. Artists like Red Horse are resisting the dominant narrative, the white male mythology that endows Custer and his so-called Last Stand with great cultural power.
>
> This myth is cracked once Native Americans refuse to be complicit with the conquest-submission storyline;
>
> The story about the frontier, democracy, and the inevitable march of civilization on the fateful days of June 25 and June 26, 1876, when Custer was killed for his sins.
>
> In refusing to honor this racist mythology, Red Horse and his colleagues open the door on a counter-narrative, a narrative of resistance, a true decolonizing story.
>
> Utopian visions!

Speaker One: **Coyote 1**

> So with Red Horse's drawings we can begin to imagine another telling, another version of the Last Stand, or telling of the Custer myth.
> Red Horse demands that Native Americans be allowed to claim their natural, inalienable rights of self-recognition, self-governance, of survival, self-autonomy, life, liberty, the pursuit of happiness, and sovereign authority over their own lands.
> This turns Custer on his head, for he and his men were arguing that they were fighting to give white America these self-same rights.

Speaker Two: **Red Horse**

> This is why I left Custer out of my painting.
> I wanted to also anticipate and undermine
> Custer celebrations
> in the next century.
>
> You can use my drawings to criticize
> all past and future
> Custer re-enactments.
>
> In this form of historical theater,
> Custer and the Seventh Cavalry would be
> pushed aside, ignored.

In their place, performers would enact a disruptive theatre—as they do in my drawings,

reclaiming and celebrating
the inalienable rights of Native Americans
to own and control their own history,
and the stories that are told about it.

ACT TWO, SCENE FOUR

Let's Be Disruptive

Speaker One: **Sherman Alexie**

Hey, Red Horse. Let's get crazy!

We could stage community
performances where all these celebrated Custer paintings—
Adams, Mulvany, Paxson, all of them—
are exhibited
alongside
your drawings.

And the stage would be
surrounded by the ghosts and works of Kevin Red Star,
Fritz Scholder, Earl Biss, and John Nieto.

And Lakota fancy dancers would
dance around the artists

Lakota and Cheyenne drummers
would make sounds

so loud
your ear drums hurt.

Speaker Two: **Coyote 1**

These performance texts would be occasions for indigenous peoples to write their way into a new version of Western history, an invitation to offer their stories and narratives about the effects of Custer on their ancestors and on themselves.

Speaker One: **William Least Heat-Moon**

> These tellings would recover buried history,
> moments, representations, like ancient pictographs
> that write across "all of us—red, white, mixed"
> (Least Heat-Moon, 1999, p. 217).
>
> This theater would represent
> Custer and the American military
> as colonizers whose "undaunted courage"
> will no longer be recognized,
> or honored or celebrated.

Speaker Two: **Coyote 2**

> These historical performances—that is, the paintings by the great white painters—treat Custer and the past as if there were things that could be fixed in time, as performances that can be unproblematically staged in the present. Indeed, historical re-enactments of the Last Stand endow it with special powers. It stands outside time. One of white America's worst military defeats is reconstituted as a victory by these painters.

Speaker One: **Walter Benjamin**

> Memories are never innocent. In their own tangled ways, our memories embed us in history, culture, ideology, and politics. What the members of a social group remember is always over-determined, structured by the artifacts of political culture.

Speaker Two: **Barbara Kirshenblatt-Gimblett**

> I agree with Walter. To remember is to assemble a set of circumstances, pictures, music, costumes, and performances that re-creates a representation and a memory of what has happened before.
>
> But each remembering, each re-enactment of a last stand, is a new interpretive act.

Speaker One: **Sigmund Freud**

> Yes, Barbara, memories are social constructions.
> We remember, we re-create
> what we want to remember.

> We clothe these ghostly figures from the past
> in the dress of the times.
>
> We give them a language,
> a racial politic and an environmental ethic
> that fits our model of who we want to be
> in this new century.

Speaker Two: **Coyote 1**

> This is all self-serving.
> Let us take note.
> Remembering this way is
> how white society keeps racism alive
> and well in the present.

Speaker One: **Sherman Alexie**

> Custer and his Last Stand
> have fitted the white man's needs
> very well since 1876.
> It is getting close to 140 years.
>
> When white America honors white men who
> fought at the Last Stand,
> it honors men who were committed
> to implementing the violent political
> agenda of a host of nineteenth century
> American presidents:
> Jefferson, Jackson,
> Lincoln, Grant.
>
> This agenda included
> taking the land
> from and killing
> Indians, and enacting a
> form of democracy
> that was
> ethnically exclusive.

Speaker Two: **Narrator**

> So there is great danger
> in these historical masquerades.

The past is frozen in time.
Particular versions of whiteness and
white history are performed.

The sins of the past are ignored,
a peaceful bond between the imagined past and
the present is forged.

In this nostalgic space,
the benign past-ness of Custer comes alive.

Speaker One: **Coyote 1**

In turn, his historic journey of conquest
and his defeat are celebrated.
A territorial and cultural politic is honored.
The white community owns this land, this place, these meanings.

The white community and its city fathers
have the right to re-create on this land,
and in these cultural spaces their version
of the past, their version of how Custer
and his fallen soldiers helped
win the West for White America.

Speaker One: **Coyote 2**

Under such a utopian scenario, redemption for the handful of sins committed by Custer is sought and easily given. Indeed, redemption gives way to celebration, to a displacement of guilt, which never really existed.

Speaker Two: **Narrator**

This has been a theme throughout the last two chapters. Custer did no wrong. The visual imagery of Custer as the fallen hero reinforces this belief. He was killed by an unworthy enemy.

Speaker Two: **Coyote 2**

In producing this performance text, this celebratory reading of Red Horse and his drawings, I have attempted to disrupt history.
I have performed an alternative version of the Last Stand project (see Denzin, 2008, p.79).

ACT THREE, SCENE ONE

White Swan Goes Rogue?

Speaker One: **Narrator**

Min-a-tehas, Strikes Enemy, or White Swan. He was a Crow artist, and a scout for Custer.[9] He lived from 1851 to 1904.

Speaker Two: **Coyote 1**

He was assigned to Major Reno's troop.[10] He created a series of ledger drawings and hide paintings[11] for naturalist and artist Ernest Thompson Seton (Bradley, 1991, p. 2; Cowles, 1982, p. 54; Miller, 1957; Seton, 1897).

Speaker One: **Coyote 2**

He got famous this way.
He was a scout first,
then an artist.
Here is how one version
of the story goes.

Speaker Two: **Narrator**

White Swan was one of five Crow scouts who participated in the Little Bighorn fight on the skirmish line with the Reno column.

Speaker Two: **Douglas E. Bradley**

Around 2:30 p.m. on the 25th of June, 1876,
White Swan and the other Crow scouts
rode under the charge of Major Reno down
the Valley of the Little Bighorn River
toward the Indian camps.

They had orders to disperse the horse herd
in order to deprive the Lakota and Cheyenne
of battle mobility.

They completed this mission.
They returned to the picket line
drawn up by Reno.
They engaged in the ensuing battle.

White Swan was wounded by
a bullet that "ripped through his right hand and into
his right knee and thigh" (Bradley, 1991, p. 5; Crow, 1999, p. 117).

Speaker One: **Young Hawk**

I rescued White Swan from the thicket on the east side of the river. We were under attack by the Lakota.

Speaker Two: **White Swan**

My friends saved me. They tried to put me on a horse, but ended up putting me on a travois. They carried a white flag to identify us to the other scouts and troopers as we climbed the slope.

Speaker One: **Young Hawk**

Looking west, we saw that the Custer fight was over.

Speaker Two: **White Swan**

I had a limp for the rest of my life from this wound. A large part of my lower right hand had been shot away.

My hearing was also damaged. In 1898, I was awarded a pension of $17 a month from the U.S. Pension Agency (Bradley, 1991, p. 7).

ACT THREE, SCENE TWO

What White Swan Painted

Speaker One: **David Cowles**

White Swan painted scenes from this battle for the rest of his life. The Battle of the Little Bighorn appears in nearly all of his drawings (1982, p. 53).

Speaker Two: **John Medicine Crow**

His major work could be said to be this watercolor, ink, and pencil drawing on muslin cloth, measuring 35 by 87 inches.

(Stage left, a spotlight shines on reproductions of White Swan drawings from Crow, 1999, pp. 116–117; Cowles, 1982, pp. 52–53.)

Speaker One: **Tonto**

He paints himself into his paintings, unlike Red Horse.

Speaker Two: **Coyote 1**

Yes. He signed all his paintings with a drawing of a white swan, and he is always part of the action.

Speaker One: **Tonto**

Autoethnographic.

Speaker Two: **Douglas Bradley**

When a man had demonstrated his valor in battle and gotten enough battle trophies, known as coup, it was socially acceptable for him to paint them as a record, or pictograph, traditionally on a large hide. The record was worn around his shoulders as a cape, or hung in his tipi (1991, p. 8).

Speaker One: **David Cowles**

Doug is right. White Swan was a
skilled painter, he knew
how to use color, show action,
fill blank space and use diagonals,
repetition, overlapping sequences,
starkly drawn figures
(Bradley, 1991, p. 12; Cowles, 1982, p. 54).

Speaker Two: **John Medicine Crow**

It is a magnificent work.
It is more than a smaller version
of Red Horse's drawings.
It is narrative art, as all ledger art is.

A large encampment of tipis stands
at the center of this drawing.

At the lower right side
of the drawing White Swan is

shooting a Lakota
or Cheyenne warrior
who is on a horse.

White Swan is then chased across
the battlefield by enemy warriors,
also on horses.

We see red footprints
on the ground.
It is very dramatic.

He is shot.
He receives wounds
to his hand and leg.

On the right side of the drawing
are three vignettes.

In the first White Swan
is looking through
a telescope or spy glass,
spying on the Lakota
and Cheyenne camp.

In the second vignette
he is being taken from the battlefield
on a travois,
led by a soldier
holding a bugle.

In the bottom right scene
White Swan, on horseback,
is killing a Lakota
(Bradley, 1991, pp. 5–6; Crow, 1999, pp. 116–117).

Speaker One: **Coyote 1**

So why did you say,
White Swan goes rogue?
Is it because
he fought on
Custer's side?

Speaker Two: **Narrator**

> Yes. But I know it is never clear-cut in matters such as this. The Lakota and Cheyenne were enemies of the Crow Nation.

Speaker One: **Coyote 1**

> Surely Custer regarded all Indians as the enemy, even though he hired Crow scouts. Did White Swan really believe Custer would help the Crow get their lands back?

Speaker Two: **Tonto**

> Never mind. So what do we make of this Crow Indian artist and his drawings? He seemed to be on the side of Custer. He tried to kill Cheyenne and Lakota warriors. In the end, his people, the Crow Nation, met the same fate as the Lakota and Cheyenne.

Speakers One and Two (in unison): **Douglas Bradley** *and* **David Cowles**

> Listen, his work has been exhibited in major museums, including the Denver Art Museum, the Heard Museum in Tucson, and the Southwest Museum in Los Angeles.

Speaker One: **Douglas Bradley**

> He was a celebrity artist. People bought his
> paintings. He was also known as a "good Indian;"
> he stayed and fought with Reno, after all.
>
> When he died, August 11, 1904, he left no descendents.
>
> The patrimony of White Swan lies
>
> in his paintings, which speak louder
>
> and longer than any of his descendents (Bradley, 1991, pp. 14, 20).

Speaker Two: **Narrator**

> A museum with his name on it stands at Little Bighorn Battlefield National Monument. He was on the wrong side.

ACT THREE, SCENE THREE

Amos Bad Heart Buffalo, or Eagle Lance (1869-1913)

Speaker One: **Eric von Schmidt**

Aren't you done with these Indian artists?

Speaker Two: **Narrator**

Hold on! Let's briefly consider Amos Bad Heart Buffalo, or Eagle Lance, as he was known by the Oglala Lakota. He was a tribal historian, a painter, and he devoted his life to recording the Oglala Lakota way of life. He did a series of paintings about the Battle of the Little Bighorn (Blish, 1967).

Speaker One: **Leslie Tillett**

I also used the artwork of Amos Bad Heart Buffalo in my book, *Wind On the Buffalo Grass* (1976). I build my book around the Battle of the Little Bighorn and the issues the Indians of the Plains were fighting for (1976, p. x).

Speaker Two: **Coyote 1**

But Eagle Lance, nee Amos Bad Heart Buffalo, was born in 1869. How could he report on the battle?

Speaker One: **Leslie Tillett**

He inherited the position of band historian from his father, but his main informants were his two uncles, He Dog and Short Bull.[12] They told him stories about the battle and the band's history.

He was a self-taught artist and learned English from the soldiers at Fort Robinson. He enlisted as a scout in the U.S. Army in 1890. According to legend, he bought a used ledger from a clothing dealer in Crawford, Nebraska, in which he began his 415 drawings, using black pen, pencil, red ink, and blue, yellow, green, and brown crayons.

He worked on this project for two decades. It was divided into three sets. The third set narrates the battle of the Little Bighorn (Blish, 1967; Tillett, 1976, p. xiii).

Speaker Two: **Lakota Elder**

Eagle Lance was our historian (Tillett, 1976, p. xiii).

Speaker One: **Coyote 1**

Show me the drawings.

Speaker Two: **Coyote 2**

They are interspersed throughout Leslie Tillett's wonderful book. Nowhere does it say Amos looked at the work of White Swan or Red Horse, but there are clear parallels, and his drawings are located alongside many of the Red Horse drawings.

(Project images of "Indians leaving the battleground" drawings by Amos Bad Heart Buffalo and Red Horse.)

Speaker One: **Coyote 1**

The two drawings tell the same story: victorious Indians riding away from battle. Red Horse's style is more elaborated, more detailed. Together, the narratives give the battle a happy ending.

ACT THREE, SCENE FOUR

Whose Ending?

Speaker One: **Leslie Tillett**

But it was the beginning of a sad ending that was to come. Amos's drawings document the sadness, namely the murders of Crazy Horse and Sitting Bull by the Army, the ill-fated Ghost Dance Movement, the Battle at Wounded Knee.
He painted the end.

Speaker Two: **Richard A. Fox Jr.**

Not a real end. The Lakota and Cheyenne did end with the move to a reservation. But it is clear that Indian artwork about the battle has been largely ignored, in no small part because it does not reinforce conventional Last Stand imagery; that is, the gallant, defiant, last stand of history (1977, p. 161).

Speakers One, Two, and Three (in unison) **White Swan**, **Amos Bad Heart Buffalo**, *and* **Red Horse**

There is another last stand.
That is the last
stand we painted!
Our warriors were
gallant, defiant
and brave.

CHAPTER FIVE

Here Fell Custer:
An Autoethnography of a Painting

ACT ONE, SCENE ONE
Father and Son

Speaker One: **Narrator**

"Here Fell Custer An Autoethnography of a Painting" is a two-act play. Its topic is nostalgia, historical romance, realism, honoring dead white men. It offers a detailed interpretation of Eric von Schmidt's 1976 *Here Fell Custer*, which is the official National Park Service painting of the Battle of the Little Bighorn.[1] I contrast von Schmidt's painting with the anti-Custer artworks of Red Star, Biss, Scholder, Nieto, Mardon, White Swan, and Red Horse; I invoke the Adams-Becker painting. Its location in the Custer Battlefield Museum places it next to von Schmidt's painting; indeed, the Anheuser-Busch poster also hangs in the Little Bighorn Battlefield National Monument (Stekler, 1994, p. 281). What these paintings mean for Native Americans and their place in our national imagination is at issue.

Speaker Two: **Coyote 1**

Mr. Narrator, can you help me out? What do you want to show me?

Speaker One: **Narrator**

Thanks for the question, Coyote. It's pretty simple. Von Schmidt (1931–2007) claims that his painting is superior to all the paintings that came before his, including those of Adams, Paxson, and Red Horse. Yet he steals from all of these painters, contending that his realistic painting is more accurate than anything that came before.

I want to contest von Schmidt's artistic aesthetic while showing that his painting and his story about it mask the genocidal intent of Custer and the military. His painting stands outside history, and minimizes the place of the Lakota and Cheyenne in this battle.

Eric wrote a widely reprinted article about how he did the painting (von Schmidt, 1976, 1992). The article is an autoethnography of the painting and his relationship to it. His painting, and his autoethnography, keep the myth of Custer alive, and this is dangerous. This is what I want this play to show.

Speaker Two: **Brian W. Dippie**

"White artists . . . have constructed their versions of the battle, some imposed constraints on themselves—fidelity to dress, weaponry—some have gone beyond visual realism to psychological realism, capturing the horror . . . despair . . . hopelessness in the faces of the doomed soldiers. Eric von Schmidt's *Here Fell Custer* is a case in point" (Dippie, 1996, p. 213).

(Stage right, a spotlight shines on a reproduction of Here Fell Custer, *see http:// www.friendslittlebighorn.com/battle-art.htm; also von Schmidt, 1992, pp. 50–51.)*

Speaker One: **Eric von Schmidt**

For as long as I can remember I have had
a dream, as old as time. In it I am fleeing
for my life; I try to hide; I am discovered; I am killed.

Speaker Two: **Narrator**

Amazing, Eric, that is some dream. What does this dream have to do with your painting?

Speaker One: **Eric von Schmidt**

In order to create my painting, I had to paint myself into it. Like the little boy in the dream, I was running and hiding, afraid of being killed. Once I got myself into the picture, all the other pieces fell into place.

※ ※ ※

Bumper Sticker, or Painted Letters as if Scrawled on a Car

(Projected onto a screen in white letters on a dark background.)

> # CUSTER OR BUST HER

Speaker Two: **Narrator**

I've had a dream like yours, Eric. I'll talk about my dream in chapter seven. But in it, I am lost, I cannot find my bicycle. I am walking in darkness. I fall through space.

Speaker One: **Eric von Schmidt**

Fair enough.

Speaker Two: **Western Art Critic**

Most artists have been faithful to the higher truth of heroism on the grand scale perfectly expressed by Eric's father, Harold von Schmidt (1893–1982), in his painting *Custer's Last Stand,* reproduced in *Esquire* magazine in 1950 (Dippie, 1996, p. 213).

Speaker One: **Narrator**

Because there were no white survivors of Custer's Last Stand, the white Custer artists were free to draw on their own imaginations.

Speaker Two: **Coyote 1**

The Indians, like Red Horse and White Swan, left vivid pictographic records.

Speaker One: **Erie von Schmidt**

Yeah, but as I said before, those Red Horse drawings had very little detail, and unlike my father's painting, Red Horse made no effort to interpret the meaning of the battle.

Speaker Two: **Coyote 1**

> Sorry, Eric. In the last chapter we pretty much demolished the myth that Red Horse did not interpret the battle.

Speaker One: **Coyote 2**

> Good point. I've also noticed that Eric is pretty complimentary about his father's painting. He says it combines elements of the romantic frontal and nostalgic styles.

Speaker One: **Coyote 1**

> He says he even posed in his dad's Custer painting as both trooper and Indian.

Speaker Two: **Coyote 2**

> Yeah, but he also says there are inaccuracies in his father's painting. The uniforms and equipment of the soldiers are wrong. Cavalry were not issued blue shirts during this time period. But there are other authentic touches, such as Custer's short barreled pistols (von Schmidt, 1976, p. 2).

Speaker One: **Eric von Schmidt**

> My father thought Custer a glory-hunting ass
> (von Schmidt, 1976, p. 2). I showed him my
> unfinished painting. He studied it for
> several minutes.
> "There is no black in nature," he said.
> It was his way of saying, "put in more
> atmosphere."
> I admit I had hoped for a
> bit more (von Schmidt, 1992, p. 60).

Speaker Two: **Coyote 1**

> Dad was not being very nice!

Speaker One: **Eric von Schmidt**

> "My painting took over five years of work to complete. The actual canvas was moved ten times, in and out of three different states. . . . One and a half divorces resulted" (von Schmidt, 1992, p. 59).

As you know, there are at least one thousand depictions of the fight—Adams, Becker, Fuchs, Steinegger, Cary, Waud, Paxson. But in all the pictures, the viewer's vantage point was that of the attacking Indian . . .

I felt it was important to give the viewer a sense of what the troopers were experiencing as their individual deaths pressed in upon them. Dad didn't do this (1976, p. 2).

Speaker Two: **Coyote 1**

So this is a father-son thing. Who paints the most accurate painting?

Speaker One: **Robert Utley**

Of the hundreds of Last Stand paintings, Eric's stands out as the most haunting and evocative of what it must have been like at that very moment on Custer Hill. No glory here, only death and tragedy.[2]

Speaker Two: **Eric von Schmidt**

Dad could have said something like that!

Speaker One: **Charles Rankin**

Eric's painting captures the true scale of the battlefield, giving the viewer the visceral sense of being there, of what it must have been like for the soldiers.

He re-creates the qualities of confusion, lost cause. This makes the painting so disquieting. A realism that is so real, *that* real—and with it the horror, the hopelessness that Custer's men faced.

We will never know what it was really like on that hill that day, but Eric has brought us closer to the genuine actuality than anyone else ever has, or ever will.

Speaker Two: **Coyote 2**

Genuine actuality, real reality? What does he mean? Whose version of genuine?

ACT ONE, SCENE TWO

This Eric von Schmidt?

Speaker One: **Coyote 1**

Is this Eric von Schmidt the same guy who composed folk songs, inspired the folk song movement, was friends with Bob Dylan, Joan Baez, and Pete Seeger, and appeared with Bob Dylan in the Newport Folk Festival in 1965, the year Dylan went electric?

Speaker Two: **Tonto**

Same man. He also created album covers for Baez and Cisco Houston and Pete Seeger.

Speaker One: **Bob Dylan**

He was a good friend. A mentor. Many times he invited us into his glad, mad, sad, biting, exciting, frightening, crabby, happy, enlightening, hugging, chugging world.

On the cover of my album *Bringing It All Back Home,* there is a picture of one of his records.

I wrote in the liner notes for one of his albums, "He could sing the bird off the wire."[3]

Speaker Two: **Art Critic**

And von Schmidt tries the same thing with his big Custer painting. You mean, take on the hard assignment, paint the impossible.

Speaker One: **Coyote 2**

I guess so. But I don't get it. Why would a lefty, a progressive, a 1960s civil rights activist like von Schmidt paint the battle from the soldier's perspective?

Speaker Two: **Narrator**

Why even paint the battle?

Speaker One: **Coyote 1**

It's a daddy thing. But then, isn't it always a daddy thing?

Speaker Two: **Tonto**

So now Bob Dylan and von Schmidt's father are in the painting, too?

Speaker One: **Eric von Schmidt**

Twenty years after dad's painting for *Esquire,* I caught that damnable Custer fever that rises off the Little Bighorn (1976, p. 2).

Speaker Two: **Coyote 2**

Go figure?

ACT ONE, SCENE THREE

Correct Details

Speaker One: **Eric von Schmidt**

I read everything I could get my hands on. I began to feel that there was something missing in all the other paintings, how it felt for the soldiers. But there was more.

Speaker Two: **Narrator**

What else was missing?

Speaker One: **Eric von Schmidt**

Historical detail is missing. The previous painters had their facts all wrong. They had not studied military history.

Speaker Two: **E. S. Paxson**

Hold on, Eric. I studied military history. I interviewed soldiers. I wrote Godfrey. I worked twenty years to get the details right.

Speaker One: **John Mulvany**

Hey, like Edgar, I visited the battlefield. I studied the dress and equipment of the cavalry, looked at photographs. I studied Indian dress. I went back to the battlefield. I worked two years on this painting (Taft, 1953, p. 135).

Speaker Two: **Eric von Schmidt**

Yeah, but you guys got the headgear and uniforms all wrong. You had the Indians in the wrong place. The terrain was inaccurately depicted. Like the other Custer painters, your theory of the battle was wrong.

The soldiers were not outgunned—the entire village had only a small number of repeating rifles. The soldiers' guns did not malfunction. Custer was not killed by arrows. He was shot in the left temple and left breast.

Speakers One and Two (in unison): **Paxson** *and* **Mulvany**

And you base these assertions on what? Whose evidence? You think you were more accurate than we were?

Speaker One: **Tonto**

Eric, are you going to answer this question? What else did the white guys get wrong?

Speaker Two: **Eric von Schmidt**

They put Custer in the wrong place. They forgot the village. They put the battle in the wrong place. They did not know how to center the action in the painting.

Speaker One: **Tonto**

The first paintings, as Eric notes, had Custer in the center of the battlefield scene, on Custer Hill, in the foreground, a kind of poster treatment, dramatic, vivid, a large event on a small canvas.

Speaker Two: **Coyote 1**

For the white painters, this painterly, frontal style changed around the turn of the twentieth century. Custer and his gallant men moved to the background, wild swirling Indians became foreground (von Schmidt, 1976, p. 2).

Speaker One: **Narrator**

I'm not sure on this. Is this what Eric says? I stood in front of Paxson's painting for an hour last summer and I sure saw a lot of soldiers, front and center.

I look at *Here Custer Fell* and Custer is only slightly off-center in the painting, surrounded by dying men, with attacking Indians in the distance, charging up Custer Hill.

Speaker Two: **Eric von Schmidt**

I mean the older paintings lacked realism, and an accuracy of detail. These elements did not come together until after the poster and frontal styles were abandoned.

This gave painters like me the opportunity to play with landscape, the placement of the village, the ridge, viewpoint, horizon, the middle distance (von Schmidt, 1992, p. 52).

Speaker One: **Curator**

Eric, whose realism? The older painters followed the style of their times, and did it pretty well. How can you criticize them for doing something that had not yet been created?

Speaker Two: **Coyote 1**

Don't let Eric off the hook. He does not have to trash the nineteenth century painters in order to produce his painting.

Speaker One: **Eric von Schmidt**

Not so hard! Give me a break! I persuaded a western painter friend to take some black-and-white Polaroid snapshots of me running around dressed as either cavalryman or Indian.

(Stage right, spotlight shines on photographic reproductions of eight Polaroid shots of von Schmidt posing for his painting. von Schmidt, 1992, pp. 54–55).

Speaker Two: **Coyote 1**

And this is realism. You dress up like an Indian and have a friend take your picture.

Speaker One: **Curator**

Coyote, do you really understand what realism is? Realism is an ideology. It involves the belief that the world, a thing, can be accurately, objectively recorded, painted, photographed, transcribed, performed.

> Realism is the bedrock assumption of historical art. It enforces an authoritarian or God's-eye-view of reality. Realist texts underwrite official versions of history.
>
> In realism, reality is established via the consensus of a group that has power. The realistic text has transparency, immediacy, visual authority, authenticity.
>
> The realist text has detail, nuance, color, perspective. It invokes everydayness, the taken-for-granted world, appearances as they should or would be.
>
> It is located *in* history and invokes historical detail. It relies on first-person accounts, witnesses, direct reporting of events, photographs (Denzin, 1995, pp. 21–22).

Speaker Two: **Coyote 1**

So this is the war of the realists. Eric von Schmidt says his realism is better than everybody else's realism.

Speaker One: **Narrator** *(to audience)*

For the white painters, these Custer paintings take a long time. Paxson, as we said, labored twenty years. Mardon took several years to complete the *Battle of Greasy Grass*. John Mulvany needed two years.

Speaker Two: **Coyote 1**

Red Horse made his drawings in less than one year, in 1881.

Speaker One: **E. T. Sutton**

White Swan made his drawings for me in one day, August 31, 1897 (Bradley, 1991, p. 7).

Speaker Two: **Eric von Schmidt**

Yes, but those Indian paintings were not realistic (von Schmidt, 1976, p. 1).

Speaker One: **Tonto**

So they don't meet your criteria of realism.

Speaker Two: **Eric von Schmidt**

> I got a better sense of the battle from the Cassilly Adams painting and Otto Becker lithograph. My first viewing was in a barroom in Durango, Colorado, in 1946. The Anheuser-Busch copy of *Custer's Last Stand* hung over the mirror behind the bar. I was underage and thirsty (von Schmidt, 1976, p. 1).

Bumper Sticker, or Painted Letters as if Scrawled on a Car

(Projected onto a screen in white letters on a dark background)

CUSTER OR BUST HER

ACT ONE, SCENE FOUR

Eric Gets to Work

Speaker One: **Narrator** *(to audience)*

> In his essay "Sunday at the Little Big Horn with George," Eric tells us how he made his painting. This gives us a unique vantage on the work, for few other Custer painters offered autoethnographies of their work.

Speaker Two: **Eric von Schmidt**

> It seemed like a good idea when "I rashly tacked up the canvas—all five by thirteen feet—in the summer of 1970. Rashness was quite in keeping with the subject—George Armstrong Custer. Why not do an epic-scale painting, and perhaps, at long last, *get it right?*"
>
> As the months wore on and I learned more, the empty canvas became a deadening reflection of my state of mind.
>
> Every day the canvas got bigger, like Melville's great white whale (1992, p. 52).

Speaker One: **Narrator**

It seems that the project developed through several phases and stages, starting in the summer of 1970, and completed in 1976 (von Schmidt, 1992, p. 52).

Speaker Two: **Coyote 1**

Do we really care?

Speaker One: **Eric von Schmidt**

I had a 3-by-5-inch black-and-white reproduction of the earliest photograph of the battlefield that I could find. I had no sketches.

Speaker Two: **Coyote 1**

Eric does not say if it was John Fouch's July, 1877 photo.[4]

Speaker One: **Eric von Schmidt**

On New Year's Day, 1971, I got up and painted until the sun set that night and half of Montana was on that blank 5-by-13-foot canvas. I got up the next day. I was stunned. It was beautiful. I had left nothing out. I was blocked. There was no way to get back in.

Speaker Two: **Tonto**

So Eric, what did you do?

Speaker One: **Eric von Schmidt**

I read some more, wrote some letters to experts about weapons, buttons, saddlebags, trivia. I visited the Smithsonian and looked at those Red Horse drawings.

Speaker Two: **Coyote**

This must have been about the time when you played dress-up, and had your friend take your picture of you running around as an Indian.

Speaker One: **Eric von Schmidt**

Yes, all that running around gave me a way to get back in the painting.
In one of Elizabeth Custer's books, I came across the lyrics to "Garryowen," including:

We are the boys no man dares dun
If he regards a whole skin.⁵

   I knew this was the guidon to follow. I had to be true to that song. I had to take the viewpoint of the troopers on the ridge. I had to let my lovely landscape go.

Speaker Two: **Coyote 1**

So he let Custer's wife and that dumb song talk him into going in this direction. She spent her entire life after the battle defending her husband, and now Eric climbs on that bandwagon, defending Custer, rewriting the Last Stand, making each dead soldier a hero.

Speaker One: **Elizabeth Custer**

You hush up. My husband was a great man. President Grant tried to make a scapegoat of him, blaming him for the massacre. But my husband was a great man, a brilliant leader of men. He and his men fought against overwhelming odds. They were wiped out defending their position, country, and the U.S. flag to the last man.

Speaker Two: **Tonto**

So von Schmidt places himself right back inside the Last Stand discourse, aligning himself with the pro-Custer camp.

Speaker One: **Coyote 1**

He says the Lakota and Cheyenne warriors "swarmed like stinging ants" (von Schmidt, 1976, p. 3).
   That is not very complimentary.

ACT ONE, SCENE FIVE

Eric Paints Himself into His Painting

Speaker Two: **Eric von Schmidt**

I wanted to get it right. I wanted to tell the story from the soldiers' point of view. Like I said, I had to get rid of the landscape. Reading the lyrics to "Garryowen" helped get me back in the painting.

164 Chapter Five

Speaker One: **Eric von Schmidt**

Then I had my dream again, the one about fleeing for my life, trying to hide, being discovered and killed.

Oddly, the little Polaroid photos of me running around dressed as a trooper captured this sense of dread and loss I felt in my dream.

There was something about the image of that trooper, his gait, his look; he was a marked man, doomed.

So I painted my little running man—me—dressed up as cavalry at the far right of the canvas (1992, p. 52).

Speaker Two: **Coyote 1**

Who is painting whom? Who and what is being drawn into this painting, the event, the battle, history? Or is the painting *painting* the painter? This is starting to sound more and more like a visual autoethnography and less and less like a realist portrayal of the battle.

Speaker One: **Coyote 2**

I'd say the painting has taken control of the painter.

Speaker Two: **Eric von Schmidt**

Shut up! Putting my little running man into the canvas shattered the purity of the painting. My beautiful landscape no longer worked. You could say penetration, a rape had occurred.

The landscape had been defiled, the battle had begun.

Speaker One: **Ms. Coyote**

Hold on one minute. A rape happened just because you painted yourself into your blankety-blank painting? *Rape. Rape. Rape.* I can't believe you are talking this way.

Your white soldiers raped, plundered, and destroyed my people, and you think you can use the word *rape* to describe what happened in your painting when you put your little running man into the scene?

Give me a break!

Speaker Two: **Coyote 2**

Eric, you have some explaining to do.

Speaker One: **Eric von Schmidt**

Hey, I'm sorry. I did not mean it this way. Even after I put the little guy in there, the painting was still a mystery. I had no clue where to go next (1992, p. 53).

(Project a 1974 photo of Eric von Schmidt in his studio in Henniker, New Hampshire. He is seen standing in front of photographs of Native American and military scenes. See http://www.friendslittlebighorn.com/images/ericvonschmidt/ evspainting-2.jpg)

Speaker Two: **Red Horse**

> I know you came to the Smithsonian and looked at my drawings. But you did not like them. You said I gave you no clues on dress, weapons, uniforms. But you do not understand. My paintings were about my people and how they experienced the battle. That is what our art is all about—a historical record for a community.
>
> I was telling the story of the battle for my people. Whether their coats were blue or red is not important.

Speaker One: **Eric von Schmidt**

> Mea culpa, Red Horse. I forgot about how pictographic narratives work. However, I was struck by all the tipis you painted. They seemed to go on for page after page. You were telling us that the Indian village was huge, it extended for over three miles. So there must have been a lot of tipis.

Speaker Two: **Red Horse**

> I did not make my drawings for white people! I don't care about how little you learned from them. And yes, Custer underestimated the size of our village.

(Stage right, a photographic reproduction from Red Horse tipi drawings—Plate XI, Indian Camp, from von Schmidt, 1992, p. 56.)

Speaker One: **Eric von Schmidt**

> Early morning, June 25, 1876. From their vantage point fifteen miles away, the advance scouts could not see the Indian camp. All they could see was smoke rising from the valley of the Little Bighorn, then the immense sprawl of grazing horses came into view, the Lakota horse herd (1992, p. 57).
>
> Red Horse did not paint this herd; he just had rows and rows and rows of tipis.

ACT ONE, SCENE SIX
Eric Hits Another Roadblock

Speaker One: **Eric von Schmidt**

I returned to my studio in Florida convinced that I needed to show as much of the encampment on the west side of the river as possible.

Speaker Two: **Narrator**

Mardon did this, too, but Mardon makes the distance between the camp and the soldiers much smaller. Eric pushes the camp to the upper edge of his painting, and places the soldiers at a great distance from the encampment.

Speaker One: **Eric von Schmidt**

I wanted to capture the psychological effect on the soldiers of seeing this huge camp on the near horizon. I'm the first painter, in the thousand-plus paintings, I believe, to show a trooper taking his own life.

Speaker Two: **Running Man**

Hey, he turned me into a dead man. At first, I was running across the lower right corner of the painting, escaping. Then he got back to Florida and he turned me into a kneeling suicide! How would you feel if he did that to you?

Speaker One: **Eric von Schmidt**

Come on, Running Man, I had no choice. I was acknowledging historical reality. It must have been terrifying for those men. Besides, by killing him this way, I stopped the left-to-right movement across the canvas. This allowed me to get greater control over the painting and where it was going.

Speaker Two: **Red Horse**

Eric says I ignored the fact that the Indians said they could see very little because of the smoke and the dust. He's right. I did not do this. The smoke and dust did not bother our braves, nor stop them.

Eric says I was giving a pictorial account of the battle, not the actuality of the battle. He says this is why I did not show diminished visibility.

He is wrong. I drew pictures of the battle as its significant moments unfolded, attack, counterattack, attack, dead soldiers, dead Lakota, dead horses, leaving the battlefield, aftermath.

My drawings, like Mardon's painting, reflected the whole battle, a twenty-four hour period.

Eric collapses the story into thirty minutes, maybe less. How can you claim to tell the whole story when you leave out so much of it?

Speaker One: **Tonto**

And that is the point. There were two different battles: the one Eric valorizes, and the one Red Horse, White Swan, and others drew.

Speaker Two: **Coyote 1**

It is more than apples and oranges. It is more than who got it right and who got it wrong. The question truly is: Whose story are you going to tell, and whose story are you going to believe and honor?

Speaker One: **Tonto**

And whose story is the official story? Remember, Eric's painting is on the official National Park Service brochure, not Red Horse's.

Speaker Two: **National Park Service Ranger**

Hold on. On our website, we reproduce a ledger art drawing by Wooden Leg depicting him seizing a soldier's carbine during Reno's retreat. We also have a link to the Indian Memorial, "Peace Through Unity."[6]

Speaker One: **Tonto**

Yeah, but your official story of the battle is von Schmidt's, who was born fifty years after the last dead were buried. Why not from someone who actually lived through it?

Speaker Two: **Eric von Schmidt**

I had my story to tell. I went back to Red Horse. He had all those dead troopers, "grotesque tumbled flesh" (1992, p. 57).

I needed a white man's counterpoint.

Speaker One: **Tonto**

But there were no white men there.

Speaker Two: **Eric von Schmidt**

There were tons of burial reports, testimonies, even some consensus on who was where on the hill. I was able to visualize who was where on the ridge. This helped me see where I would place them within the framework of the composition (p. 57).

Speaker One: **Archaeologist**

Why didn't you go back to Doug Scott's study, and other studies of what happened, based on the find spots of bullets, bones, and other remains? That would be more accurate than anyone's half-remembered report.

Speaker Two: **Tonto**

Of course, every other white painter who came before Eric had figured out who was where, because they all read the same inaccurate reports. Adams and Becker named the figures along the bottoms of their paintings. It's not like Eric was working from scratch.

Speaker One: **Coyote 1**

Still, it is amazing. Amazing. Eric knew who was where on the ridge.

Speaker Two: **Eric von Schmidt**

Yup. Two days after the battle, burial parties identified men found near Custer—Smith, Tom Custer, Col. Yates, Martin, Hughes, Cooke.

This information gave me the psychological concept of the painting, the viewpoint of the trooper. But the pictorial concept of the painting was still unclear.

Speaker One: **Coyote 1**

Eric doesn't get Tonto's sarcasm. I don't think he heard what the archaeologist was saying, either.

Speaker Two: **Coyote 2**

Back to Eric. The pictorial concept of the painting would not be an issue for Red Horse. He told his story from the point of view of the warriors, moving from one scene of destruction, or victory, to the next.

Speaker One: **Tonto**

Eric's problem is that he stops time. He freezes the battle into one moment, one time, the time just before death. This is the difference between Western figurative art and Indian pictorial art. But the National Park Service decided to privilege the Western version.

Speaker Two: **Eric von Schmidt**

Give me a break. Let me tell you how I worked this out. You are right. I'm painting the end of the battle, the denouement.

So if it was really close to the end, then Custer would be down, dying. He had a serious chest wound; there would be blood.

Speaker One: **Coyote 1**

You said he was shot in the left temple and left breast.

Speaker Two: **Eric von Schmidt**

Now I had to put the parts of the painting together. In my painting, I've singled out only those known to have been found near Custer.

The figure of Sgt. Hughes holding the guidon came first. He is in the front center of the painting. Then came Custer, buckskin jacket, hatless on one knee, wounded.

Then, left to right in the painting are: Lieutenant A. Smith, wearing a vest, behind a dead horse; crawling, Captain Thomas Custer; down the slope, Captain George W. Yates, wearing a buckskin jacket and black hat. Farther down the hill are Lieutenant William Riley, near the sage brush clump, and Trumpeter Henry Voss. The man just above the horse's head is Lieutenant W. W. Cooke (von Schmidt, 1976, p. 3; 1992, p. 59).

Speaker One: **Tonto**

Wow! Is this what you white folks call historical accuracy? *This* is being true to reality? But you are making it all up. Nobody was there! Besides, lots of people were dead. Nobody could accurately write how they were positioned.

Speaker Two: **Coyote 1**

I just looked at Paxson's painting. You know, your placement of figures is pretty much just like his!

Speaker One: **Eric von Schmidt**

Hush! I was putting this together myself. Once I got the foreground into place, I was able to move farther down the slope. I painted in nameless dead soldiers, dead horses, and scattered equipment (1992, p. 59).

Speaker Two: **Coyote 1**

Yeah, but Eric, your placement is exactly the same as Paxson's. This can't have been an accident?

ACT ONE, SCENE SEVEN

Stuck Again

Speaker One: **Coyote 1**

Eric, so where were you going with this?

Speaker Two: **Eric von Schmidt**

I got stuck again. I slogged along like this for about two years. The painting had become my personal reality.

It haunted me. I could not escape.

Every day I looked into the forsaken eyes of those dying men. I stared at their "broken, crushed, smashed, trampled bodies. I saw an obscene jumble of twisted shapes, stripped of dignity, devoid of hope" (1992, p. 59).

And this is what I had painted! I was stopped dead in my tracks. I had the pictorial concept: these pitiful men. But what next?

Speaker One: **Narrator**

And your father was no help. He told you to put in more atmosphere.

Speaker Two: **Tonto**

So you had these twisted, dead, and wounded bodies on the top of the hill. This was your painting? Here fell Custer? That was your story, your concept? This is how the official story should read?

Speaker One: **Eric von Schmidt**

Yup, and I was just plain bored and I was tired of painting white people (1992, p. 60).

Speaker One: **Coyote 1**

Really? Why, for heaven's sake? You were only telling the white man's version. How could you be tired?

Speaker Two: **Eric von Schmidt**

I just had to paint me some injuns! (1992, p. 60).

Speaker One: **Tonto**

INJUNS!

Speaker Two: **Eric von Schmidt**

> I went back to pictures some friends had taken of me riding horses, when I was growing up. In many of them, I was wearing only a breechcloth.

(Stage right, a spotlight shines on a photograph of von Schmidt on horseback dressed as an Indian model (1992, p. 59).)

Eric von Schmidt dressed as Indian model, courtesy of Caitlin von Schmidt and Montana Historical Society

Speaker One: **Coyote 1**

> Was this when you were playing cowboys and Indians with your friends?

Speaker Two: **Eric von Schmidt**

> I could not figure out how to fill in the space between the top of the ridge—with Custer and his boys—and the Indian village and the tipis across the river.
>
> So I started painting Indians in that big space in the middle of my canvas.
>
> I just couldn't stop painting Indians. Once you've painted one, you've got to paint more (1992, p. 60).

172 Chapter Five

Speaker One: **Coyote 1**

> Really, I feel the same way about painting white people. Once one of them shows up in your neighborhood, you can expect a flood of others.

Speaker Two: **Eric von Schmidt**

> I kept studying the old photograph. Why didn't that old photographer do something about scale? Why didn't he send an assistant down to the bottom of the ridge?

Speaker One: **Tonto**

> Maybe he didn't have your obsession.

ACT ONE, SCENE EIGHT

Custer or Bust Her

Speaker One: **Coyote 1**

> So how did you solve your little problem?

Speaker Two: **Eric von Schmidt**

> "My new bride and I were in Mexico. I decided I had to go back to the battlefield. We drove her little Volkswagen—with CUSTER OR BUST HER written across the trunk—straight from Mexico to the battlefield and arrived at dusk."(p. 61)
>
> It looked just like the old photograph. I ran down the hill, right into that old black-and-white print.
>
> I spent the next five days sketching and taking pictures. I solved the distance problem by painting an accurate "landscape that matched the view of the old photograph." (p. 61).
>
> Then I asked the park ranger and his wife to ride down the slope, toward the river, stopping about every fifty yards, so I could sketch them.
>
> When they reached the river, my scale problems were over.

Speaker One: **Tonto**

> So you painted in the missing details in the old photograph. Didn't you start out with this photo in 1970? Wow! What does correct mean here? Correct in whose eyes?

Speaker Two: **Eric von Schmid**t

> If you put it that way, I was back to square one. Yes. But there was a lot more to it.
>
> I discovered I had too many Indians. I'd painted in forty Indians, you know, with loving care and detail.
>
> When I got back East, I discovered they were twice as big as they should be, given the scale of the painting.

Speaker One: **Coyote 1**

> Wow, even though it was 5 by 13 feet! I mean, there were three thousand in the village and you painted only forty.

Speaker Two: **Coyote 2**

> How did you know you had too many Indians?

Speaker One: **Eric von Schmidt**

> Don't be snippy. I had forty men, forty horses. That was way too many men, and way too many horses.
>
> One hundred and sixty hoofs. Six months of lost labor.

Speaker Two: **Coyote 1**

> What a pity.

Speaker One: **Eric von Schmidt**

> Then, one boozy evening, I was still looking for the middle distance. I stabbed a finger on the canvas, and said, RIGHT HERE. And here it was, the middle point.
>
> Two men, one standing, one sitting on a white horse. They are barely bigger than the head of pin (p. 61).

Speaker Two: **Narrator**

> I see them—they are below and to the left of Hughes, who is holding the guidon.

Speaker One: **Coyote 2**

> So you were slightly drunk, knew you had too many Indians, and as luck would have it, a paint-smeared finger found the right spot on the canvas.

Speaker Two: **Eric von Schmidt**

So that's how you guys do it. Drink a little whisky and jab a finger at the canvas.

And you said Red Horse was not realistic enough in terms of historical detail.

Speaker Two: **Eric von Schmidt**

Hold on. Once these two little men were in the right spot, I could bring the Indians and their horses back into the picture.

Speaker One: **Coyote 1**

So it took white bodies to define the space for brown Indian bodies.

Speaker Two: **Eric von Schmidt**

And I say to those of you who want to be painters: don't, for God's sake, become a painter of historical themes on a grand scale (p. 61).

Speaker One: **Coyote 2**

Eric, you have not responded to me or Coyote. Maybe you should sip a scotch instead, but do you have no answer? You call this being realistic?

Speaker One: **Tonto**

Indeed. You can sure say that again. Maybe there should be another rule. White men should not paint Native Americans.

ACT TWO, SCENE ONE

Making Sense of Eric

Speaker One: **Narrator**

Let's summarize. Where are we in this little anatomy of a painting?

Speaker Two: **Tonto**

Let's start with the title. "Here Fell Custer."

Speaker One: **Eric von Schmidt**

This is no last stand. By the time Custer dies, the battle is over. So I painted a scene of death, not a scene of struggle.

Speaker Two: **Narrator**

> Your title places your project outside the thousand earlier Last Stand paintings. Those paintings were about a battle that was ongoing—a last stand, bitter to the end.
>
> In your painting, the battle is over. The title says it all.

Speaker One: **Tonto**

> So why the Indians? Why did you even paint us into the frame?

Speaker Two: **Coyote 1**

> I have the same question. You have us on horses, racing around, up and down the hill, back and forth from river to the ridge.

Speaker One: **Coyote 2**

> You do have the village with our tipis arranged in camps across the river. That was nice of you.

Speaker Two: **Tonto**

> But you don't paint us with any detail at all.
> We are fuzzy figures in the painting:
> no headgear, nobody is dressed in
> proud war regalia, no colored headdresses,
> or bright loin cloths, or beaded jackets,
> or beaded leather leggings, or
> colorful war shirts.

Speaker One: **Coyote 1**

> We are a bland presence on the canvas.
> And our women and children are missing.

Speaker Two: **Eric von Schmidt**

> I needed Indians to fill in that big center gap on my canvas. All the other painters before me had the Indians on Last Stand ridge, but in my version they would have been gone when Custer fell.

Speaker One: **Coyote 2**

> So if your Lakota and Cheyenne are gone before Custer falls, then you aren't showing the battle.

Speaker One: **Tonto**

> So this is not the battle, which Red Horse painted so gloriously. You don't even have soldiers fighting Indians. Indeed, your soldiers have their backs turned away from the attacking Indians. Not very smart soldiers—or not very accurate painter.

ACT TWO, SCENE TWO

The Center of the Painting

Speaker One: **Narrator**

> Now I get it. Eric tells us he had a traditional academic background as a painter. A painting is a composition. A painting, in the classic sense, has to follow rules. It has to have a pictorial content, a center, a focus.
>
> It has to be an accurate, realistic representation of something. That thing has to be placed on the canvas in terms of another set of rules, including distance, spacing, perspective, horizon line, and action.
>
> Furthermore, a painting has to have a central psychological concept, or a point of view, both for the viewer of the painting and for the person or object(s) in the painting itself. The point of view must draw the person into the psychological center of the painting.

Speaker Two: **Eric von Schmidt**

> The psychological point of view in my painting is that of the dying men on the ridge—what they saw and how they felt about it. That is, once they saw the size of the Indian camp, they knew they were dead men. I knew this was what I wanted to paint.

Speaker One: **Coyote 1**

> Eric claims to be reproducing reality. But he is abiding by the old rules of the game which don't necessarily reproduce reality, whatever that may be. He can't have both. He is fooling himself.

Speaker Two: **Narrator**

> Coyote, you are right. We see this in the way that Eric talks about the composition of the painting—what would go where—as being difficult, especially the distance between Indians, and their camp and the ridge.

Speaker One: **Coyote 2**

> The old photograph was important for him. He seemed to have wanted a painting that matched that picture.

Speaker Two: **Tonto**

> But Coyote, we know photographs are not to be trusted.

Speaker One: **Eric von Schmidt**

> But there was nothing in the photograph, just the ridge and the river far below.

Speaker Two: **Narrator**

> So the painting unfolds in steps. We can offer the steps as a list.

※ ※ ※

(Stage right, a spotlight shines on a list of steps involved in von Schmidt's painting.)

1. The painter paints an original semiabstract landscape;
2. The painter studies historical materials;
3. The painter dreams his way out of his dream into his painting as a little running man;
4. The painter studies Red Horse's drawings;
5. The painter takes Polaroid snapshots of himself in various poses;
6. The painter visualizes where the men were on the ridge. This helps him elaborate the psychological concept of the painting;
7. The painter uses an eight-by-ten glossy of the panoramic view from the hill to the river;
8. The painter brings the pictorial and psychological contends of the painting together;
9. The painter paints the Indians (Injuns) into the painting;
10. The painter and his new wife return to the battlefield and take more photos;
11. The painter removes Indians from his painting; and
12. Intoxicated, the painter finds the middle distance in the painting and paints in the two little figures.

Speaker One: **Curator**

This took five years. Was he working with *The Law of the Golden Section?* I understand the law established by the ancient architect called Vitruvius, and it states:

"For a space divided into equal parts to be agreeable and aesthetic, between the smallest and largest parts there must be the same relationship as between this larger part and the whole space" (Parramon,1990).

Speaker Two: **Coyote 1**

This means he had to divide the spaces between the ridge and the river into equal, or agreeable parts. Since there was no photograph showing what was in that space, he had to fill in the blank spaces with Indians, horses, and soldiers. The terrain gave us cover from Custer's men, and we used it.

Speaker One: **Eric von Schmidt**

Right. It was a question of balance, unity, and proportion. If the focus was on Custer and his men at the top of the ridge, then everything below the ridge had to be in balance, size-wise. For the sake of the composition, I also needed the psychological middle distance.

Speaker Two: **Tonto**

And of course, that would be two white men.

Speaker One: **Coyote 2**

Fortunately for us, Red Horse and White Swan were not governed by this painterly aesthetic. Maybe that is another reason that Eric did not like Red Horse's drawings.

—※—※—※—

Bumper Sticker

(Projected onto a screen in red letters on a white background)

> **CUSTER DIED FOR HIS SINS**

—※—※—※—

ACT TWO, SCENE THREE

What if Custer Did Not Fall Here?

Speaker One: **Narrator**

Let's go back to Eric's title, *Here Fell Custer.*

Speaker Two: **Coyote**

Yeah.

Speaker One: **Tonto**

We have to assume, for the sake of historical accuracy, that he died or fell on this ridge.

Speaker Two: **Coyote**

There is a monument on Custer Hill that reads:

> G.A. CUSTER
> BVT. MAJ. GEN.
> LT. COL.
> 7TH U.S. CAV.
> FELL HERE
> JUNE 25 1876

Speaker One: **Narrator**

Eric didn't have to go very far to find the title for his painting.

Speaker Two: **Tonto**

More than a few Native Americans and archaeologists dispute the point that he fell here. Some suggest he died closer to the Little Bighorn River and the Medicine Tail Coulee ford (Brust, Pohanka, & Bernard, 2005, p. 8; Scott, 1999, p. 171).

Speaker One: **Coyote**

So what if Custer did not fall here? If he didn't, then Eric and all those other painters would have to change their paintings.

Speaker Two: **Tonto**

> Why does it matter where he fell? What makes this so special?

Speaker One: **Park Superintendent**

> Well, if he didn't fall here, we'd have to move all those little white markers that show where the other soldiers fell. We are pretty sure we got this right!

Speaker Two: **Coyote**

> It's this white man thing about death and hero worship.

ACT TWO, SCENE FOUR

What is Missing Here?

Speaker One: **Coyote 1**

> Look again at his painting.

Speaker Two: **Tonto**

> Yeah? What am I supposed to look for?

Speaker One: **Coyote 1**

> What don't you see?

Speaker Two: **Tonto**

> Native Americans. I see a white man's story. The entire focus is on Custer and his men.

Speaker One: **Coyote 1**

> In this respect, it is no different from any of the other thousand Custer paintings.

Speaker Two: **Tonto**

> It honors the Seventh Cavalry. It holds Custer up as a fallen hero. It honors and names the men in his company who died closest to him. It honors white history's version of the event.

Speaker One: **Coyote 2**

It marginalizes Native Americans. Don't forget—in his story about the painting, he says we "swarmed like stinging ants."

Speaker Two: **Coyote 1**

Hey, first he paints us in, then he takes us out, then he puts us back in but changes where we are.

Speaker One: **Tonto**

Makes you think they could almost tell this story without us.

Speaker Two: **Narrator**

Sure makes you wonder. As we noted earlier, when you drive into the National Park Service's Little Bighorn Battlefield National Monument, Eric's painting appears on one of the roadside exhibits. It is also portrayed on the heading of the National Park Service brochure.

Speaker One: **Tonto**

So you enter this national monument through the Custer narrative, not the Native American story.

Speaker Two: **Coyote 1**

But I thought *we* won the battle.

Speaker One: **Narrator**

And if you travel a few miles south to the Custer Battlefield Museum in Garryowen, you will find that a reproduction of Eric's painting hangs next to a reproduction of the Adams-Becker painting.

Speaker One: **Coyote 1**

I feel like a character in a Bob Dylan song.
 "There must be some way out of here,
 said the joker to the thief.[7]"

Speaker Two: **Tonto**

Who's the joker and who's the thief?

Speaker One: **Coyote 1**

Eric is the thief. He stole his story from our people. We're jokers, if we buy into it.

Coda

It matters to archaeologists, painters, photographers, National Park Service superintendents, and Custer re-enactment companies where Custer fell. For the rest of us, it matters very little, except to know that Custer's Hill is a perfect place to go if you want to see how white America re-enacts its version of how Custer won his battle. It's a perfect place to go to see how myth lives on through realist narratives, to see which dead soldier fell where on Custer Hill, to learn which caliber bullets were found along Reno Ridge, or Medicine Tail Coulee Ford of the Little Bighorn River.

It even matters to some when each event in the battle occurred, and there are detailed chronologies of that fateful two-day battle (Brust, Pohanka, & Barnard, 2005; Michno, 1997; Scott, Fox, Connor, & Harmon, 1989). It matters to others which battlefield markers are spurious, which artifact descriptions are correct or incorrect, whether radiocarbon sampling, human osteological analyses, and nonhuman vertebrate faunal remains confirm which nineteenth century reports. There are volumes upon volumes authenticating these facts. Annually, Custer's Last Stand re-enactments take place in Hardin, Montana, and at the Custer Battlefield Museum in Garryowen. The past and its facts come alive in these performances.

—*—*—*—

But where did they lay to rest the dead bodies of Red Horse, White Swan, Crazy Horse, Sitting Bull? Who has done radiocarbon testing of their remains? The places where these bodies fell are not the sites of national monuments and national parks, nor are they places where tourists take their children. These red bodies appear to lie outside history. Oddly, of course, they are part of history, integral to it, but only when they are foils for telling how Custer fell.

This is why counter-hegemonic histories—the paintings of White Swan, Red Horse, Fritz Scholder, Earl Biss, Kevin Red Star, John Nieto, Allan Mardon—are so important. They bring Custer down off his pedestal. Biss, Nieto, and Red Star turn Custer into a vain, pompous, self-centered figure. They strip him of his military honors. They will not honor him by recognizing his actions on the battlefield. In their paintings, there is no Last Stand Hill.

The counter-hegemonic paintings contest von Schmidt's painting and the narratives he attaches to it. They question his dismissals of Red Horse. They challenge his use of the phrase, "Paint me some Injuns." They contest his minstrelsy, his dressing up like a Native American model and riding bareback, wearing only a loincloth. They wonder what he means by the "real" battle. They doubt his ability to reduce the conflict between Native Americans and whites to a representation focused on a single point in time. While willing to grant him his artistic license, for them it was a two-day event, a series of skirmishes, battles, attacks, counterattacks, aftermaths, death rituals, celebrations. It would make no sense to them to spend five years getting a single painting right—whatever right might mean.

Bumper Sticker

(Projected onto a screen in red letters on a white background)

> **BUT IT WAS GENOCIDE**

Underlying these aesthetic, painterly differences is a fundamental contradiction. It hinges on war and genocide. On June 26, 1876, the Seventh Cavalry was on a mission to destroy a Native American community, to first kill old people, women, and children, burn their tipis, and then kill Lakota and Cheyenne warriors. This is what the soldiers were doing. Custer was their leader. These men knew they could die. They understood this. They also understood that their mission was to kill Native Americans. On this there was no uncertainty.

There is something disingenuous, a fundamental dishonesty about Eric von Schmidt and his mission. He said his task was to show how the soldiers felt when they knew they were going to die. He takes some of his inspiration from Elizabeth Custer and her use of words from the old Irish drinking song, "Garryowen." While other painters would list the names of Native Americans and soldiers along the bottom of their paintings, von Schmidt put the lyrics from a drinking song along the bottom of his. This underlies his commitment to tell the story from the soldiers' point of view, and perhaps something more. And, his aha! moment was in a drunken state. Of course, the soldiers knew they could die at any moment; they were soldiers. So what made death at this event any different? Clearly, their dying was about more than a soldier dying on the battlefield.

Obviously for von Schmidt and the other white painters, the soldiers' deaths were fraudulent and unfair. Custer should not have lost. Indeed, Custer should not have been challenged. He and his men should not have been killed. The Native Americans should have laid down their weapons, surrendered, run, or died during the attack. But they refused to do this. They refused to die, to willingly submit to the Seventh Cavalry and its genocidal mission.

So the Last Stand is about an unfinished battle, victory deferred. And in a few short years, victory would be certain. The Lakota and Cheyenne nations would lose their land and be on reservations, Custer's mission accomplished. The Last Stand paintings are cultural re-enactments, mythical restagings, performances that say the U.S. military did not lose that day. In glorifying the fallen soldiers, painters from Adams to von Schmidt aligned themselves with America's genocidal mission to destroy Native Americans. These paintings, as revisionist history, are just as fraudulent and dishonest as any real life re-enactment that takes place at Hardin or Garryowen.

So with von Schmidt, like all the other painters who came before him, we have a painter and a painting that insert themselves into history. Together, painter and painting bring history alive. Indeed, as he paints himself into his painting, von Schmidt becomes more important than his painting. He is the painting, and the painting is who he is. His story is more important than the story told by the painting. Still, together, painter and painting authorize history. Together they reinforce the myth that Custer was victorious. They perpetuate the view that Native Americans—Injuns, the barbarians—are less than human.

Racism is hidden, trumped by the claim of artistic realism. The painter's obsessive attention to detail, scale, dress, weaponry, body placement, and distance from ridge to river ensures the viewer that history is being told correctly. On these points the painter has kept a promise to himself and honored his contract to the viewer. He set out to show how Custer fell, and he has done so within the aesthetic guidelines of classical, historical representational art, painting done on a grand scale, painting done about monumentally important historical events.

CHAPTER SIX

Custer's Last Rally[1]

ACT ONE, SCENE ONE
Meet Buffalo Bill Cody

Speaker One: **Narrator**

"Custer's Last Rally" is a three-act historical drama, a minstrel show of sorts, a night in the museum, a play within a play. It moves across several sites, from the Last Stand paintings exhibited in the Whitney Gallery in the Buffalo Bill Historical Center to Custer's presence in William Cody's, aka Buffalo Bill, Wild West show in which he appears as a character in a play called "Custer's Last Rally." In the play, Cody plays Custer and Sitting Bull plays himself. Cody re-enacts, and hence keeps alive the Custer epic, the story of eternal youth.

(Stage right, a spotlight shines on an 1886 advertisement for "Custer's Last Rally" from p. 282 of Welch, 1994.)

—*—*—*—

Buy your tickets for "Custer's Last Rally," being the re-enactment of a single, profound event in American history, that is, the murder of General George Armstrong Custer, America's foremost martyr, to Indian conquest staged by Buffalo Bill Cody, the man who avenged General Custer's death by killing and scalping Chief Yellow Hair (Warren, 2005, p. 268).

—*—*—*—

(Project picture of Buffalo Bill Cody in a stage outfit in which he killed Yellow Hair, as found on page 170 of Warren, 2005.)

Speaker Two: **Narrator**

> Allow me to introduce the famous William F. Cody, performer extraordinaire. He still rides today, across our imagined horizon . . . huckster, entertainer, celebrity, myth-maker.
>
> Cody embodied the westward-moving, industrially modern American. He believed fervently in capitalism. He was devoted to his Indian friends whose relatives he fought and killed.
>
> He loved the world of the stage, theater, and performance. And all his life he straddled both sides, theater, nontheater, Indian, anti-Indian.
>
> He displayed a remarkable unwillingness to choose sides. He had a talent for creating dramatic spectacle that made it possible for him to avoid doing so, and the worldwide public, who shared his beliefs, flocked to his shows for over a quarter-century (Warren, 2005, pp. 542, 548).

(Project photo of William Cody and Sitting Bull found on page 86 of Reddin (1999). Also found at http://www.historicalstockphotos.com/images/xsmall/2441_william_f_cody_buffalo_bill_standing_with_sitting_bull.jpg)

Speaker One: **William Frederick Cody** (1858)

> "I killed my first Indian when I was twelve years old.
> I was an Indian fighter for Johnston's
> Army. We were hired to put down a
> Mormon rebellion in Salt Lake City.
>
> I was on patrol. Presently the moon rose, dead
> ahead of me, and painted boldly across
> its face was the figure of an Indian.
>
> He wore this war bonnet of the Sioux, and at
> his shoulder was a rifle pointed at someone
> in the river bottom; in another second, he would
> drop one of my friends." (p.43)
>
> I raised my old muzzle loader and fired.
> The figure tumbled down the bank and fell
> in the water.

"Little Billy's killed an Indian" called McCarthy,
"all by hisself" (Cody, 1910/2001, p. 43).

I created my little Wild West show to tell
the story of the Indian wars, General Custer and
Little Bighorn, the four epochs of American history,
the Drama of Civilization: Primeval Forest before
the arrival of Columbus; the arrival of two Indian tribes
—Sioux and Pawnee; the Prairie epoch buffalo hunters;
the Cattle ranch cowboys; the Mining Camps,
Pony Express, and Deadwood Stage
(Warren, 2005, pp. 267–268).

I added one more episode: "Custer's Last Rally" in 1886.

Speaker Two: **Brian Dippie**

"As you can see, the Custer epic is ritual drama. Custer is eternal youth. The ritual of re-enactment holds out the promise that there really is no Last Stand, for its self-sacrificing heroism assures that the Last Stand will flourish forever in memory, enjoying perpetual life" (Dippie, 1976/1994, p. 89).

ACT ONE, SCENE TWO

Cody, Custer, and the Western Minstrel Show[2]

Speaker One: **Tonto**

What's the point of this play?

Speaker Two: **Coyote 1**

You keep asking this question.
Nobody wants to die.
Cody keeps Custer alive.

Speaker One: **Narrator**

Everything this book is about comes together in Buffalo Bill's Wild West show, from the Cassilly Adams painting, which was incorporated into the show as a landscape panorama, to the Busch beer commercials. Not to be overlooked are the show's re-enactments of violence toward Native Americans, culminating in performances of "Custer's Last Rally," which was intended to perpetuate the Custer myth, to show Little Bighorn really was not the Last Stand.

(Project image of Cassilly Adams's Custer's Last Fight found at http://www.philaprintshop.com/images/custer.jpg)

Speaker Two: **Tonto**

This helps.

Speaker One: **Narrator**

I have to return to the beginning, to the question that has been examined in every chapter in this performance. How do the re-enactments of the battle on June 25–26, 1876, between the Seventh Calvary and the Lakota and the Cheyenne, perpetuate racist, discriminatory discourses about Native Americans and their place in American culture?

Speaker Two: **Coyote 1**

Or, how could something so entertaining, so dramatic, so realistically pleasing, so historically "accurate," be so cruel to Indians?

Speaker One: **Tonto**

Hey, it's all make-believe.

Speaker Two: **Coyote 1**

But it goes beyond make-believe. It's about the unquenchable desire of Americans to consume minstrel shows and racialized spectacles that keep the illusions of the Wild West alive.

Speaker One: **Narrator**

When I was little, when my brother and I were not playing cowboy and Indian, he was Buffalo Bill and I was Wild Bill Hickok, then he was Roy Rogers and I was Gene Autry.

Speaker Two: **Coyote 1**

You know Roy Rogers played Buffalo Bill in a 1940 movie.

Speaker One: **Coyote 2**

> I forgot that. Charlton Heston, Paul Newman, and Eminem all played Buffalo Bill. Errol Flynn played Custer.

Speaker Two: **Coyote 1**

> That's just like Hollywood to use famous actors to play famous people. Western minstrel shows are all about the ability of Americans to be racist and seemingly nonracist at the same time, a talent Cody cultivated. He created dramatic racialized spectacles and sold them to audiences around the world as authentic history, history as entertainment. This is what his Wild West show was all about.

Speaker One: **Coyote 2**

> Cody and his audiences consumed these racialized frontier fantasies. This made it possible for everyone to feel good about being patriotic supporters of Custer's project.

Speaker Two: **Narrator**

> Cody's presentation of Native America is an extension of Custer's views. Let's get this straight. Cody is Custer, and Custer is Cody.

(Project excerpts of the timeline for William F. Cody found in Appendix C.)

ACT ONE, SCENE THREE

Ned Buntline Creates Buffalo Bill

Speaker One: **Coyote 1**

> You could say Cody lived a fun-filled life. Was he ever not performing some version of a manufactured, mythical West?

Speaker Two: **Coyote 2**

> It's said Cody got the nickname Buffalo Bill because of his contract to kill buffalo and supply meat to the military; thus began the myth of Cody. And don't scold me for using the term *buffalo*; it's what I'm used to. The correct term is now accepted to be *American bison*.

Speaker One: **Coyote 1**

Understood. Clearly, part of the Cody myth came about because of Ned Buntline, aka Edward Zane Carroll Judson (1813–1886). Ned and Bill were made for each other (Johannsen, 1950; Pond, 1919).

(Project public domain photographic portrait of Ned Buntline available from Wikipedia at http://en.wikipedia.org/wiki/Ned_Buntline)

Speaker Two: **Ned Buntline**

Bill and I met each other in 1869 at Fort McPherson, Nebraska. I was lookin' for a model for a character named Buffalo Bill. Bill Hickok turned me down, and suddenly I saw Bill Cody. He was perfect!

Speaker One: **Coyote 2**

So Cody fit the character Buntline had in mind—a white Indian, a buffalo hunter, a military scout. Buntline went on to write a series of dime novels about Bill, the first and the most famous of which was *Buffalo Bill Cody—King of the Border Men*.

Speaker Two: **Ned Buntline**

Bill and I became fast friends. I wrote a play based on him called "Scouts of the Prairie." It opened in Chicago in 1872 and Bill starred in it. It was a financial success and launched Bill onto the national stage as a performer of Wild West stories.

Speaker Two: **Buffalo Bill**

During the summer of 1872 I received numerous letters from Ned, urging me to come East and go upon the stage to represent my own character. "There's money in it," he said, "and you will prove to be a big card, as your character is a novelty on the stage" (Cody, 1910/2001, p. 284).

Speaker One: **Ned Buntline**

Bill left the show that summer of 1872. He wanted to make more money.

Speaker Two: **Buffalo Bill**

The next season, 1873–1874, Texas Jack Omohundro and I organized our own company, the "Buffalo Bill Combination," and convinced Wild Bill Hickok to join us. We had a variety of acts and stunts. We did

"Scouts of the Plains" and performed as a company for the 1874–1875, and 1875–1876 seasons (Cody, 1910/2001, pp. 294–295, 304).

Speaker One: **Ned Buntline**

Bill was called back into the military in the summer of 1876. Indeed, at the Battle of Warbonnet Creek, he avenged Custer's death. Showman that he was, he saw an opening for greater fame and took it.

Speaker Two: **Narrator**

Hold on folks, this story is getting ahead of itself.

Act One, Scene Four
Cody Kills Indians and Meets Custer

Speaker One: **Buffalo Bill**

As I said earlier, I killed my first Indian when I was twelve. If you worked for the army, that's what you did—you killed Indians.

I was a white Indian. I was a scout for the Army. I was a buffalo hunter, a rider for the Pony Express. I killed Indians and buffalo, and that is how I met General George Armstrong Custer.

Speaker Two: **Narrator**

What is a white Indian?

Speakers One and Two (in unison): **Philip Deloria** *and* **Louis Warren**

The term conflates heroic scout and white man. The white Indian adopted Indian fighting methods, but he was not a savage.

He embodied the values of civilization. Unlike the members of the Boston Tea Party, the Western frontier White Indian did more then play Indian or Injun, he killed injuns (Deloria, 1999, p. 11–12, 41–42; Warren, 2005, p. 82).

Speaker One: **Custer**

You could say I was a white Indian. I killed Indians. I had to learn how to be a buffalo hunter. The first time I tried to kill a buffalo, I shot my horse in the head and killed him instead. The buffalo trotted away

(Warren, 2005, p. 133). I quickly learned how to do it. I watched Bill Cody. Soon I was guiding wealthy tourists who wanted to kill buffalo, just like Cody was.

Speaker Two: **Louis Warren**

Bill Cody and George Custer filled the same mythic space: the white Indian guide, "avatar of wilderness for gentlemen hunters" (2005, p. 134).

In the summer of 1869, Custer guided two aristocrats and one hundred-fifty tourists on a buffalo hunt near Fort Hayes.

He arranged for the party to be accompanied by the Seventh Cavalry regimental band, which played "Garryowen" along the way (Warren, 2005, p. 135).

Speaker One: **Eric von Schmidt**

Darn! Isn't that the song they played at Little Bighorn? That's the song that influenced me when I was doing my big painting.

Speaker Two: **Coyote 1**

This is ironic. Eric used to dress up like an Indian. It is kind of disgusting, though, when you think of it. Custer thought he was an Indian. He had a fringed buckskin suit matching the color of his hair. He'd jump on his horse, give a war whoop, go racing off at full gallop (Warren, 2005, p. 135).

Speaker One: **Eric von Schmidt**

Hold on, Coyote. Dressing up like an Indian helped me finish my masterpiece.

Speaker Two: **Buffalo Bill**

I learned from George Custer how to lead a hunt for wealthy patrons. You needed a band, officers, soldiers, a cavalcade of wagons, extra horses, some Chinaman to do laundry, and at least three darkie cooks. It helped if you had Indians riding along, too.

Speaker One: **P. T. Barnum**

Believe it or not, I staged the first buffalo hunt in New Jersey in 1843. I went on a real hunt with Custer in the summer of 1870. We were treated like visiting royalty.

Speaker Two: **Custer**

> Listen, P. T., you may have started these hunts, but I teamed up with Bill Cody, and on many an occasion, we gave each other tips on how to kill buffalo and guide wealthy people.

Speaker One: **Buffalo Bill**

> In the summer of 1867, nine years before the Battle of the Little Bighorn, George and I went on a ride across the plains together. I guided Custer and his men through a difficult "sixty-mile stretch between Fort Ellsworth and Fort Larned"(Warren, 2005, p. 136).
>
> The general thanked me for having brought him straight across dangerous country without any trial (Cody, 1910/2001, p. 119).
>
> We became fast friends after this. The general promised to get me an assignment, and indeed I got a job as chief scout with the Fifth Cavalry in 1868. In 1869 I was involved in the Battle of Summit Springs.

Speaker Two: **Louis Warren**

> This was an imaginary friendship, although there is a documented 1873 meeting between the two men when they conducted a buffalo hunt for the entertainment of the Grand Duke Alexis from Russia (Warren, 2005, p. 136).

Speaker One: **Coyote 1**

> Hey, it's all made up for these two performers! It's all imaginary.

Speaker Two: **Coyote 2**

> Did you know that the general, the great Indian killer, took a Cheyenne woman named Monahsetah as his mistress after the Battle of Washita in 1868?

Speaker One: **Elizabeth Custer**

> Listen, Coyote 2. Some say she had a child by him, but that is not true. George would never have done that. He loved me. None of his men would ever have taken an Indian woman as a concubine (Warren, 2005, p. 237).

Speaker Two: **Coyote 1**

> I'm sorry, Libbie. I don't know Indian mistresses. But your husband was an arrogant, petty tyrant, a cruel man. He would order his troops

flogged for minor offenses, and other offenders had half their hair shaved off. Now, come on.

Speaker One: **Narrator**

I can pick up on what Coyote says. George resented anybody who got more attention than he did. He resented Bill Cody's rise to fame. He'd take jabs at Bill, calling him "Antelope Jim" and never mentioning him in his books, even though he praised other scouts, including Wild Bill Hickok (Warren, 2005, p. 139).

Speaker Two: **Buffalo Bill**

Mr. Narrator, I liked the general. I know he was jealous of me. He had a hard time, enemies from all sides, in the army and in the press. As a white Indian, I tried to stay neutral.

I was just opposed to Indian savagery. I killed wild animals. I helped clear the land for the settlers, and the march of civilization and capitalism across the plains.

Speaker One: **Coyote 1**

Wild Bill, this is pretty self-serving stuff. How could you not take sides?

ACT ONE, SCENE FIVE

Cody Avenges Custer by Killing Chief Yellow Hair

(Stage right, a spotlight shines on the following newspaper headline.)

―✻―✻―✻―

TRIBUNE EXTRA

Bismarck, Dakota Territory. July 6, 1876
General Custer Killed.
No officer or man of 5 companies
left to tell the tale.
Country up in arms.

―✻―✻―✻―

Speaker One: **Newsboy**

Get your *Tribune* here. Custer is dead!

Speaker Two: **Jack Crawford**

I wrote this poem for General Custer and for William Cody. It was published in 1879.

The Death of Custer

Did I hear news from Custer?
Well, I reckon I did, old pard;
It came like a streak of lightnin',
And, you bet, it hit me hard . . .
But I'll bet my bottom dollar
Ye had no trouble to muster
A tear, or perhaps a hundred,
When ye heard of the death of Custer.
He always thought well of you, pard,
And had it been heaven's will,
In a few more days you'd met him,
And he'd welcome his old scout, Bill. . . .

And I reckon ye know his record,
For he was our guiding star . . .

But I tell ye the day is approaching—
The boys are beginning to muster,
That day of the great retribution—
The day of revenge for our Custer.
(Crawford, 1879, pp. 79–82)

Speaker One: **Second Newsboy**

President Grant vows revenge, orders Fifth Cavalry to attack Cheyenne warriors involved in Battle of the Little Bighorn.

Speaker Two: **Narrator**

As you know, Cody serves as a lead scout for the mission, which included five hundred men and horses (Cody, 1910/2001, p. 308).

Speaker One: **Buffalo Bill**

How could I not have stepped forward? When the general and his men were massacred, the entire nation was up in arms. That's why I got involved in the July 17, 1876, Battle of Warbonnet Creek against the Sioux and Cheyenne.

The battle went fast.

We were chasing the Indians, who were about to attack two of our men. The Indians turned on us. One of them was handsomely decorated with all the ornaments usually worn by a war chief. He called out to me, "I know you, Pa-he-haska[3]; if you want to fight, come ahead and fight me (Cody, 1910/2001, pp. 309–310).

He was ridging back and forth in front of his men, bantering, challenging me. I accepted the challenge. We rode at each other at full speed. When we were only thirty yards apart, I raised my rifle and fired, and killed his horse.

Suddenly my horse stumbled and went down. I sprang to my feet. The Indian was upon me, we were both on foot, scarcely twenty feet separated us. We fired at each other at the same time. He missed me, but my bullet hit him in the chest.

He fell. He was bleeding. I was upon him. I had my knife out. And I drove it to its hilt into his heart.

I scientifically jerked his war bonnet off his head in about five seconds.

Speaker One: **Coyote 1**

Hey, Mr. White Indian, what do you mean, scientifically scalped him?

Speaker Two: **Buffalo Bill**

Coyote, I mean it was neat and clean.

No fewer than two hundred Indians were rushing at me. Thankfully, the men of the Company saw what was happening. They came to my rescue. As they got close to me, I swung the Indian chieftain's top-knot and bonnet in the air, and shouted (Cody, 1910/2001, pp. 310–311): *"The first scalp for Custer!"*

Speaker One: **Coyote 1**

Nice work, little big man. Real brave . . .

Speaker Two: **Buffalo Bill**

I was fighting for Custer's honor. I was fighting for the honor of every American, for every soldier who died at Custer's Last Stand.

Speaker One: **Coyote 1**

You knew this would secure your national reputation. I bet you were already planning how to work this into your Wild West show.

Speaker Two: **Buffalo Bill**

No, no, no. There had to be payback. That is why I took the first scalp for Custer. That's why I killed and scalped Chief Yellow Hair. There had to be retribution. We could not just accept the slaughter of Custer and his men.

Speaker One: **Coyote 1**

Slaughter? Slaughter? Custer wanted to destroy an entire Indian village.

Speaker Two: **Coyote 2**

Hey Bill, didn't the father of Yellow Hair ask you to turn over his war bonnet, guns, ornaments, weapons? Didn't he offer you four mules, and you said you could not do that? And you never did give them back (Cody, 1910/2001, pp. 311–312).

Speaker One: **Coyote 1**

Pretty heartless, Bill.

Speaker Two: **Buffalo Bill**

I'm sorry. I just got real busy.

Speaker One: **Coyote 2**

Too busy? *Too busy?*

Speaker Two: **Buffalo Bill**

Yeah, real busy. Remember, that day we drove off more than seven thousand Indians.

Once my Wild West show was established, I made the scene where I scalped Yellow Hair a regular part of the show.

Sometimes it was part of what we called "Custer's Last Fight," which was another segment in the show.

I always admired Custer as a man, an officer, a martyr. He was a national hero (Warren, 2005, p. 135–136).

Speaker One: **Narrator** *(to Buffalo Bill)*

Bill, many say you made Custer a national hero after he died by giving him such a prominent part in your Wild West show. Indeed, at times you even played Custer—the two of you were folded into one another, the perfect simulacra. In the end, you were both shadows following one another around.

ACT TWO, SCENE ONE

Cassilly Adams and Buffalo Bill's Wild West Show

Speaker One: **Buffalo Bill**

After the Battle of Warbonnet Creek, I returned to the stage, performing "Scouts of the Plains." I immediately added a new scene, "Buffalo Bill's First Scalp for Custer." In another part of the show, we did "Custer's Last stand." I played General Custer.

Speaker Two: **Louis Warren**

When Cody impersonated Custer, he wore a wig and carried a sword. In later years Buck Taylor played Custer, and Cody played himself doing a mad dash to save Custer at Little Bighorn. Then he would follow this episode with a "First Scalp for Custer" re-enactment (Warren, 2005, pp. 272–273).

Speaker One: **Narrator**

According to our timeline, Cody formed Buffalo Bill's Wild West show in 1882.

Speaker Two: **Louis Warren**

That is correct. His show rode the wave of Custer's Last Stand paintings (Warren, 2005, p. 261). By 1886 he had worked into this show a visual presentation of the Battle of the Little Bighorn.

It was based on Cassilly Adams's 1884 painting, *Custer's Last Stand* (Warren, 2005, p. 261).

Speaker One: **Buffalo Bill**

For the show I needed panoramic backdrops, landscapes, smoke, mirrors. I needed cycloramas, colored canvases, pictures of the Wild West, buffaloes, Indians, stage coaches, tipis, a moving picture show before movie pictures had really taken off.

So we had props: guns, saddles, stagecoaches, buffaloes, Indians, whips, a plywood set of mountains, paintings of forests, trees, pictures of the Little Bighorn, all as backdrop to live re-enactments.

Speaker Two: **Coyote 1**

This is realism at its finest? This is like E. S. Paxson hiring Lakota and Cheyenne warriors to be models in his Last Stand painting.

Speaker One: **Buffalo Bill**

Coyote, listen, for my Custer performances I needed to use a Last Stand painting.

Speaker Two: **Narrator**

Well, you had a lot of paintings to pick from. I mean, just look at the list I put together [in Appendix B[4]]. It makes good sense, though, that you picked the Adams painting.

Speaker One: **Buffalo Bill**

These were all excellent paintings. I could have used any of them. I liked Mulvany's, too. I chose to use Cassilly Adams's painting because it was big, and it had been created as a traveling exhibit. It showed Custer as a man and as a child. By 1888, it was getting a lot of publicity because of the Busch advertisement.

It was like its own cyclorama. When Becker turned the Adams painting into a lithograph, he incorporated a view of the Little Bighorn River that I needed for my show (Warren, 2005, p. 261). So it worked nicely for our purposes, too.

But I had to talk with my friend Adolphus Busch before the deal was signed, sealed, and delivered.

ACT TWO, SCENE TWO

A Play Within a Play: A Brewery Buys a Painting

Speaker One: **Coyote 1**

I heard Cody had to get permission from Adolphus Busch to use the painting in his show.

Speaker Two: **Narrator** (*as cultural cynic*)

The Adams-Becker print has been seen by a greater number of viewers than any other picture in American history. Paul Andrew Hutton is right. This picture helped Anheuser-Busch become a global corporate giant and promoted Custer as a heroic legend.

This was a partnership that must rank as one of the greatest triumphs of American capitalism (see Hutton, 2004c, p. 405).

Speaker One: **Coyote 1**

Who can argue? When Cody picked up the painting, that was pretty good advertising, too.

Speaker Two: **Coyote 2**

It worked two ways. You could say the picture also helped Cody's Wild West show become so popular and so profitable.

Speaker One: **Narrator** (*as jokester*)

There is a backstory here about nineteenth century robber baron capitalists and how they used Western art to get rich. This is also the story of Jay Cooke and Thomas Moran's famous painting, *Grand Canyon of the Yellowstone* (Denzin, 2008).

But let Mr. Cooke tell the story.

Speaker Two: **Jay Cooke** (*in redface*)

I was a good friend of Adolphus Busch. He and his family used to stay at my estate outside Philadelphia. He shipped thousands of barrels of his beer on my Northern Pacific railroad line.

I told him about my success with Thomas Moran, the artist who painted *Grand Canyon of the Yellowstone*. I paid for that painting, and I sponsored Moran's trip.

I used his painting in advertisements for my railroad line. I told Aldophus he could do the same thing, if he could get hold of Adams's painting of *Custer's Last Fight*.

Speaker One: **Adolphus Busch**

This is exactly what I did. I bought the rights and then hired Mr. Becker to turn it into a lithograph.

But there is more to the story. In 1879 I launched a national advertising campaign to make Budweiser—pasteurized, bottled, and served cold—America's national beer. My ads said it was "American" to drink Budweiser beer.

In an effort to nationalize my product, I connected Budweiser to the American military, and the men who served in the military.

Cassilly's battlefield painting was perfect for my purposes. It was all about fallen soldiers and American honor. Americans were up in arms about the Custer massacre. They were still grieving over the deaths of the soldiers.

The nation applauded when Cody avenged Custer's death at Warbonnet Creek.

Speaker Two: **Coyote 1**

Not to get too far off track here, but this reminds me of Americans cheering when George W. Bush invaded Iraq and captured Saddam Hussein; some kind of payback was going on here, too.

Speaker One: **Adolphus Busch**

Good point, Coyote. But then I always said, there is money to be made in being patriotic.

Speaker Two: **Buffalo Bill**

There is nothing wrong about a painting advertising beer, or Wild West shows, for that matter. This kind of foreshadows what we see today—liquor and beer advertisements at sporting events, with sports teams bearing names like Braves, Indians, Redskins.

Speaker One: **Adolphus Busch**

That lithograph became the first Anheuser-Busch promotional item in 1896.

I was happy to work with Bill Cody. I was glad that he could make good use of the lithograph in his Wild West show.

It was good business for both of us.

Speaker Two: **Buffalo Bill**

Adolphus was easy to work with. I told him that we'd see to it that our boys drank his beer after our shows. And they did.

Speaker One: **Narrator**

Soon, every time a drinking man turned around, he saw the Budweiser ad and that battlefield above the Little Bighorn River with bloodthirsty Indians killing Custer and his men.

And so was launched a 125-year-plus history of Anheuser-Busch support for the U.S. Armed Forces (Navy League of the United States, 2003).[5]

Is it too cynical to say the success of Anheuser-Busch started with the Battle of the Little Bighorn, a painting called *Custer's Last Fight*, which was then incorporated into Cody's Wild West show?[6]

Speaker Two: **Narrator** *(as art historian)*

Agreed. Buffalo Bill Cody helped, too. He took that painting all across America and Europe.

Speaker One: **Adolphus Busch**

Busch gave the painting to the Seventh Cavalry in 1895. It kept getting lost and was destroyed in a fire at Fort Bliss in 1946 (see Appendix A Timeline).

Speaker Two: **Narrator**

This adds an element of irony and comedy to the story. Of course, the lithograph reproductions of the original continued to circulate.

Speaker One: **Coyote 1**

Not to be blunt, but the fact that the original kept getting lost maybe speaks to the inability of the army to win the original Battle of the Little Bighorn.

Speaker Two: **Coyote 2**

Could you be a little subtle? It's just a painting.

Speaker One: **Narrator** *(as doubting Thomas)*

When Adolphus Busch bought Cassilly Adams's painting and hired F. Otto Becker to turn it into an advertisement, he fused three ritual images into one frame: beer-drinking; male companionship in the civic spaces of the public tavern; and public spectacle that mourned and celebrated the violence involved in *Custer's Last Stand*.

Good citizens honored Custer's violent death by drinking Busch's beer and going to Cody's Wild West show!

Locating the battle in his taverns, Busch froze Native Americans in this violent frame, and at the same time valorized the fallen American soldier. And this frame would hang behind the bar in thousands of pubs and taverns, to be seen by millions of Americans.

Bumper Sticker

(Projected onto a screen in red letters on a white background)

Custer Died for Your Sins—Vine Deloria

ACT TWO, SCENE THREE

Libbie Custer Plays Coy

Speaker Two: **Coyote 1**

I understand that in 1888 the Boston Company created a fifty-by-four-hundred-foot cyclorama called "The Battle of Little Big Horn," and it incorporated elements from the Adams-Becker print. I understand they asked Mrs. Custer to write a few words about it and she was unable to. To be a commercial success, they felt they needed her endorsement.

Speaker One: **Coyote 2**

Buffalo Bill invited Mrs. Custer to his show in 1886. And she refused.

Speaker Two: **Elizabeth Custer**

Dear friend William Cody, I cannot even consider for a moment what you suggest in calmness. My shattered nerves will not allow me to see how you, such a loyal friend of General Custer, honor him in your show.

I have, accordingly, asked Capt. E. S. Godfrey to go in my place and he has agreed (Dippie, 1996, pp. 209–210).

Speaker One: **Coyote 1**

So no official endorsement by Mrs. Custer on these Custer performances.

Speaker Two: **Coyote 2**

Yup. It was just too much for her to take on.

Speaker One: **Buffalo Bill**

Well, Coyote 2, I accepted Libbie's judgment. I went forward. By this time, I had secured rights to use the Adams-Becker print.

Speaker Two: **Elizabeth Custer**

Actually, I did go to Mr. Cody's show. It just took me a while. I attended the Madison Square Garden performance in January, 1886.

Speaker One: **Publicist**

The presence of Custer's widow at the premiere insured its acceptance by the public as an accurate and respectful representation (Warren, 2005, p. 272).

ACT TWO, SCENE FOUR

Getting Ready to Perform Custer's Last Rally

Speaker One: **Frank Richmond** (*as off-stage announcer*)

(*A cowboy band plays the* Star-Spangled Banner *in the background for an audience of 20,000 people.*)

Good evening, folks. You will experience something unique tonight: an authentic Wild West experience.

Please welcome Buffalo Bill's Wild West and the Congress of Rough Riders of the World, in order:

- Miss Annie Oakley, sharpshooter;
- Race of the Races—a race between a cowboy, a Cossack, a Mexican, an Arab, a Gaucho, and an Indian;
- U.S. Artillery Drill by Fifth Regiment veterans;
- A cowboy camp is attacked by marauding Indians who are repulsed by Buffalo Bill;
- A Pony Express rider delivers the mail;
- Mexicans perform lasso tricks;
- Arab horsemen demonstrate their style of horsemanship;
- Indian boys race;
- Indians—Sioux, Arapahoe, Cheyenne—do war dances;
- Veterans from the Sixth U.S. Calvary do military exercises;
- A Deadwood stage coach is held up;
- The Rough Riders of the world ride;
- Colonel W. F. Cody performs sharpshooting stunts, riding at full speed;
- A buffalo hunt with real buffalo;
- The Battle of the Little Bighorn, with Colonel W. F. Cody playing General George Armstrong Custer;
- The Battle of Warbonnet Creek, when Colonel W. F. Cody takes the first scalp for Custer; and
- Curtain: A cowboy in Dodge City, 1882.

Speaker One: **Buffalo Bill**

I built my show around the Last Stand; the climax was the re-enactment of Custer's Last Stand, and then my killing of Chief Yellow Hair.

Speaker Two: **Tonto**

So you are a hero, two times over. You are a slain martyr, a man who gave his life for his country. Then you became the savior, the man who brought justice to the battlefield, and honored the dead by killing an Indian chief.

Bumper Sticker

(Projected onto a screen in red letters on a white background)

> **CUSTER DIED FOR HIS SINS**

ACT TWO, SCENE FIVE

Using a Painting to Work the Audience

Speaker One: **Coyote 1**

Bill, you and your troupe give a powerful performance. You sure stir up the audience with this patriotic stuff—soldiers, veterans, Army drills, buffalo hunts, attacks on stage coaches—then you kill Custer. Then you kill an Indian in retribution.

Speaker Two: **Narrator**

This is just like a Shakespeare tragedy; a flawed but admirable protagonist commits a fatal error. His death is avenged, and his reputation redeemed by an equally attractive protagonist.

Speaker One: **Ned Buntline**

In staging this drama over and over again, Cody brought the essence of classical drama into his show, affirming for the audience the timelessness of Custer's story, and affirming the belief that justice does prevail. This is the model I used in my stories and plays.

Speaker Two: **Sherman Alexie**

So in essence, like the *Night at the Museum* movies, Cody's play within a play brings a painting, or exhibit, alive.

Historical characters, like figures in a museum diorama, step out from behind the glass and talk to the audience, as if they were alive and real.

Speaker One: **Ben Stiller**

Hold on! Custer is in my movie. He is played by Bill Hader, who saves me while riding a bicycle. Custer works closely with Sacajawea, and tells her his battle plans.

He is portrayed in his Civil War days. He has long hair and is referred to as a general. He wears a major general's shoulder boards and double-breasted frock coat with the correct number of buttons.

He also has his trademark red scarf.

Speaker Two: **Buffalo Bill**

See, Custer lives! Buffalo Bill lives!

Speaker One: **Cassilly Adams** *(to Buffalo Bill)*

Listen, Bill, those filmmakers could have used some of my advice when they put the general in their *Night at the Museum: Battle of the Smithsonian* movie.

You needed my painting because you needed to see how to stage that battle, how to dress Custer, how to dress his soldiers, even to dress the Indians. You needed my painting to see how to depict the battlefield, including how to show the Little Bighorn River, where to locate the tipis.

Most importantly, you needed to see how to stage the Last Stand as an event.

My painting was a roadmap. It served as a metaphor for your show.

It was the template for staging re-enactments of the Last Stand; it stood in as a representation of the show itself.

Speaker Two: **Coyote 1**

But all those details were made up!

Speaker One: **Cassilly Adams**

Hey, I did my best to be accurate.

Speaker Two: **Adolphus Busch**

Cassilly, Coyote. Don't forget me. Colonel Cody also needed that little lithograph I paid Mr. Becker to make.

Speaker One: **Sherman Alexie**

Holy smokes, all that and more! Too bad Billy Boy never looked at the Red Horse or White Swan drawings. But then, he had no desire to tell our side of the story.

Speaker Two: **Narrator**

Sherman, remember that Buffalo Bill presumably takes the name "Custer's Last Rally" from John Mulvany's 1881 painting of the same name. That is a grim painting. We talked about it at great length in Chapter Two.

Mulvany's Custer, as Taft said (1953, p.136), is fearless. Custer knows he is facing death. He shows hatred for the Indians, but love for his men.

Speaker One: **Brian W. Dippie**

Good point. In fact, Cody used Mulvany's painting in a 1904 poster, "Custer's Last Stand as Presented by Buffalo Bill's Wild West" (Dippie, 1996, p. 218).

An 1896 Cody poster used Mulvany's title, but borrowed from the Adams-Becker–Anheuser-Busch lithograph (Dippie, 1996, p. 219).

Speaker Two: **Coyote 1**

The story here is simple. In staging his Wild West shows, Buffalo Bill used the Adams and Mulvany paintings. They served as backdrop, as copy for advertisements, and as models for staging performances of the Last Stand.

ACT TWO, SCENE SIX

Performing Custer's Last Rally

Speaker Two: **Buffalo Bill**

Let's get started. Remember, we have two Last Stand plays to perform—"Custer's Last Rally" and "Buffalo Bill's First Scalp for Custer," also called "Duel Between Buffalo Bill and Yellow Hair" (Reddin, 1996, p. 76).

Speaker One: **Custer**

Bill Cody performed me in "Custer's Last Rally." I am very grateful for that, even though he did wear a wig and wave a sword around in the air.

Speaker Two: **Coyote 1**

Yeah. So just what did "Custer's Last Rally" look like?

Speaker One: **Sherman Alexie**

The Indians were ferocious-looking. They usually appeared stripped to the waist, in paint, with feathers, headdresses, and armed to the teeth. They scalped fallen soldiers at will. These were Indians playing being Indians (Reddin, 1996, pp. 75–76; Deloria, 1998).

Speaker Two: **Eliza**[7]

I swear, when I seen Mr. Cody come on stage, with his back and hips, he was built exactly like the Ginnel. I said, "Well, if he ain't the 'spress image of Ginnel Custer in battle, then I never seed anyone that was (Warren, 2005, p. 274).

Speaker One: **Elizabeth Custer**

I thanked Mr. Cody for teaching the youth of the country how our noble soldiers, officers, and scouts had sacrificed so much for our country.

Speaker Two: **Buffalo Bill**

When we debuted in 1887 in New York, I used an all-white army. This reinforced the general idea that westward expansion was a white, Anglo project (Warren, 2005, p. 97).

Speaker One: **Ned Buntline**

Sometimes Bill called it the "Battle of Little Bighorn." "Custer's Last Rally" was intended to show how the Indians, with strategic cunning—allow me to quote from the program—"Ambushed the gallant Custer and remorselessly annihilated the entire command and were scalping and gloating over their captives, and a heap of dead soldiers and horses" (Reddin, 1999, p. 141).

In some versions, the actor playing Custer claimed to be riding the war horse of the late Chief Sitting Bull.

Speaker Two: **Elizabeth Custer**

I watched the rehearsals for the Madison Square Garden performances. They had a huge number of scenes. Colonel Cody directed the tragic mock fight with the Indians. The actor playing my husband was always the last man to fall dead.

Speaker One: **Sherman Alexie**

According to white myth, "Custer's Last Rally" represents the nation's most famous Indian battle. In this play, the death of America's most famous martyr is avenged by its most famous performer, the man who avenged his death.

Speaker Two: **Coyote 1**

Heavy stuff, dude!

Speaker One: **Elizabeth Custer**

The show has a series of short scenes.

Scene One: General Custer's encamped troops, dressed in blue uniforms, are preparing to go on a march in pursuit of Indians.

Scene Two: A scout discovers a Sioux village where Sitting Bull and his warriors are engaged in innocent activities. The scout returns and informs Custer of the large Indian village.

Scene Three: The bugler blows his horn. The Indians prepare an ambush.

Scene Four: Custer's troops rush onto the stage. The bugler sounds the charge. Custer waves his sword and races forward on his horse, followed by his men. They charge the Indian village.

Scene Five: Custer and his men are overwhelmed by the Indians in hand-to-hand combat. Soldiers are scalped. Custer is the last man killed. He dies only after slaying many Indians and performing great acts of bravery and valor (Warren, 2005, p. 269).

Speaker Two: **Ned Buntline**

These scenes were always very exciting to watch. Buffalo Bill usually followed this part of the show with the story of his battle with Yellow Hair.

Speaker One: **Sherman Alexie**

The "Duel Between Buffalo Bill and Yellow Hair" reduced White-Indian affairs to a single combat, a single violent moment. This is very Western, and it is classic Greek drama: a single combat determines the outcome of a nation. Think Achilles versus Hector. Buffalo Bill and Ned Buntline had this down cold.

Speaker Two: **Wild West Show Announcer**

This battle actually occurred during the play called the "Sitting Bull War." It tells the story of the first scalp taken in retribution for Custer's murder. The play has several short scenes.

Scene One: Cowboys and Indians are riding toward one another. Cody is in the foreground.

Scene Two: Yellow Hair challenges Buffalo Bill. The two men gallop toward one another. The cowboys and other Indians assemble on the side of the stage, forming an audience for the battle that is about to start.

Scene Three: The two men dismount and fire their guns. Cody grasps his knife. Yellow Hair has a spear. Cody knifes Yellow Hair, then he leaps up, holding the scalp of Yellow Hair in his right hand. Yellow Hair falls dead.

Scene Four: The Indians charge back on stage and attack the cowboys. A violent battle ensues. The Indians are defeated. They slink off into the darkness.

Scene Five: Buffalo Bill returns to the center of the stage. The Master of Ceremonies steps forth and praises him for his bravery, patriotism, and his part in clearing the way for civilization (Warren, 2005, p. 76).

(The Curtain Comes Down)

Speaker One: **Narrator**

We've reviewed these two morality plays and the paintings that stand behind them. They enact myth and an imaginary history. They reproduce racist discourses about Native Americans, and totally ignore the fact that the events represent how whites were destroying at least two Indian nations.

Speaker Two: **Sherman Alexie**

And no mention that the U.S. government has violated its treaty agreements with the Lakota and the Cheyenne.

Speaker One: **Narrator**

Right, Sherman. As fate would have it, Custer and Cody meet again.

ACT THREE, SCENE ONE

Wild Bill Dies and a Town Creates a Museum

Speaker One: **Narrator**

William Cody died on January 10, 1917, eleven years after his show closed. Within a few months of his death, the town of Cody, Wyoming, (named after him) began construction on a museum, the Buffalo Bill Historical Center, to honor Cody and his memory and to celebrate the spirit of the American West and Cody's place in this history (Bartlett, 1992).

Speaker Two: **Coyote 1**

The center quickly added two central wings, or sites, one devoted to Western Art called the Whitney Gallery of Western Art, and a second focusing on Buffalo Bill, his life, his Wild West show, his writings, and its relations to a third exhibit site, The Cody High Style.

Speaker One: **Richard Bartlett**

In due time, the Center, soon called the Smithsonian of the West (Dickinson, Ott, and Aoki, 2005, p. 87), would expand, to also include wings devoted to nineteenth century Plains Indians, Western Fire Arms, and the Natural History of the Greater Yellowstone Region, plus the McCracken Research Library and the Greever and Braun Statue Gardens which display statues of Sacagawea and Crazy Horse as well as the *Unknown* and *Male Warrior with Loincloth* (Denzin, 2008, p. 111).

A life-size statue of Cody greets visitors as they enter the center. A life-size statue of Cody on a horse, called *The Scout,* standing atop a huge concrete plinth, can be seen from the windows at the west end of the Whitney Gallery (Bartlett, 1992, p. 47).

Speaker Two: **Curator**

In the years 2006–2007, we launched a small exhibit of Custer paintings. You have talked about this exhibit in this book. Then we extended the exhibit in 2010 and 2011.

So we have Custer paintings in one wing, and Cody memorabilia in a wing practically next door. I mean, you can't have Cody without Custer, and you can't have Custer without Cody.

Speaker One: **Narrator**

By "Custer paintings," you mean the paintings by Paxson, Mardon, Scholder, Biss, and Weighorst?

Speaker Two: **Curator**

Yes. Custer lives, so to speak, in these paintings in the Whitney Gallery.

Speaker One: **Ben Stiller**

It's like another *Night at the Museum* movie. Cody and Custer could walk out of their respective sites in the Buffalo Bill Historical Center and have dinner. In fact, let's imagine them doing this.

ACT THREE, SCENE TWO

Ghosts in the Museum: Cody and Custer, side by side

Speaker One: **Buffalo Bill**

George, they won't let us die. They've turned us into tourist attractions.

Speaker Two: **Custer**

Well, folks keep painting pictures of me and my boys at the Last Stand. They've named national forests, towns, newspapers, and high schools after me. They do annual re-enactments of my Last Stand.

But nobody has made a name for himself painting your picture. What do you think of that, Mr. Wild West showman?

Speaker One: **Buffalo Bill**

Actually, they named a town and a historical center after me, and Disney performs a version of my Wild West show in Paris and in Orlando.

That kind of attention you have been getting doesn't bother me, George.

But then nobody ever called me a coward, and Indians didn't kill me. I killed them, to avenge your death, remember?

Anyway, they've made movies about both of us.

Speaker Two: **Custer**

Let's stop this bickering. We were both showmen, and we both needed the Indians for our stories.

I needed Crazy Horse and Sitting Bull so I could be remembered as the general who gave his life in the most important Indian War in the nineteenth century.

Speaker One: **Buffalo Bill**

Some people would say you needed me, too. My Wild West show helped salvage your reputation.

But along with me, you had a lot of other help. There were those painters, there was Mr. Busch and his beer advertisement.

There were the poets, like Longfellow and Whitman, who helped turn you into a national hero. Eventually, Hollywood got into the act.

Speaker Two: **Custer**

Don't forget my dear wife, Libbie. She helped a lot.

Speaker One: **Buffalo Bill**

George, look at these paintings. Which one do you like best: Biss, Paxson, or Mardon?

Speaker Two: **Custer**

I gotta go with the Paxson. I come out looking pretty good in that painting. I'm heroic, brave, flanked by Cooke and my brother. Crazy Horse is in the background along with those other savages. I kinda like the Biss painting, too.

Speaker One: **Buffalo Bill**

So you don't like the Mardon painting?

Speaker Two: **Custer**

No! First of all, you can barely find me on the canvas. He gives more attention to Sitting Bull and Crazy Horse than to me. It's like I'm an afterthought. And this is *my* story.

Speaker One: **Buffalo Bill**

I see what you mean. Last summer, they moved the paintings around in the museum. Now you can stand in one spot and see both the Mardon and the Paxson paintings at the same time.

Speaker Two: **Coyote 1**

　It's about time they brought Mardon right up against Paxson, because he tells the story as the Lakota and Cheyenne saw it. His version is closer to what Red Horse is telling.

Speaker One: **Custer**

　But he doesn't show the battle from the point of view of the soldiers, and that is what Paxson did so well.

Speaker Two: **Coyote 1**

　Maybe we have been telling the wrong story.

ACT THREE, SCENE THREE
Another Ending

(Spotlight shines on poster)

CUSTER DIED FOR HIS SINS

Speaker One: **Sherman Alexie**

　Let's imagine a new ending to this play.

Speaker Two: **Louise Erdrich**[8]

　Can we get rid of the violence and the war talk?

Speaker One: **Elizabeth Cook-Lynn**[9]

　And Native Americans playing Indians?

Speaker Two: **Vine Deloria Jr.**

　Maybe nobody has to die for anybody's sins any longer.

Speaker One: **Sherman Alexie**

Let's get rid of cowboys and Indians. No more War Dances?

Speakers One and Two: **Louise Erdrich** *and* **Elizabeth Cook-Lynn**

Let's imagine a space of hope and love, let's go back to that big Indian village on the banks of the Little Bighorn. Before Custer and his soldiers charged us.

Our children were playing and swimming.
The elders were digging for roots, cooking.
The warriors were grooming their horses.

Speaker One: Vine **Deloria Jr.**

Nobody wanted to fight that day. We wanted to live in harmony with the world. But our warriors had no choice. They fought to protect a way of life, to save a village.

Speaker Two: **Sherman Alexie**

Hold on. Let's go back into the Buffalo Bill Historical Center. Let's tear down the walls that separate white culture and Indian culture. Let's put some of the Plains Indian exhibits in the Whitney Gallery. Let's move the guns someplace else.

Speaker One: **Coyote 1**

Sherman, when you tear down the walls, remember that visitors to the Buffalo Bill Historical Center are already experiencing white Western culture alongside Plains Indian art and artifacts. Moving walls will not change this fact.

Speaker Two: **Coyote 2**

Don't forget Custer betrayed the Lakota Sioux, the Cheyenne, and the Crow nations. The U.S. government had no intention of ever giving land back to them. So if you think everything can be smoothed over, you are wrong.

Speaker One: **Coyote 1**

But we need a utopian vision, a way out of this tangled, violent history.

Speaker Two: **Coyote 2**

I got it, Coyote! Let's get the painters back together. Let's bring in Red Horse, Eric von Schmidt, and Allan Mardon. We can commission them to collaborate on a monumental painting of the event as the "official" painting. Let them imagine a new ending and a new beginning.

Speaker One: **Coyote 1**

Great idea. This could replace the von Schmidt painting that the Park service now uses on its brochures. It would be the painting every visitor drives past on the way to the Little Bighorn Battlefield National Monument.

Speaker Two: **Coyote 2**

And it would hang in the Buffalo Bill Historical Center, right where that big Paxson painting is now exhibited.

Speakers One and Two: **Louise Erdrich** *and* **Elizabeth Cook-Lynn**

Let's do it! A world with peace, harmony, love, caring, justice, peace. No more war. No more war paintings.

Speaker Two: **Coyote 2**

Maybe a painting can change the world.

THE END

CHAPTER SEVEN

The Last Stand

What Americans believe about the West is as significant as what actually happened in these storied landscapes.[1]

"I'm running through the dark. I run toward the sound of laughter. I am standing in the middle of a gigantic Indian camp. And I don't mean some Disneyland, Nickelodeon, Rollercoaster, stuffed animal, cotton candy Indian Camp.

Nope.

I am standing in the middle of a real Indian camp, complete with thousands of real Indian tipis, and tens of thousands of real old-time Indians.

These are how Indians used to be, how Indians are supposed to be. Justice always talked with admiration about Indians like this. . . . Even the dogs seem to be barking in Indian" (Alexie, 2007, pp. 59–60).

Like that huge Indian camp along the banks of the Little Bighorn River, before the Battle of Greasy Grass. (Denzin)

"She promised, she'd be there with me when I paint my masterpiece" (Bob Dylan, 1971).[2]

Rescripting

Custer On Canvas has been about nostalgia, memory, imaginary pasts, traveling Wild West minstrel shows, Indians playing Indians, whites playing Indians, artists and their Last Stand paintings, soldiers, generals, scouts, ritual dramas, eternal youth, self-sacrificing heroes, buffalo hunters, dime novelists, a myth that will not die. Custer is eternal youth. The Last Stand implies an ending. There was no last stand.

It has been about how an event and a set of paintings, when combined with a Wild West show and an advertisement for beer, freezes forever a people in an imaginary racist past. It is about how that past lives in the present through paintings, performances, movies, commercials, and museum exhibits.

It has been about storytelling. The Custer narratives are stories about "storying," and my narrative, as argued in Chapter 1, has been an attempt to problematize the concept of the Custer "script" itself. This book is a subversive response to a script we have all been handed through the Last Stand paintings. In rescripting the grand narrative, I have attempted to undo the Last Stand. This is because there is no last stand. There was no stand. Indeed, there is no last. To repeat, as Eric von Schmidt discovered when inscribing the Last Stand, there is nowhere to stand. There is no true vantage point. The Last Stand is a social construction, pure and simple. My dramatic format throughout has been intended to leave you, the reader, with nowhere to stand, except to understand that what you knew before can no longer be taken as true. The story I tell here is but one more version of the "real" last stand.

In challenging the concept of an objective rendering of the Last Stand I create a space for alternative tellings, most importantly, Red Horse's forty-one drawings. These drawings, like those of White Swan, Amos Bad Heart Buffalo, Mardon, and Scholder, challenge the official history embedded in the so-called canonical paintings, from Adams through Mulvany, and Paxson to von Schmidt. These official stories present Native Americans as uncivilized, violent barbarians. They are part of the Custer myth.

The alternative narratives challenge this myth. They anticipate and record the death of the Indian Nation. They bring care and remorse to these tragic endings, emotions excluded in the dominant white narrative. They offer a counter-narrative, turning the Last Stand into a process, into a sequence of interconnected events. They give Custer a small part in the larger play. He is just another dead soldier, not a grand hero or tragic figure.

The Native American ledger artists, using the methods of pictographic narrative, treat the battle as a victory. They paint themselves into their autobiographical drawings. The drawings cover familiar themes: warrior-soldiers, dead cavalry, dead Indians, Indians in pursuit of cavalry and horses, Indian prowess over disorganized cavalry. This art records painful memories while honoring those who died. It obviously refused the racist mythology of the white artists and their drawings. Red Horse and his associates paint their way into an alternative history, a counter-resistance narrative, a decolonizing story.

The early Anglo-American paintings and lithographs (1876–1899) were based on a realist nineteenth century aesthetic. This aesthetic presumably guaranteed historical accuracy and authentic detail, often leading the painter to fill his studio with artifacts that would then be painted into his masterpiece. Persons were named in these paintings, as if to give them a name gave the work greater credibility. Of course, these staged versions of the Last Stand were produced in the studio. Turned into lithographic reproductions, the paintings were then available for mass consumption. The Custer myth, the Last Stand narrative, is all-consuming, especially so for white painters, from Paxson to von Schmidt. The project takes control of their lives. They labor over their paintings, taking years to complete them. They anguish over detail, point of view, nuance, horizon, the middle distance, historical accuracy. If asked by the right person, they made changes or additions, as when E. S. Godfrey spoke to E. S. Paxson about his painting:

Godfrey *to* **Paxson**

Ed, the general's personal yellow silk flag is missing from your painting. It needs to be there.

Godfrey *to* **Reader**

I came back to his studio eight years later, and there was the flag in the painting. I thanked him, and so did Mrs. Custer the next time she saw him.

The white painters struggle to capture the dying soldiers' experience, to catch their dread, fear, and pain. They make repeated trips to the battlefield, taking photographs of themselves in various locations on the site, from the river to the Last Stand monument. They paint on giant canvases, suggesting that an event so important demands huge space. This is quite unlike the tiny ledger art of White Swan or Red Horse. The white painters thoroughly buy into the Custer myth, including its tellings by Libby Custer, and reject the drawings of Native Americans. Racism is erased by an aesthetic of realism, a belief that a well-trained painter can render objects in reality objectively, nonemotionally, free of personal bias.[3] The artist was dedicated to this objective aesthetic. This meant the painter painted the world correctly, in terms of historical, empirical, and psychological detail. This involved visual realism, a fidelity to dress, uniform color, weapons, and so on. In turn, visual realism authorized attempts at psychological realism, including capturing the fear of death for the dying soldiers.

This version of the historically accurate painting is taken to the theatrical stage in the traveling minstrel event called the Wild West show (Reddin, 1999). Custer's Last Stand became a centerpiece in Cody's extravaganza. It was all there in Cody's show, and before the show in those paintings, too: soldiers, cowboys, Indians, violence, death, a last stand to defend democracy and civilization for white settlers. The paintings provided the backdrop for the performances, and the performances brought the paintings alive. Indeed Cody, Tom Mix, and others turned the paintings of Adams and Becker into posters advertising their shows (Reddin 1999). And Mr. Busch used them to sell his beer.

A tighter fit between fabrication, history, vengeance narratives, and reality could not be found. The Wild West, like the paintings it was based on, became a performance: tourism for traveling European aristocrats; racialized spectacles with white Indians, buffalo hunters, mythic spaces on the frontier; the Wild West for hire, sometimes with traveling painters and photographers. Kill and scalp an Indian for Custer. Bill Cody reenacts Custer's death. A museum and a town bring the two men together through an art exhibit. Art imitates life. Life imitates art, sometimes. The Wild West showman and his museum performing the Wild West.

BUT CUSTER DIED FOR HIS SINS
CUSTER OR BUST HER

The Custer painters were not trained to paint Indians, in the manner of Catlin or Remington. They offered, instead, stereotyped depictions of Native Americans.

Consider any of the paintings of Native Americans by George Catlin. The Last Stand artist's primary focus was on the heroic white men who died that day in that battle, at the hands of barbarians. The national poets—Longfellow, Whitman—got into the act, using their poetry to validate the paintings and the tragedy the artists rendered in such graphic detail.

Recall these comments from Walt Whitman (1881) on John Mulvany's 1879 Custer's Last Rally:

Walt Whitman

> "I went today and spent over an hour in front of John Mulvany's vast canvas. There are no tricks . . . altogether a Western autochthonic phase of America, the frontiers . . . heroic . . . nothing in the books like it" (1876, pp 592–593).

And remember these lines from the other nineteenth century national poet.

Henry Wadsworth Longfellow

> "By their fires the Sioux Chiefs
> muttered their woes and griefs . . .
> And Rain-in-the-Face, in his flight,
> Uplifted high in air . . .
> The brave heart, that beat no more,
> Of the White Chief with yellow hair.
> from 'The Revenge of Rain-in-the-Face'"

Using the name Battle of Greasy Grass as a counter-name for the Battle of the Little Bighorn helps to challenge these poetic interpretations. Yet no poets have stepped forward to honor Red Horse's heroes. Only Allan Mardon gives Crazy Horse and Sitting Bull the due they deserve.

This book has been about personal memory, my life as it intersected with the Vietnam War, Dee Brown's 1970 Bury My Heart at Wounded Knee, and my attempt to write my way back into a space Brown occupied in

1970. Can we use our words to rewrite history? Dee Brown was able to do this, and Allan Mardon's Battle of Greasy Grass provides a powerful set of counter-images to all the pro-Custer paintings, from Adams through Paxson and von Schmidt. And this is not solely an American issue, for the cowboy and the Indian, Custer and his Last Stand and Buffalo Bill Wild West shows are global phenomena, exported to New Zealand and Australia, Africa to India, Europe to Asia, South America to Canada (Hollick, 1992; Nash, 1992). If the Wild West, cowboys and Indians, Buffalo Bill, and Custer's Last Stand had never existed, Europe and the other nations of the world would have had to invent them. The Wild West and all its accoutrements was a traveling minstrel show that could not be contained in the United States, and William Cody helped make this so.

Consider the following excerpt from a modern (November 2010) exhibit in Auckland, New Zealand. (Refer to photos from the Auckland War Memorial Museum/Tamaki Paenga Hira exhibit, "Educating the Wild Child.")

In the Wild Spaces, playing without restraint, children developed and learned games and outdoor pursuits that became part of the universal fabric of childhood in New Zealand. . . . This space 'in between' school and home is where children invented their own games.

Wild Child shows the toys children made—knuckle bones, hoops, stilts, peashooters, spud guns, and bows and arrows. It shows the costumes they wore, modeled after cowboys and Indians, Hopalong Cassidy, the Lone Ranger.[4]

A cowboy and Indian outfit, complete with toy pistol, cowboy hat, chaps, vest, and Indian headband with feathers hangs below these words.

Imagine white children playing cowboys and Indians, doing their versions of a Wild West show in the Wild Spaces between home and school in 1970s New Zealand.

Consider the wide reach of a Buffalo Bill Wild West Vintage Poster, approximation of 1885 Cody Poster. This poster is available for sale in the Buffalo Bill Historical Center gift shop in Cody, Wyoming, and in poster shops in New Zealand.

―※―※―※―

Norman's Dream

Like Eric von Schmidt, for as long as I can remember, I have had a dream, which "must be as old as time" (von Schmidt, 1992, p. 53). In the dream I am lost. I have ridden my bicycle somewhere, parked it, locked it up, gone inside, walked around. When I come back outside my bicycle is missing. I look everywhere. I have doubts about where I parked it. I walk in circles, I walk around the block. I look in alleys. I go two streets over and look for it. It gets dark. I become fearful. I have forgotten where I parked my bicycle, and now I am tumbling through space. I am acting irresponsibly. I feel guilty, ashamed. How did this happen? Sometimes I do not fall. I just walk around lost in darkness. I never find my bicycle.

Several years ago, I drove to Milwaukee to attend the annual meetings of the Midwest Sociological Society. I parked my car in a parking lot and went into the convention hotel. Three days later I checked out of the hotel but could not remember where I had parked my car. I had lost the ticket given to me by the parking lot attendant. I walked and walked, for over an hour, up and down streets, before I stumbled on my car, in a lot two blocks from the hotel. I had no memory of driving into that lot and leaving my car there.

My Milwaukee experience mirrors the recurring dream. Once again I have lost something, and have forgotten where I put it. The experience and the dream are about memory, loss, forgetting, recovering something that I have been responsible for. The dream and the experience are about finding a place where things are certain, where bicycles and cars are not lost, where memory does not fail, leaving me falling through space.

In the dream I blame myself for the loss, for the forgetfulness, like the singer in "Bob Dylan's Dream" (1962). I rework those lines ever so slightly, with this dream:

I dream a recurring dream that becomes a nightmare
concerning myself and the memories I have lost.
With half-closed eyes I stare into a room, but
no one is there.
Time passes and the dream
and the nightmare remain.
I cannot dream my way back to that moment where loss is absent.
My dream stays with me
My dream moves with me into the museum,
Into the spaces of Custer's Last Stand and
William Cody's Wild West show.

⁕ ⁕ ⁕

When we were young, my brother and I
wore cowboy outfits and rode a swayback horse
named Sunny, deaf in one ear and blind in one eye.
I have a picture of this moment.

When I was little, in the 1940s, living in
south-central Iowa, our grandmother told
us stories about Indians.

When I was nine years old, I played Squanto
in my class's Thanksgiving play.

When I was not yet ten,
One Sunday Mother and Dad
took my brother and me to see a powwow
Being performed in the Mesquaki Reservation
In Tama, Iowa.

⁕ ⁕ ⁕

I stand with the granddaughters in front of the Paxson and Mardon paintings.

It is like being back in my dream.
I am lost, I have no firm grounding.
I cannot explain these paintings to them.
I feel irresponsible, guilty, I
remember playing Squanto when I was nine.

But Squanto is not in this room.
And I have no memory, other than a
fake childhood
memory of playing Indian in a school play
and dress-up with my brother
to build on, no place to stand.

Whose Last Stand?
Who was Custer?
Little Bighorn?
I lived a childhood based on fake Last Stands and
pretend Wild West shows.

This is outrageous.
These childhood games taught me
that anyone could be an Indian for a day,
in a play.
These mini-minstrel shows,
like the Custer paintings and Wild Bill
Cody's Wild West shows
taught me that "Indianness" was something
You put on and took off.

The reality of that lie confronted me that day when I stood in front of these paintings with my granddaughters.

Memories, Paintings, and Museums

I turn around and walk back into the museum. I stand again in the large exhibit room. I confront the huge Paxson painting and glance across at the Mardon Battle of Greasy Grass. It suddenly becomes clear. Like my dream, the Last Stand paintings are about memory and loss. Painters like Paxson want to recover what has been lost, namely Custer, his men, and the American dream of white supremacy. Custer should not have been killed. He should not have lost that battle. He should have been able to destroy the Indians. But this is not the case for Mardon. And now irony enters the picture, for Mardon's painting brings Custer down to earth and refuses to valorize him. The viewer, like Naomi, does not know where to stand. What do these two, totally different paintings mean?

Back to Paxson and his obsession with death. The horror of the battle that he paints is not about the fear in the men's eyes. The horror operates at a higher level, at the level of a nameless, bottomless fear, a nightmare. If Custer was killed, any other white American could be killed. Hence the painter must show that while Custer died with dignity, in fact, he is still alive. This must not be forgotten. For the myth to prevail, memory must hold firm, details must be accurate.

This is why Buffalo Bill's re-enactment of the moment when he scalped Yellow Hair was so important. It restored order to the dream that was out of balance.

I scalped Yellow Hair to avenge Custer's death.

—William Cody

―――✳―✳―✳―――

But the order that Cody restores for Custer is undercut by Mardon. His braves, by and large, are filled with joy and the thrill of victory. And they did not scalp Custer.

―――✳―✳―✳―――

Fuchs, Adams, Paxson, Mulvany, Remington, Russell, and von Schmidt are looking for a place to paint from. Fearful that memory will fail them, they seek a stable site that will allow them to render the event in accurate detail. They go back to the battlefield, over and over again. They fill their studios with objects, bows, arrows, guns, old uniforms, headdresses. They interview survivors, study old paintings, hire live subjects. Nothing must be forgotten. If they can get it right, then Custer lives forever, remembered, not forgotten, remembered in loving, if painful, detail.

The painters, like the dreamer in my dream, are responsible for not losing what has been given them; namely a myth, in one form or another, about control, loss, and identity. Lost Bicycles and dead generals and painters are no different at this level.

―――✳―✳―✳―――

This project started in a museum inside a museum, the Whitney Gallery of Western Art inside the Buffalo Bill Historical Center. And the Whitney is located— geographically and symbolically—midway between the Cody Firearms Museum and the Plains Indians Museum. There would have been no Last Stand without the use of some of the guns exhibited in the Gun Museum. Of course, those guns were used against the Indians, whose lives are re-presented in the Plains Indians Museum. Conveniently, then, the Whitney displays the paintings that were produced by the historical event that brought Indians and guns together, that fateful day, June 26, 1876.

Museums, of course, are about more than collections of artifacts and pictures. Museums like the Buffalo Bill Historical Center are cultural centers, sites of experience for cultural tourists. Museums are about memory, the recovery of the past through the assembling of objects, pictures, photographs, paintings, sculptures, statues, videos, guided tours, performances, tourists, curators. Museums are laboratories for creating new knowledge. In this sense, they are memory palaces, places to mourn and celebrate, stages for the re-enactment of political ideology. And, they are embedded in a tourist economy, complete with cafes, and gift shops, and book stores" (Kirshenblatt-Gimblett, 1998, p.139; Luke, 2002; Sather-Wagstaff, 2010).[5]

Dark Tourism

A cultural site like the Buffalo Bill Historical Center offers the Western tourist a set of narratives, stories, pictures, and performances about the New and Old West. Sather-Wagstaff (2010) calls these productions memoryscapes, images that evoke memories, meanings, and connections to historical, cultural, political, and geographical places and spaces. The heritages of the West, or the western heritage,[6] is embodied in these narratives, in the paintings, sculptures, and statues, and in the interactive videos that are ever present in places like the Buffalo Bill Historical Center.

In these productions the spirit of the New West is made real by "looking West," to use John Dorst's phrase (Dorst, 1999). And this is the mythical, fictional, but still historical West, the West manufactured in dime novels and Wild West shows, complete with cowboys, Indians, the military, guns, warfare. This is the Wild West as entertainment (Lukes, 2002, pp. 11–12). All of these elements are present in the memoryscapes that circulate in the Buffalo Bill Historical Center. In them, the tourist emotionally experiences the Buffalo Bill Cody version of the Western heritage.

Underneath it all is a hidden truth. The Buffalo Bill Historical Center offers the tourist a trip into the spaces of dark tourism, a historical trip into the places of death and suffering (Sather-Wagstaff, 2010). However, the museum aesthetic sanitizes this space, death and suffering are transformed into historical art, into historically important historical art, no less! Paintings are carefully separated on sterile white walls, often out of historical context. Native Americans would never present art in this way, nor would most cultures outside the European world (see Loendorf, 2008; Tilley, 2008).

The dark spaces of the Buffalo Bill Historical Center are right there, front and center, for all to see in Paxson's huge painting—blood, gore, scalps, arrows sticking out of chests, men writhing in pain, dead and dying horses. This is the dark but valorized side of the West, the version that hurts and is deadly. The paintings and the exhibits and the contradictions that circulate between them help the tourist navigate, construct, and give meaning to this sublimated violence. All of the Custer, and many of the other paintings in the Buffalo Bill Historical Center, are about death, violence, and genocide. But they are not presented as such. They are presented as historical works of art, the essence of the western Heritage. And this is how one form of dark tourism in the New West works.

Truth, Myth, and Imagination: Art of the Battle of Little Bighorn[7]

A Short One-Act Play

It is time to go back into the museum. I'm standing in front of the Paxson and Mardon paintings once again with Naomi and Sylvia. It is the summer of 2010. Christine C. Brindza (2010) has arranged a small exhibit of work depicting the Battle of the Little Bighorn. A number of painters, including Red Horse, White Swan, William Cary, Cassilly Adams, E. S. Paxson, F. Otto Becker, Allan Mardon, Earl Biss, Fritz Scholder, Kevin Red Star, and John Nieto have joined us for a conversation. Custer and Cody, Vine Deloria Jr., Sherman Alexie, John Dorst, Coyote 1 and Coyote 2, and Tonto are also here. They are trying to imagine how the Buffalo Bill Historical Center could present Last Stand exhibits differently. This also involves how the West, and cowboys and Indians, should be presented in the various sites in the Center. You could call this an exercise in critical museum studies (Dorst, 1999, p. 225; Lukes, 2002).

ACT ONE, SCENE ONE

Another Night at the Museum?

Speaker One: **Coyote 1**

What is this, another night at the museum?

Speaker Two: **Narrator**

No, not yet, anyway. I want to look at the paintings again, the painted hides, the ledger art, the big and little canvases—Red Horse, White Swan, Paxson, Mardon, Scholder, Biss.

Speaker One: **Sherman Alexie**

Can we go back to what I said in the last chapter? Remember, I proposed that we do a major reconstruction of the museum, that we tear down the walls that separate white culture from Indian Culture.

Speaker Two: **Vine Deloria Jr.**

Yes. YES! This would involve moving the exhibits of white and Indian culture into different spaces.

Speaker One: **Coyote 1**

You'd have to move the Cody Style Rooms, the Western Gun Museum, and the Whitney Gallery. Where would you put them?

Speaker Two: **John D. Dorst**

Call this critical museum studies, the construction of a consciously reflexive or meta-museum.

Speaker One: **Coyote 2**

In the meta-museum, displays and arrangements critically comment on themselves. A display is not an end in itself, it is not something that stands outside time, place, politics, and history (Dorst, 1999, pp. 225–226).

Speaker Two: **Tonto**

This would mean a reimaging of the Museum and how it re-presents the West. The Buffalo Bill Historical Center believes that what Americans believe about the West is as significant as what actually happened there.

Speaker One: **Coyote 2**

So how does a museum separate fact from fantasy, myth from reality?

Speaker Two: **Stuart Hall**

It can't. There is only a politics of representation. So whose politics—which objects, paintings, stories, and narratives—will the Buffalo Bill Historical Center tell?

Speaker One: **Buffalo Bill Historical Center Staff**

The McCracken[8] staff collaborates with curators, scholars, students, writers, and filmmakers to reveal the American West in all its human and natural complexity. *The last word on the West* defines the mission—to preserve the written and visual record.

Speaker Two: **Coyote 1**

Whose texts, whose records? Whose last word? So let's get on with it, Mr. Critical Museum Curator.

Speaker One: **Tonto**

Let's go back to the paintings.

Speakers One and Two: **Custer** *and* **William Cody** *(in unison)*

Hold on. You can't get to the paintings without going through us. This is Bill's museum, and there would be no Last Stand paintings without George.

Speaker One: **Coyote 1**

And these are not just Last Stand paintings. These representations provide an essential iconography of the Wild West, complete with cowboys, Indians, and appropriate western regalia.

Speaker Two: **John D. Dorst**

Bill and Coyote are both right. Bill's Wild West show is the first clear moment in which the West as a staged spectacle is packaged for mass consumption. And his show, with Custer and Sitting Bull, creates the automatic pairing of cowboys and Indians (Dorst, 1999, p. 31).

Speaker One: **Coyote 1**

So the Last Stand paintings are about cowboys and Indians.

Speaker Two: **Coyote 2**

Are you saying it is impossible to escape this cowboy-Indian Wild West motif, no matter where you put the walls in the reconstructed Buffalo Bill Historical Center?

Speaker One: **John D. Dorst**

Yes. It's all tangled up.

Speaker Two: **Sherman Alexie**

Remember, Cody brought Sitting Bull and the other Indians into his show, and located them in his play about Custer, so now you have Indians and soldier-cowboys performing together.

Speaker One: **John D. Dorst**

At this level, you have a reconciliation between the red man and the white man—assimilation to white culture, white history, an endorsement of white ideology (Dorst, 1999, p. 29).

Speaker Two: **Coyote 1**

This is the look of the New West! Why this assimilation motif, why reconciliation?

Speaker One: **Coyote 2**

When does this New West Show start?

ACT ONE, SCENE TWO

The New Wild West Museum

Speaker One: **Christine C. Brindza**

Let's go into the Whitney Gallery and look at the exhibit we ran last summer. We've got a painted deer hide depicting the Last Stand. We have the Paxson and Mardon paintings. Off the main room we have paintings by Biss and Scholder, and sketches Paxson made for his huge painting.

We believe that artists choose their own version of history when painting their version of the Battle of the Little Bighorn. Sometimes they provide information mistaken for truth (Brindza, 2010, p. 5).

Speaker Two: **Coyote 1**

Can we start with the Native American paintings?

Speaker One: **Coyote 2**

Yes!

Speaker Two: **Christine C. Brindza**

Actually, Coyote, we've just opened the new Museum of Native American Art. This complements the Museum of Plains Indians, which has cultural artifacts.

In this new museum we have a large collection of Native American paintings about the Battle of Greasy Grass.

We have the works of nineteenth and twentieth century Native American painters, many of the ones Norman has been writing about: Red Horse, White Swan, Amos Bad Heart Buffalo, Earl Biss, Fritz Scholder, Kevin Red Star, John Nieto.

We have ledger art at the front of the exhibit. We also have the work of contemporary Native American women photographers.

Speakers One and Two (in unison): **Red Horse** *and* **Native American Deer Hide Painter**

Say what you want. Our drawings of the battle are based on first-hand observations. We were there. None of the white painters were there. Our drawings are about brave warriors protecting their village. Our drawings show that Custer and his men were very disorganized. We also show them setting fire to our tipis. We show them attempting to kill our women, children, and elders. They were murderers.

Speaker One: **Fritz Scholder**

In my two big paintings *Custer and 20,000 Indians* and *American Landscape,* I refuse to honor the myth surrounding Custer as a heroic figure. I turn him into a caricature of the valiant military leader.

He is pompous, filled with self-importance, and his men are gun-toting cartoonlike figures.

Speaker Two: **Kevin Red Star**

In my painting, *Rain in the Face,* I honor the man who is alleged to have killed Custer. I did this because he needs to be seen, honored, and validated.

Speaker One: **Earl Biss**

I took a slightly different path from Kevin. Like Fritz, I wanted to pull Custer down off his high horse. My photograph-like painting presents a perplexed, puzzled, vain Custer.

Speaker Two: **John Nieto**

I had the same project. In my *Custer Suite,* an insolent Custer is surrounded by four proud Native American warriors.

Speaker One: **Narrator**

The noble warriors are looking forward, directly into the eyes of the viewer. Custer, in contrast, has his head turned, as if being unable to look the viewer in the eye.

Speaker Two: **Allan Mardon**

Custer was a weasel!

Speaker One: **Assistant Curator**

With this new wing, we wanted to show a different version of the Last Stand story. We are putting the big Paxson painting in storage for the time being because it needs restoration work. Perhaps this is symbolic; the painting is aging.

We'll keep Allan Mardon's *Battle of Greasy Grass* in this exhibit space. Remember, he includes in his painting people usually ignored by other painters.

He has Kate Bighead, who saw the battle from a distance, and Isaiah Dorman, the African American scout and interpreter who was killed near the river.

He paints in Mark Kellogg, the *Bismarck Tribune* reporter who was also killed on the battlefield. He shows Kellogg with papers scattered around his body, suggesting that his account was lost for all time (Brindza, 2010, p. 8).

Speaker Two: **Coyote 1**

Which means that no immediate first-person white account of the battle ever existed.

Speaker One: **Tonto**

You have to admire Allan's painting. Listen to what Mindy Besaw[9] says about it.

Speaker Two: **Mindy A. Besaw** *(reading a letter dated January 10, 2010, to* **Allan Mardon***)*

"Dear Allan,

Your painting, *The Battle of Greasy Grass,* with its colors, abstracted figures, flattened spaces, repetition of shapes, and interplay of text and image, seizes and holds my attention.

I would argue that the painting is rooted in the great historical movements of the past—the Fauvres, the Cubists, Native American hide paintings and ledger art.

It's easy to argue that your interpretation of the Battle of the Little Bighorn provides a new perspective on this moment in history.

It asks us to rethink age-old stories and myths about the battle. *The Battle of Greasy Grass* is a masterpiece and we are lucky to have it in our museum" (Besaw, 2010, in Mardon, 2010).

Speaker One: **Coyote 1**

Hey, this is high praise. But she is a curator.

Speakers One and Two (in unison): **Coyote 1** *and* **Tonto**

Hey, Mindy, you could say the exact same thing about the narrative art of our painters—from Red Horse to Red Star.

Speaker One: **Mindy A. Besaw**

You guys are right.

Speaker Two: **Assistant Curator**

The New West Museum is set up to tell a different story about the Last Stand, about cowboys and Indians, a different story, too, about memory, about what we remember, including how we represent violence.

Speakers One and Two (in unison): **William Cody** *and* **Custer**

This New West Museum tells a different story, alright. It undercuts the stories surrounding us, my Wild West show and your Last Stand.

Speaker One: **Coyote 2**

The paintings in the New West Museum leave Custer and Cody fans with a new problem, for there was no real Last Stand. The history of the new Old West must be rewritten.

Speaker Two: **Assistant Curator**

If you look beyond the Mardon painting, you will see another exhibit space. We have been working with groups of Native American photographers. Some of their work critiques the "vanishing race" genre of romantic photography, so popular with the revival of the work of Edward Curtis and other photographers of American Indians.

We have a series of photographs by Native American women photographers who use their photographs to tell stories. We have included the work of Pena Bonita and Pamela Shields.

They tell stories about Native American women and their relations to American culture.

They do not reproduce the vanishing race genre, a major legacy of the Last Stand narratives.

—※—※—※—

In struggling to find my own place in the Last Stand narratives, I learned that these paintings and the stories they tell, like the postmodern West itself, exist only as a multiplicity of conflicting representations, distorted pictures, memories, fictions, romantic myths. Two themes are central to this romantic mythology: Native Americans and cowboys as iconic representations of the Wild West, and Custer and the Battle of the Little Bighorn as a site for commemorating a white version of western history. Since 1876, these two themes have been folded into a series of cultural performances, including museum exhibits of Last Stand paintings and historical re-enactments of the Battle of the Little Bighorn. I have attempted to write my way into and alongside these cultural formations, reading them from the standpoint of personal memory and critical theory.

It is not enough to criticize these myths. We need utopian alternatives, paintings, photographs, performance events, and public ceremonies that honor counter-memories of grief, loss, a politics of possibility that can turn history around. Indigenous representations must be heard and seen. This is what Allan Mardon is calling for when he says we need to fill the museums and art galleries with Native American paintings of the Battle of the Little Bighorn.

Indigenous performance narratives help unravel the knot that insists on connecting idealized versions of Native Americans with the landscapes of the West. The knot links consumption with the Western tourist identity, and locks Native Americans forever in a violent but romantic western pastoral narrative. This is the heart of the Western Heritage—cowboys, Indians, horses, buffaloes, bows and arrows, dude ranches, the outdoors, mountains, raging rivers, forests, and Western theme parks.

These identities and activities stand outside time, frozen in place. They are kept alive in Hollywood movies [10] and enacted in family summer vacations to Yellowstone, with side trips into Custer Country and stops in Cody, Wyoming for a quick look at firearms and paintings in the Buffalo Bill Historical Center.

The idealized West is in trouble. The rivers are polluted, the Indians are poor, and some are alcoholic, like the cowboys. The ranches are owned by big corporations. The forests are being cut down. The New West is destroying itself in the name of progress. But it holds to a small set of performances that live on in the Wild West show, on the rodeo circuit, and in Last Stand re-enactments in Garryowen, Montana, every June 25 and June 26, without fail.

I seek a critical politics of representation that recognizes the brutal U.S. colonization of Indian nations, but does not naïvely idealize Native Americans. A new set of performance narratives about Native Americans and the New West is required. As I have argued previously (Denzin, 2008, p. 204) these performances would draw audiences and performers into interactive relationships. It would move us away from the spaces of consumption tourism, trophy collections, and cultural voyeurism. It would lead us away from those staged performances that idealize Native Americans by turning them into fancy dancers, drummers, basket and blanket weavers, and makers of turquoise jewelry.

It is necessary to say one more time that the American West was stolen from Native Americans. The reservations are a direct result of the Indian Wars of resistance to the nineteenth- and twentieth-century colonial efforts to seize native lands and resources, including the first last stand at the Battle of Greasy Grass. The story of the West, at this level, is not a story of native self-determination, sovereignty, and indigenousness. It is a story of theft, genocide, violence, and tyranny (Cook-Lynn, 2007, p. 95). What kind of postmodern self wants to anchor itself in this cultural space? How can you attend a Last Stand re-enactment and not confront these harsh realities?

Returning over and over again to Last Stand paintings, I have examined questions of memory, race, and violence against Native Americans. Even as perceptions of Native Americans have changed, the majority culture clings to a reading of the Last Stand that honors Custer and his men. It is as if we can only begin anew by returning to a racist beginning, the Last Stand one more time. This is what the Custer paintings do. They keep the battle alive. They draw a line in the sand. They say this is where the end began, the last stand.

CUSTER DIED FOR HIS SINS

Custer died, not for his sins. He died so that our nation would renew its commitment to conquer Native Americans, and claim the West for its vision of justice, democracy, and civilization. In calling these representations and interpretations into question, I have attempted to imagine another set of performances, those anchored in the point of view of Native Americans, hoping, that someday, as Bob Dylan suggests, when a new masterpiece is painted, everything's gonna be different. How to make that so has been the topic at hand. Sherman Alexie can have the last word.

ACT ONE, SCENE THREE

Coyote Speaks out Against Revenge

Custer and his men are still alive.
Custer never died.
He was in my dreams last night.
I was by the river.
A white soldier cut my throat.
Another soldier scalped me.
"And now my father wants revenge.
And he wants me to want revenge" (Alexie, 2007, p. 75).

I can't do this any longer.
It's not my battle.

I'm no redskin Johnny Cash,
Crazy Horse, Sitting Bull,
Lone Ranger, Tonto, Red
Rider, Tom Mix, Bill Cody,
Gene Autry, Sky King,
Annie Oakley. Calamity Jane,
Wonderman cowboy
who is gonna go out and get
revenge for what happened
to my drunken father's drunken
father's grandfather.

If I kill a white soldier
THEN A WHITE SOLDIER
WILL HAVE TO KILL ME.

Is revenge a circle inside a circle
inside a circle?

Can I get outside the circle
into another circle?

Is there a circle of forgiveness?
Can we have paintings about forgiveness?

Can we start over?
No more Last Stands.

A world without end.
A new beginning.

    Amen.

APPENDIX A

Timeline:
The Plains Indian Wars (1860–1890) and the Battle of Many Names (1876)

This timeline may be projected as well as spoken.

1862	Homestead Act is passed, giving 160 acres of western land to anyone who could cultivate it for five years.
1862	Dakota War, or "Sioux Uprising," between the United States and the Lakota, primarily in Minnesota.
1864	Sand Creek Massacre: Local militia in southeast Colorado kill and mutilate an estimated 150 Cheyenne and Arapaho.
1863–1869	Transcontinental railroad is completed.
1868	Federal government gives the Black Hills to the Lakota forever.
1868	Custer's Seventh U.S. Cavalry attacks Black Kettle's Cheyenne village on the Washita River, killing 250 men, women, and children.
1870	Massacre on the Marias River. A total of 173 Blackfeet men, women, and children slaughtered by U.S. soldiers on January 23.
1871	Jay Cooke ignores 1871 Treaty of Fort Laramie and moves the Northern Pacific Railroad into Sioux land.[1]
1872	Sitting Bull's men kill 42 soldiers and warn U.S. military against incursions into the Yellowstone Valley.
1872	Yellowstone National Park is established. Native Americans are pushed out of the park to make it safe for tourists.
1875	Army expedition led by George A. Custer confirms reports of gold in Black Hills, sacred ancestral homeland of the Lakota.
1875	Sitting Bull and Crazy Horse oppose selling any Black Hills land to the government.
1875	In November, Secretary of War warns of trouble in Black Hills.

244 Appendix A

1876–1877	Black Hills War, or Little Bighorn Campaign. The Lakota under Sitting Bull and Crazy Horse fight U.S. military over violations of 1868 Treaty of Fort Laramie, including Battle of the Rosebud (1876) and Battle of the Little Bighorn (1876).
February 7, 1876	War Department authorizes operations against the "hostile" Lakota, including the bands under Crazy Horse and Sitting Bull.
March 17, 1876	General Crook's advance column under Col. Reynolds attacks and destroys a large, peaceful, Native American camp on the Powder River.
June 17, 1876	Crazy Horse has a dream about how to fight the Blue Coats (Crook's men), and they win a battle—the Battle of the Rosebud—that day. After this battle, the chiefs move west to the Valley of the Greasy Grass (Little Bighorn).
June 24, 1876	Custer's Seventh Cavalry moves toward the large, three-mile-long Indian encampment in the Valley of the Greasy Grass. Sitting Bull, the one old man chief of all the camps, did not believe Crazy Horse's dream that the Blue Coats would fall into the Indian camp. By this time, Sitting Bull's traveling village had nearly 2,000 fighting men (Welch, 1994, p. 127).
June 25, 1876	Custer discovers the large Indian village. At roughly 12:15 p.m., he divides the Seventh Cavalry into four groups. The first fighting begins about 3 p.m. and lasts until about 5:25 p.m., with no survivors from the battalion led by Custer. Some reported that the fight involving Custer lasted less than one-half hour (Miller, 1957, p. 158). It is estimated that the warriors outnumbered the Seventh Cavalry about 3 to 1, or roughly 1,800 against 600, and in Custer's actual fight, 1,800 against 268 (Ambrose, 1975, p. 444).
June 25, 1876	Deaths: 36 Native Americans[2], 268 U.S. troops. There may not have been a last stand, per se; rather, the troops were overwhelmed by a single charge (Michno, 1997, p. 215).
June 26, 1876	Indians continue to fight other members of Custer's cavalry.
June 27, 1876	Relief troops reach the battle site. The Native American dead have been removed from the field. The bodies of the troops are naked, scalped, and mutilated except for Custer, who had been shot in the left temple and left breast. His naked body is posed between the naked bodies of two soldiers (Welch, 1994, pp. 175–177).
June 28–29, 1876	The dead Seventh Cavalry members are buried. The bodies of nine officers were recognized and their locations marked by stakes, but the available evidence concerning where anyone fell and died is incomplete (Brust, Pohanka, & Barnard, 2005; Gray, 1991, p. 411; Scott, 1999).

July 5, 1876	Gen. Terry's report of the massacre is telegraphed all across the country.
July 6, 1876	National newspapers carry the first accounts of the massacre.
July 22, 1876	All Native Americans in Lakota country are treated as prisoners of war.
August 15, 1876	Native Americans are forced to give up all rights to the Powder River country and the Black Hills.
September 5, 1877	Crazy Horse is stabbed and dies outside Fort Robinson
1877	Chief Joseph and Nez Perce War in Yellowstone Park region
1878	Bannock Indian Wars in Yellowstone Park.
1878–1879	Cheyenne, Sheepeater, and Ute Wars
1879	Little Bighorn battlefield is preserved as a national cemetery to protect the graves of the Seventh Cavalry buried there.
1885	Sitting Bull travels with Buffalo Bill's Wild West show, helping stage performances of "Custer's Last Battle."
1887	Buffalo Bill's Wild West show stages "Custer's Last Stand" in London for Queen Victoria and the Prince of Wales.
December, 1890	Wounded Knee Massacre
December 15, 1890	Sitting Bull is shot and dies immediately at Wounded Knee.
1917	U.S. Tenth Cavalry involved in firefight with Yaqui Indians. End of Indian Wars.
1946	Custer battleground redesignated as Custer Battlefield National Monument.
1991	Battlefield renamed Little Bighorn Battlefield National Monument.
1991	Indian Memorial authorized by Congress at Little Bighorn Battlefield National Monument.
2003	Indian Memorial officially dedicated on June 25, 2003, 108 years after massacre.
2007–2008	A mini-exhibit, "The Battle of Many Names," opens at the Whitney Gallery of Western Art at the Buffalo Bill Historical Center with the Custer Last Stand paintings of Scholder, Biss (1995), Mardon (1996), Paxson (1899), and Weighorst.
2007–2008	The Hardin Area Chamber of Commerce & Agriculture, which stages Custer's Last Stand re-enactments, posts a Custer's Last Stand photo gallery on its website with collections of photos of Sitting Bull, Lewis and Clark, Sacajawea, Custer scouts, mountain men, and pioneers. See www.custerslaststand.org

APPENDIX B

Timeline: Paintings of the Battle of Many Names[1] June 26, 1876

This timeline may be projected as well as spoken.

July 19, 1876 William M. Cary, *The Battle on Little Big Horn River—The Death Struggles of General Custer*, New York Daily Graphic, full-page depiction (Dippie, 1974, p. 64).

1876 Alfred R. Waud, *Custer's Last Fight*, illustration in *Frederick Whittaker, A Complete Life of Gen. George A. Custer*. New York: Sheldon & Company, p. 606.

1876 Feodor Fuchs, *Custer's Last Charge,* the first color lithograph of the battle

1878 H. Steinegger, *Custer's Death Struggle*

1879 E. S. Paxson announces desire to paint his version of the Battle of the Little Bighorn.

1881 Chief Red Horse, forty-one color drawings

John Mulvany, *Custer's Last Rally*

J. W. Buel, *Death of General Custer*

1883 Barnsley, del., (name incomplete in documentation), *Custer's Last Fight on the Little Big Horn*

1884 John Elder, *Custer's Last Charge*

1884 William M. Cary, *Battle of the Little Big Horn: Death of Custer,* illustration for poem by Frederick Whittaker in Charles J. Barnes and Marshall Hawkes (Eds.) *National Fifth Reader.* New York: American Book Company.

1884 Cassilly Adams paints the first version of the painting known as *Custer's Last Fight*. It measured 16 feet 5 inches by 9 feet 6 inches and was painted on a wagon canvas for a traveling exhibit. There were two end panels; one depicted Custer as a young child, and the second showed Custer dead on the battlefield (Taft, 1953, p. 143; Kemmick, 2002).

1888	E. Pierpont, *Cyclorama of Gen. Custer's Last Fight*
1888	Adolphus Busch has an idea for an advertising campaign based on the Battle of the Little Bighorn. He acquires Adams's Custer painting, which hung on the wall of a St. Louis tavern owned by John C. Furber (Taft, 1953, p. 335).
1889	Busch employs the Milwaukee Lithographing Co. to make prints of Adams's painting. The lithograph is copyrighted in 1896.
1889	Rufus Zogbaum, *The Last Stand*
1890	Paxson completes research for his painting.
1890	F. Remington, *Custer's Last Stand*
1891	Williams, *Custer's Last Battle*
1895	F. Otto Becker, an employee of the Milwaukee Lithographing Co., is hired by Busch to make a master painting of *Custer's Last Fight*, from which the famous advertising lithograph would be created. Busch pays for the painting but never takes possession of it; it remains in Becker's hands. Becker's lithograph differs from the Adams's painting in terms of detail and emphasis (Taft, 1953, pp. 144–146).
1895	Cassilly Adams's *Custer's Last Fight* is presented to the Seventh Cavalry at Fort Riley by the Anheuser-Busch Brewery.
1896	Gen. Edward S. Godfrey, a member of the Custer burial party, writes E. S. Paxson saying he hopes he corrects the errors in Adams's painting.
1897	E. L. Blumenschein, *We Circle All Round Him*
1899	H. R. Locke, *Gen. Custer's Last Battle*
1899	E. S. Paxson completes and exhibits *Custer's Last Stand*[2]
1902	E. Cameron, *Custer's Fight—Little Big Horn River*
1903	Charles Russell, *The Battle of Little Bighorn*, also called *Custer's Last Stand*
1908	J. H. Sharp, *The Custer Battlefield*
1915	W. H. Dunton, *Custer's Last Stand*
1923	T. B. Pittman, *Custer's Last Stand*
1926	Elk Eber, *General Custer's Lekte Schact*
1934	*Custer's Last Fight* is discovered with considerable damage in storage at Fort Bliss, Texas.
1934	D. Franklin, *Custer's Last Stand*
1935	Adams's painting is sent to the Works Progress Administration in Boston for restoration. It returns to Fort Bliss in 1938.
1936	Becker reassembles the eight pieces of his painting and repaints the seams to restore it to its original state.

1939	Becker sells his original painting to Anheuser-Busch for $2,000.
1939	W. R. Leigh, *Custer's Last Fight*
1946	A fire in the officers' mess at Fort Bliss destroys the Adams painting.
1950	Harold von Schmidt's *Custer's Last Stand* is reproduced in *Esquire* magazine.
1976	Eric von Schmidt, son of Harold von Schmidt, *Here Fell Custer*
1995	Earl Biss, *Custer*
1996	Alan Mardon, *The Battle of Greasy Grass*
2002	Custer Battlefield Museum becomes the first institution granted permission by Anheuser-Busch to reproduce and sell a limited edition of the original advertising lithograph of *Custer's Last Fight*.
2002	National Park Service selects Eric von Schmidt's *Here Fell Custer* as the official painting depicting the Last Stand.
2007–2008	Mini-exhibit, "The Battle of Many Names," opens at the Whitney Gallery of Western Art at the Buffalo Bill Historical Center.
2007–2008	The Hardin Area Chamber of Commerce & Agriculture, which stages Custer's Last Stand re-enactments, posts a Custer's Last Stand photo gallery on its website with collections of photos of Sitting Bull, Lewis and Clark, Sacajawea, Custer scouts, mountain men, and pioneers. See www.custerslaststand.org

APPENDIX C

Timeline: William F. "Buffalo Bill" Cody

1846	Born February 26 in LeClaire, Iowa, into an abolitionist Quaker family.
1854	Family moves to Kansas.
1858	Works as express messenger, kills first Native American.
1860	Becomes Pony Express rider.
1861–1865	Serves as scout for Ninth Kansas Volunteers and Seventh Cavalry.
1867	Serves as scout for George A. Custer.
1867	Secures contract to kill buffalo for the Union Pacific Railroad and shoots 4,280 buffalo; given nickname Buffalo Bill.
1867	Claims friendship with Custer (Warren, 2005, pp. 135–136).
1868	Chief scout for Fifth Cavalry.
1869	Takes part in victory at Battle of Summit Springs (July 11) against Cheyenne warriors.
1869–1872	Serves as guide for tourists wanting to hunt buffalo, including Grand Duke Alexis of Russia on the Great Royal Buffalo Hunt.
1869	Awarded Congressional Medal of Honor for his service to the army.
1869	Ned Buntline creates a character named Buffalo Bill.
1872	Appears in Chicago in Ned Buntline's play *The Scouts of the Plains*.
1873-1876	Joined by "Wild Bill" Hickok in tours for *The Scouts of the Plains*.
1876	Serves as scout for Fifth Cavalry and takes part in Battle of Warbonnet Creek (July 15) against Cheyenne warriors who had participated in Battle of the Little Bighorn. Cody kills and scalps Cheyenne Chief Yellow Hair.
1876	Returns to the stage and re-enacts his duel with Yellow Hair—*Buffalo Bill's First Scalp for Custer*—displaying his scalp, war bonnet, knife, and saddle.

252 Appendix C

1879	Publishes his autobiography, *The Life and Adventures of Buffalo Bill*.
1882–1833	Forms his own show. The show includes a tableau presentation of Custer's Last Stand based on Cassilly Adams's 1884 *Custer's Last Stand* painting and the 1896 lithograph of the painting produced by Otto Becker for Adolphus Busch (Warren, 2005, p. 261).
1883–1884	Hires celebrities and Lakota and Cheyenne Indians to perform in his show, including Annie Oakley, Sitting Bull, Red Cloud, and Frank North.
1883–1884	Introduces "Custer's Last Stand" as a regular part of his show. Cody plays Custer. Lakota and Cheyenne attack stagecoaches and have fights with cowboys and settlers.
1886–1887	Show performs on Staten Island for two seasons, then moves indoors to Madison Square Garden.
1885	Sitting Bull and Cody perform together in Montréal.
1886–1898	Includes "Custer's Last Rally" as irregular feature of his show. The "Last Rally" is not shown in the United States after 1898 (Warren, 2005, p. 270).
1887	Takes his show to France, Spain, Italy, Germany, Austria, and Belgium, and performs in London for Queen Victoria and the Prince of Wales.
1887–1890	Sitting Bull murdered on December 15 at Wounded Knee Creek, South Dakota.
1890	Called to the site of Wounded Knee Massacre as mediator between army and Lakota.
1892	Opens Irma Hotel in Cody, Wyoming.
1893	His Wild West show, with "Custer's Last Rally," is outstanding attraction at the Chicago World's Columbia Exposition.
1895	Helps found the city of Cody, Wyoming; Cody Road leads into Yellowstone National Park. Opens Wapiti Inn and Phaska Tepee in 1905 to accommodate travels along Cody Road.
1906	Makes final European tour.
1908	Sells stock in his show.
1910	Performs final farewell.
1917	Dies January 10 in Denver, Colorado.
1917	Town of Cody explores building a museum to honor him, to be called the Buffalo Bill Historical Center.
2010	The historical center extends for another year its exhibit of Last Stand paintings.

NOTES

Introduction

1. I thank Mitch Allen for his guiding hand throughout this chapter.
2. The Custer paintings refer to more than 1,000 paintings of Custer's last fight at Little Bighorn. For partial listings of these paintings, see Appendix A and visit the Friends of the Little Bighorn Battlefield website at http://www.friendslittlebighorn.com/custerslaststand.htm. To this list can be added the recently published "Custer Writings" by the late Norman Maclean. Maclean (2008) records a historical irony: Custer, a teetotaler, owes a good deal of his reputation to Anheuser-Busch and its reproduction of *Custer's Last Fight* (p. 55).
3. According to Brest, Pohanka, and Barnard (2005, pp. 19–24), the earliest photographs of the Custer battlefield were taken by John H. Fouch (July 1877), Stanley J. Morrow (April 1879), David J. Barry (1881, 1886), F. Jay Haynes (1882, 1894), L.A. Huffman (1916), L. Moorhouse (1901), and Edward S. Curtis (1907). The Haynes photograph seems to have been the source of Otto Becker's 1893 lithograph, which is based on Cassilly Adams's *Custer's Last Fight* (Brest, Pohanka, & Barnard, 2005, p. 208; Tilden, 1964, p. 191).
4. Russell (1968) states that the first "picture of Custer's last fight was a woodcut in the *New York Graphic and Illustrated Evening Newspaper* dated July 19, 1876. . . . [It] was drawn by Mr. W. M. Cary from 'sketches and descriptions by our special correspondent' . . . the picture centers on Custer with one foot resting on a dead horse" (p. 15).
5. Little Bighorn is frequently spelled two different ways: Little Bighorn and Little Big Horn. I will use Little Bighorn throughout the book but will retain Little Big Horn when used in quotes.
6. Philbrick argues that there are two last stands. See Appendix A, "Timeline: The Battle of Many Names," for a summary of the history (1862–present) of the American military's treatment of Native Americans.
7. See Appendix B, "Timeline: Custer's Last Stand Paintings (1876–1996)."
8. I steal from Greil Marcus (2010), who says of his forty-year interest in Bob Dylan's music: "I only wanted to get closer to the music than I could by listening to it—I wanted to get inside it, behind it, and writing about it, through it, inside of it, behind it was my way of doing that" (p. xvii).

9 *Night at the Museum* (2006) and *Night at the Museum: Battle of the Smithsonian* (2009) are both directed by Shawn Levy and star Ben Stiller.

10 Michael Yellow Bird (2004) observes the terms Indian and Native American are problematic, describing identities imposed by European Americans. He prefers First Nations or indigenous peoples (p. 47).

11 Nineteenth-century Western American art was typically figurative and action-based, telling a story about or documenting a specific or archetypical historical event, moment, person, or place. It was characterized by realism and careful attention to authentic, anatomical detail and what passed as historical accuracy. Manifest Destiny, paternalistic views of Native Americans, and nostalgic, romantic, masculine views of the past and nature were recurring themes in these paintings (Hassrick, 1983, pp. 8–9; 2007, pp. 9–11; McCracken, 1952, pp. 7–8).

12 The patrons of nineteenth century Western art were American industrialists, gilded-age robber barons, men who owned breweries, oil wells, mines, railroads, and steel factories. The names are still familiar: Rockefeller, Morgan, Vanderbilt, Carnegie, Cooke, Pabst, Busch, Schlitz, Miller, Coors. These men commissioned and consumed art as a way of demonstrating their wealth (Josephson, 1962). They hired artists to make paintings that would be turned into advertisements for their railroads and breweries. This form of art patronage continues to the present day. It includes publicly supported systems of museums and theaters, as well as the corporate sponsorship of sporting arenas and amusement parks. In each case, this is art in the service of white patriarchal capitalism.

13 See Maclean (2008, pp. 63–64) for an attempt to read Custer and the battle from within the framework of classical tragedy, casting Custer as a tragic hero (see also Weltzien, 2008, pp. xxii–xxiii).

14 Red Horse's drawings were produced in 1881 at the request of assistant army surgeon Charles E. McChesney to accompany the story of the battle as recorded in Mallery (1881). Tillett (1976) reproduces some of Red Horse's drawings, as well as those of others who were present at the battle, including Kate Bighead, Amos Bad Heart Buffalo, Kicking Bear, and Kills Two. Red Horse's drawings are reproduced in their entirety for the first time in Viola (1999c). Red Horse's drawings are housed in the Smithsonian's National Anthropological Archives (Viola, 1999c, p. 82). Taft (2004) does note Red Horse's drawings, describing them as "primitive in design and execution" (pp. 445–446).

15 The movie, directed by Yves Simoneau with a screenplay written by Daniel Giat, earned three Golden Globe awards. Its cast included Anna Paquin, August Schellemberg, Aidan Quinn, and Fred Thompson.

16 Ledger art, a term for Plains Indian narrative drawing or painting on paper or cloth, was primarily produced from the 1860s to the 1930s but also continues into the present. The term comes from the accounting ledger books that were a common source of paper for Plains Indians during the late nineteenth century.

17 Midway between the two paintings hangs Earl Biss's 39-by-30-inch *General Custer in Blue and Green* (1996).

18 In the summer of 2010, the Whitney gallery presented another small exhibit of works depicting the Battle of the Little Bighorn (Brindza, 2010, p. 4).

19 This text is an excerpt from a press release under the headline "Revisit Gen. Custer's life in historic Monroe, MI with Little Big Horn Associates on June 4, 2010." For the

full text of the press release, see http://www.prlog.org/10700560-revisit-gen-custers-life-in-historic-monroe-mi-with-little-big-horn-associates-on-june-4-2010.html

20 Minstrelsy is a nineteenth century stage form using white performers in blackface (or brown or red) as a way to represent the mannerisms, speech, dress, gender, and culture of nonwhite people, including African Americans and Native Americans. A racial masquerade lurks behind minstrelsy with white performers staging stereotyped representations of people of color. Blackface minstrelsy was the symptomatic nineteenth century stage form for an era of transnational colonial expansion. William Cody's Wild West show toured Europe, for example, with both white and Lakota performers playing Native Americans (Denzin, 2005, pp. 940–941).

21 See http://www.custermuseum.org/

22 Custer National Forest has three ranger districts spread across two states. Its 1,278,279 acres include parts of the Absaroka-Beartooth Wilderness north of Yellowstone National Park and near Red Lodge, as well as some grasslands in northwest South Dakota.

23 We started annual visits to Cody, Red Lodge, and Yellowstone in 1988. As regular "seasonals," we now spend about six to eight weeks a year in the region.

24 When the text refers the reader to an event, text, image, or painting, I have attempted to locate websites where those images can be found.

25 I return to von Schmidt and his painting in chapter 1.

26 Amos Bad Heart Buffalo (1869–1913) is an Oglala Lakota tribal historian and artist known for his pictographs (Tillett, 1976, pp. xi–xv).

27 Von Schmidt's painting is in the Little Bighorn Battlefield National Monument near Crow Agency. Von Schmidt reproduces the lines from the song "Garryowen" along the bottom of his painting.

28 "Custer's Last Rally" is the title of a play within William Cody's Wild West show and the title of John Mulvany's 1881 painting of the last stand.

Chapter One

1 Performance instructions and discussion of the identities and sequence of speakers within any scene were discussed in the introduction.

2 At least forty more films exist. For a more complete list, see Hutton, 2004b; Simmon, 2003; Welch, 1994, p. 22.

3 The Adams, Becker, and Busch dates are disputed (Taft, 1953; von Schmidt, 1976). Adams's painting was produced sometime before 1886 for two members of the St. Louis Art Club: C. J. Budd and W. T. Richards. It was financed in part by John C. Furber, a St. Louis bar owner (Taft, 1953, pp. 142–143). Budd and Richards began exhibiting and promoting the painting in 1885. It was then sold to Furber, who hung it in his saloon. Furber's saloon failed. The painting was valued at $10,000. When Furber died in 1888, creditors took over his assets, including the Adams painting. Anheuser-Busch had a $35,000 claim against the estate. Adolphus Busch acquired the Adams painting in 1888 for that sum. Busch planned an advertising campaign based on the Battle of the Little Bighorn. According to von Schmidt (1976), E. Otto Becker was hired by Busch in 1895 to paint a smaller version of the Adams painting. Busch gave the painting to the Seventh Cavalry in 1895. The Becker lithograph was copyrighted in 1896 (Taft, 1953, pp. 143–144).

4 The Custer Battlefield Museum is a nonprofit corporation located in Garryowen, Montana, on the site where Custer's Seventh Cavalry troops, under the direction of

Major Marcus Reno, attacked Sitting Bull's camp on the afternoon of June 25, 1876. The town of Garryowen is owned by Christopher Kortlander, who also operates the museum. The Tomb of the Unknown Soldier is also located at this site.

5 Deloria (1969) writes that the bumper sticker was originally meant as a dig at the National Council of Churches and "referred to the Sioux Treaty of 1868 at Fort Laramie in which the United States pledged to give free and undisturbed use of the lands claimed by Red Cloud in return for peace. Under the covenants of the Old Testament, breaking a covenant called for a blood sacrifice for atonement. Custer was a blood sacrifice for the United States breaking the Sioux treaty. That, at least originally, was the meaning of the slogan" (p. 148). An image of the bumper sticker can be found at http://www.bumperart.com/ProductDetails.aspx?SKU=2004062001&productID=3773

6 According to Christine C. Brindza, curatorial assistant at the Buffalo Bill Historical Center's Whitney Gallery of Western Art, the center and gallery had 200,000 visitors in 2007 (personal communication, February 29, 2008).

7 The Carbon County Historical Society Museum in Red Lodge is about 120 miles from the site of Custer's Last Stand. In January 2008, the museum proudly announced the acquisition of a corroded cuff button from the uniform worn by Second Lt. John J. Crittenden, the only infantry officer assigned to Custer's Seventh Cavalry. The button was exhibited next to a gun similar to those used in the Battle of the Little Bighorn (Hedges, 2008).

In 2009, promotion of Custer's battle was in full swing; I could book a Custer family vacation package that would include a visit to the oldest city in South Dakota's Black Hills and a tour of the colossal Crazy Horse monument and the famous faces of Mount Rushmore. The vacation would honor the heritage and history of the Lakota people. We could play at Flintstones, a family friendly theme park. The package included three nights of lodging in Custer, Mount Rushmore National Memorial, Crazy Horse Memorial, National Museum of Woodcarving, Jewel Cave, and Flintstones Bedrock City. Price started at $425 for a family of four (two adults and two children, 12 and under).

8 The town of Garryowen was named after the old Irish tune "Garryowen," one of George Armstrong Custer's favorite marching songs. "Garryowen" is an old Irish quickstep that can be traced back to the 1800s. The song was adopted as the regimental song soon after Custer arrived to take over the Seventh Cavalry. It was the last song played by the band for Custer's men as they rode into history. A registered historic site, Garryowen is the only town within the battlefield. It is located south of the Little Bighorn Battlefield National Monument and Custer National Cemetery.

9 Also see Appendix A and Brown, 1970; Welch, 1994.

10 Welch (1994), citing Gray (1991), argues that the whole of the battle "from Reno's charge to Custer's demise . . . lasted from 4:08 to 5:25 when the battle ended. The heavy part of the battle took thirty-five minutes" (Gray, 1991, pp. 272–273; 1994, p. 175).

11 Reno's Companies M, A, and G; Benteen's companies D, H, and K; Custer's company; and the ammunition train (Ambrose, 1975, p. 436).

12 The estimates of military deaths vary, depending on which battlefield (Custer or Reno) is being counted. The total numbers vary from 206 to 210 for Custer alone, to 253 to 268 for Custer and Reno combined (see Gray, 1991, pp. 406–408, 412–413).

13 See Wilmer "Stampede" Mesteth's 2007 CD, *The Lakota are Charging*. He performs historical Lakota songs from the battle. See http://www.wiserearth.org/user/WilmerMesteth

14 On Memorial Day 1999, the placement of markers to honor Native American warriors slain during the battle was initiated. Red granite was chosen by the tribes to contrast with the white marble markers designating the fallen soldiers. Markers have been added each year on June 25 to commemorate the sites discovered within the previous year.

15 In the Battle of the Little Bighorn, Edward S. Godfrey was a lieutenant in Capt. Benteen's force, which, with Maj. Reno's troops, was operating in support of Custer's main body. He published his account in 1892 and rewrote it in 1908 (Hutton, 2004a, p. 230).

16 There seem to be two spellings of the interpreter F. F. (Fred) Gerard's name. Welch (1994) spells it Gerard, while Godfrey (2004, p. 310) spells it Girard. I believe these refer to the same interpreter.

17 Rashomon has become a byword for any situation in which the truth of an event is difficult to verify because of the conflicting accounts of different witnesses (Heider, 1988). It is named for Akira Kurosawa's 1950 film *Rashomon*, in which a crime witnessed by four individuals is described in four mutually contradictory ways. The film is based on two short stories by Ryûnosuke Akutagawa.

18 I've stolen the above paragraphs and arguments directly from Carol Rambo, who edited an earlier version of this work.

Chapter Two

1 Color lithography technology was available as early as 1837.

2 As indicated in the introduction, copies of this painting can be purchased at the Custer Battlefield Museum in Garryowen for $39.99 (as of 2010).

3 See Appendix B for a timeline of events from 1876 to 2008.

4 This is a selection from more than one thousand paintings of the event. I draw from Hutton (2004), Kemmick (2002), McCracken (1952), Paxson (1984), Taft (1946, 1953), Tillett (1976), Viola (1999), and von Schmidt (1976).

5 Von Schmidt (1976) argues that in all of the paintings "the viewer's vantage was that of an attacking Indian" (p. 2). I don't agree.

6 In 1970, Waud's painting was altered in a McDonald's restaurant ad "so that the General's left hand now clutches a sack of McDonald's hamburgers" (Dippie, 1976, p. 56).

7 In 1969, Fuch's painting was used by the *New York Times*, advising readers that they "might locate hard-to-find details on Custer's last stand" in the *Times* index (Dippie, 1976, p. 56).

8 Viola (1999c) says there were forty-one drawings (p. 82).

9 Sometime after 1900, H. J. Heinz acquired Mulvany's painting. It hung for many years in the company's Pittsburg headquarters (Dippie, 1976, p. 56).

10 Russell (1968) says it was painted between 1878 and 1886 (p. 31). The earliest date that can be attached to the picture is April 26, 1886, when copyright No. 9562 was issued to John G. Furber for a four-page printed pamphlet descriptive of *Custer's Last Fight* (Russell, 1968, p. 31).

11 In the far lower right of the print is an image of the Peace Monument with an Indian on horseback. In the far lower left of the print is a reproduction of the insignia of the Seventh Cavalry, bugle and flags, with the name Custer. Across the very bottom of the print are these words: Limited Edition—Published by the Custer Battlefield Museum, Garryowen, Montana—"Where Battle of the Little Big Horn Began." Proceeds go to preservation of the Peace Monument and the Tomb of the Unknown Soldier.

Chapter Three

1. In summer 2010, in a separate room, the Buffalo Bill Historical Center hosted a new exhibit: "Brush, palette and Custer's Last Stand." It contained sketches for lithograph representations of the Last Stand paintings of Paxson, Mulvany, Adams, and Fritz Scholder. In the main room of the museum, Paxson's huge painting faced Mardon's painting, while Biss's Custer lurked on a side wall.
2. Oil on canvas, 29.75 by 40 inches.
3. Lithograph on paper, 30 by 22.5 inches.
4. Allan Mardon, "All Over the West." Retrieved January 18, 2011, from http://www.artworkstoo.com/mardon.htm
5. To repeat, the Whitney Gallery purchased the painting and artist sketches from the Paxson estate for $50,000 in 1963.
6. The original letter is on display in the Whitney Gallery of Western Art at the Buffalo Bill Historical Center.
7. According to Welch (1994), by the time Crazy Horse arrived at this point in the battle, most of the fighting had ended and the "troops were done for" (p. 168). This is not how Crazy Horse is depicted in Paxson's painting.
8. McCracken was curator of the Whitney Gallery when it purchased the Paxson painting in 1963.
9. Biss (Crow, 1947–1998) was a former student of Fritz Scholder at the Institute of American Indian Arts in Santa Fe. In this painting, Biss's use of deep blues and yellows shows elements of Scholder's expressionist style.
10. The work is a 39-by-30-inch oil on canvas with painted tin figures (horses and riders) around the border.
11. The Biss painting appeared in the 2010 exhibit as well.
12. See www.spartacus.schoolnet.co.uk/WWbighorn.htm
13. See www.spartacus.schoolnet.co.uk/WWbighorn.htm
14. Oil on canvas, 29.75 by 40 inches.
15. Lithograph on paper, 30 by 22.5 inches.
16. Brindza suggests that Scholder is commenting on the image of Custer in William M. Cary's "The Battle on Little Big Horn River—The Death Struggles of General Custer," *New York Daily Graphic*, full-page depiction (Dippie, 1974, p. 64).
17. Greasy Grass is the name given the Little Bighorn River by many Indian tribes including the Crow, Lakota, and Cheyenne (Welch, 1994, p. 101). An interactive video is in front of Mardon's painting at the exhibit.
18. The drawings are in the Smithsonian's National Anthropological Archives.
19. Materials from Allan Mardon are taken from interview conversations and e-mails on April 27–28, 2010. Direct commentary on his painting closely follows the discussion in the notebook provided to viewers of the painting by the Whitney Gallery. Currently, visitors to the gallery can go to a computer kiosk that highlights and describes parts of the painting. According to Christine C. Brindza, acting curator, that information is based on the booklet that was prepared by museum staff. Both documents were based on information supplied by Mardon (personal communication, May 10, 2010).
20. Allan Mardon: "That is an interesting point. I did not intend that" (personal communication, April 27, 2010).

21 Mardon says, "I have also found inspiration in the paintings of artists Joan Miro and Paul Klee, where a central subject may or may not exist but enigmatic symbols such as those that appear in cave drawings, tapestries, or hieroglyphics complete the full story. Many of my paintings have let me explore the spiritual, war and social life of the Indians . . . Through my research I have discovered that . . . Indians have lost their land, their main source of livelihood—the buffalo—and their traditional way of life. And they were dying of white man's diseases, sometimes purposefully forced upon them." Allan Mardon, "All Over the West." Retrieved January 18, 2011, from http://www.artworkstoo.com/mardon.htm

Chapter Four

1 I return to von Schmidt and his painting in the next chapter.
2 Amos Bad Heart Buffalo (1869–1913) is an Oglala Lakota tribal historian and artist known for his pictographs (Tillett, 1976, pp. xi–xv).
3 I also discussed Scholder's painting in the last chapter.
4 See Crow artist Kevin Red Star's *Rain in the Face* at HistoryNet.com at http://www.historynet.com/kevin-red-star-art-of-the-west.htm/1 and the artist's web site at www.KevinRedStar.com
5 In particular, Native American artist John Nieto's *Custer Suite:* See http://www.bluecoyotegallery.com/JohnNietoOriginalArtworkandPaintings.htm; also http://www.kenbailey.com/custer-suite-by-john-nieto.html
6 In 1881, the War Department erected a monument for the Seventh Cavalry, civilian personnel, and Indian scouts killed in the 1876 battle. In 1991 a national competition was held for the design of an Indian Memorial to accompany the change in name of the battlefield from "Custer" to "Little Bighorn" Battlefield National Monument. "Peace Through Unity" was the theme of the competition. The name change was mandated by a law signed by President George H. W. Bush on December 10, 1991. The law also ordered the construction of a privately funded Indian Memorial to be built near Last Stand Hill. In September 2001, President George W. Bush signed a bill that approved the necessary funds for the memorial construction. On June 25, 2003, the Indian Memorial Center was dedicated. It stands 75 yards northeast of the 1881 Seventh Cavalry monument. The office of the park historian on this site houses the White Swan Memorial Library.
7 To see the Red Horse drawings, go to http://collections.si.edu/search/results.jsp?q=Red+Horse+drawings&image.x=43&image.y=10
8 I thank Jim Goralski of Altamira Fine Art gallery in Jackson, Wyoming, for introducing me to the Custer paintings of John Nieto in the summer of 2010.
9 The Crow had aligned themselves with the U.S. government in exchange for a promise from Custer to return land stolen by other tribes.
10 The White Swan Memorial Library at Little Bighorn Battlefield National Monument houses the office of the park historian. This facility contains extensive research materials on the Battle of the Little Bighorn as well as other related historical events. See the national monument's website at www.nps.gov/libi/
11 They included four large multi-vignette muslin paintings, three multi-vignette hide paintings, and six single drawings on brown butcher paper (Cowles, 1982, p. 53).
12 They were army scouts.

Chapter Five

1. Von Schmidt's painting is the banner photo for every page of the Friends of Little Bighorn Battlefield website (http://www.friendslittlebighorn.com). According to the website, it is the official National Park Service painting depicting the Last Stand. It is displayed on the wayside exhibit at Last Stand Hill and in the National Park Service brochure. This was confirmed on October, 20, 2010, in an email from park ranger Jerry Jasmer: "The *Here Fell Custer* painting, by Eric von Schmidt, is portrayed on the heading of our park brochure handout. The painting also appears on one of our wayside exhibits. I hope that this has been helpful."
2. These two statements about von Schmidt's painting are from endorsements about the painting on the Friends of the Little Bighorn Battlefield website that markets prints of the painting.
3. Dylan liner notes to Eric von Schmidt, 1969 album, "Who Knocked the Brains Out of the Sky?" (SRS 67124). See http://articles.latimes.com/2007/feb/12/local/me-vonschmidt12
4. See endnote 3 in the Introduction for a list of the nineteenth century photographs of the battlefield.
5. Along the bottom of his painting, von Schmidt reproduces an edited version of the lines from "Garryowen," an old Irish drinking song that became the regimental song for Custer's Seventh Cavalry band. The Irish poet Thomas Moore wrote the words around 1807. There are many different versions of lyrics for the song. These lyrics were found on page 465 of Hutton, P. A. (Ed.). *The Custer Reader*. 1992, Lincoln: University of Nebraska Press.
6. For a sample of Wooden Leg's drawings, see the chapter "Cheyenne Memories of Little Bighorn" in Spang, Walks Alone, & American Horse Fisher, 1999, p. 37. For more background on this Cheyenne warrior who fought Custer, see Marquis (1931).
7. Permission granted, Bob Dylan, "All Along the Watchtower." 1968 by Dwarf Music; renewed 1996 by Dwarf Music.

Chapter Six

1. The title of a play within William Cody's Wild West show and the title of John Mulvany's 1881 painting of the Last Stand.
2. See endnote 20 in the Introduction for a definition of minstrelsy.
3. Also the name of a tourist lodge that Cody built and operated along the road to Yellowstone. It is still open.
4. See Appendix B for a full list of these paintings.
5. The company works with the Navy League to support an annual Navy Day Ball in St. Louis and a series of St. Louis Cardinal Company Days at Busch Stadium, when young men and women are officially recruited into the U. S. Navy (Navy League of the United States, 2003).
6. On November 18, 2008, Belgian brewer InBev completed its acquisition of Anheuser-Busch, making it the global leader in beer and one of the world's top five consumer products companies. Under the terms of the agreement, all shares of Anheuser-Busch were acquired for $70 per share in cash, for an aggregate of $52 billion (www.anheuser-busch.com/Press/Press. November 18, 2008). On December 8, 2008, Anheuser-Busch–InBev cut 1,400 U.S. salaried positions.

7   Eliza was Elizabeth Custer's black servant.
8   Erdrich is a member of the Turtle Mountain Band of Chippewa. Her recent novel, *The Plague of Doves* (2009), was a finalist for a Pulitzer Prize in fiction.
9   Cook-Lynn is a member of the Crow Creek Sioux Tribe.

Chapter Seven
1   This text comes from the mission statement for the McCracken Research Library at the Buffalo Bill Historical Center. See http://www.bbhc.org/mccracken/
2   By permission, Big Sky Music, 1971.
3   Of course these assumptions are the basis of postpositivism, and they have been severely criticized in the critical qualitative research literature (Denzin, 2009, 2010).
4   Quoted material comes from http://www.aucklandmuseum.com/296/wild-child
5   In the summer of 2010 you could buy my book *Searching for Yellowstone* in the Buffalo Bill Historical Center museum shop, which sells Western jewelry, prints, clothing, DVDs, CDs, calendars, and books.
6   For a discussion of the production of heritage in the Autry Museum of Western Heritage in Los Angeles, see Luke 2002, pp. 12–13, 235.
7   This is the title of Brindza's 2010 article in *Points West*, the official magazine of the Buffalo Bill Historical Center.
8   According to the Buffalo Bill Historical Center website, "The McCracken Research Library supports inquiry across many disciplines related to the American West. With extensive collections of rare books, historic photographs, and original manuscripts, the library offers scholars direct contact with the materials of history." See http://www.bbhc.org/mccracken/
9   Besaw is curator of the Whitney Gallery of Western Art in the Buffalo Bill Historical Center.
10 My local Comcast cable system runs Encore Western movies 24 hours a day. I can watch at least one, sometimes two John Wayne Western movies every day, including *True Grit* (1969) and *Rooster Cogburn* (1975), the former of which was remade by the Coen brothers in 2011, starring Jeff Bridges and Matt Damon.

Appendix A
1   Robber baron Cooke, also financier of the Northern Pacific Railroad, made $3 million a year in commissions for selling government bonds during the Civil War (Zinn, 2003, p. 242)
2   The reported number of Indian deaths varies widely, from fewer than 40 to between 60 and 100 (Welch, 1994, p. 184).

Appendix B
1   This is a selection from more than one thousand paintings of the event. I draw from Hutton (2004); Kemmick (2002); McCracken (1952); Paxson (1984); Taft (1946, 1953); Tillett (1976); von Schmidt (1976); and Viola (1999).
2   Taft (1946) lists Paxson's painting as appearing in 1893 (p. 375). Paxson's son (Paxson, 1984) states that his father completed "his documentary Custer's Last Stand in December 1899" (p. 43). It was copyrighted in 1900 as Custer's Last Fight (p. 115).

LIST OF PLATES AND CREDITS

Plates appear after page 128 in the text

1. Black and white photographic print of General George A. Custer, full figure in military uniform, standing three-quarter profile to camera, arms folded at chest. A draped table stands to the left. A square object lies on the floor behind his right foot. Matthew Brady photo, c.1865. Courtesy of Buffalo Bill Historical Center, Cody, Wyoming; Vincent Mercaldo Collection, p.71, 1925.3.

2. Wood engraving after drawing, William de la Montagne Cary, *The Battle on the Little Big Horn River—The Death Struggle of General Custer,* in the *Daily Graphic and Illustrated Evening Newspaper,* New York, New York, July 19, 1876. Courtesy of Buffalo Bill Historical Center, Cody, Wyoming; Don Russell Collection, Gift of Mrs. John Bissell, MS62.1.0.3.27.

3. Chromolithograph, John Mulvany, "Custer's Last Rally, 1881. LRC of print: John/Mulvany/1881. LRC of bottom in pencil: Compliments/John Mulvany. Printed LLC under print: John Mulvany, Pinxt. Bottom center: Copyrighted, LRC: National Photogravure Co. Printed bottom center under print: Custer's Last Rally./Battle of the Little Big Horn./June 25, 1876. Courtesy of Buffalo Bill Historical Center, Cody, Wyoming; Museum Purchase, 149.69.

4. Cassilly Adams, artist, Otto Becker (1854–1945), lithographer. *Custer's Last Fight,* 1896. Inscribed: The Original has been Presented to the Seventh Regiment U.S. Cavalry/By Anheuser-Busch St. Louis, Missouri, U.S.A./World's Largest Brewery/Home of Budweiser and/other Anheuser-Busch Fine Beers. Courtesy of Buffalo Bill Historical Center, Cody, Wyoming; Gift of The Coe Foundation, 1.69.420B.

5. Painted deer hide of the Battle of the Little Bighorn, c.1895. Courtesy of Buffalo Bill Historical Center, Cody, Wyoming; Gift of Robert G. Charles, NA.702.4.

6. Oil painting, Edgar Samuel Paxson, *Custer's Last Stand,* 1899. Courtesy of Buffalo Bill Historical Center, Cody, Wyoming; Museum purchase, 19.69.

7. Painting, Allan Mardon, *The Battle of Greasy Grass,* 1996. Courtesy of Buffalo Bill Historical Center, Cody, Wyoming; Museum Purchase with funds from the William E. Weiss Memorial Fund, Mr. and Mrs. Gordon H. Barrows, and the Franklin A. West Memorial Fund, 6.01.

264   List of Plates and Credits

8   Painting, Earl Biss, *General Custer in Blue and Green,* 1996. Courtesy of Buffalo Bill Historical Center, Cody, Wyoming; Gift of Mr. and Mrs. Charles B. Israel of Aspen, Colorado, 18.00. Permission to reproduce, Lou Lou Goss.

9   Painting, Fritz Scholder, *Custer and 20,000 Indians,* 1969. Courtesy of Buffalo Bill Historical Center, Cody, Wyoming; Gift of Janis and Wiley T. Buchannan III, 7.08. Permission to reproduce image, Lisa Scholder.

10   Painting, Fritz Scholder, *American Landscape,* 1976. Courtesy of Buffalo Bill Historical Center, Cody, Wyoming; Gift of Jack and Carol O'Grady, 10.00.4. Permission to reproduce image, Lisa Scholder.

11   Photograph, unknown artist, "Little Bighorn National Monument," 1994. Courtesy of Buffalo Bill Historical Center.

12   Drawing, White Swan, "White Swan Kills a Sleeping Sioux," 1897. White Swan uses a name glyph to sign his work. Courtesy of Philmont Museum-Seton Memorial Library (IMG: 3732 JPG).

13   Drawing, White Swan, "White Swan with Spy Glass Watching Sioux Tee-pees," 1897. Courtesy of Philmont Museum-Seton Memorial Library (IMG: 3716 JPG).

14   Drawing, Red Horse, "Red Horse drawing of Indians fighting Custer's troops at Battle of Little Bighorn," 1881. Local Number: OPPS NEG 47000D BW; Courtesy of the National Anthropological Archives, Smithsonian Institution (see http://collections.si.edu/search/results.jsp?q=Red+Horse

15   Drawing, Red Horse, "Red Horse drawing of dead cavalry," 1881. Local number: OPPS NEG 47001 B/W; Courtesy of the National Anthropological Archives, Smithsonian Institution.

16   Drawing, Red Horse, "Red Horse drawing of Indians leaving the Battle of Little Big Horn," 1881. Local Number: OPPS NEG 47001F B/W. Courtesy of the National Anthropological Archives, Smithsonian Institution.

17   Painting, Eric von Schmidt, *Here Fell Custer,* 1977. Courtesy of Caitlin von Schmidt and Montana Historical Society.

REFERENCES

Abourezk, Kevin. 2009. "Let This Be Custer's Last 'Last Stand.'" *Reznet News,* June 11: http://www.reznetnews.org/blogs/red-cloud/let-be-custer-last-last-stand

Alexie, Sherman. 1993. *Lone Ranger and Tonto Fistfight in Heaven.* New York: HarperCollins.

Alexie, Sherman. 1995. *Reservation Blues.* New York: Grove Press.

Alexie, Sherman. 2002. "What Sacagawea Means to Me." Viewpoint, *Time,* July 8, 42, http://www.time.com/time/2002/lewis_clark/lprocon.html

Alexie, Sherman. 2007. *Flight.* New York: Black Cast.

Ambrose, Stephen. 1975. *Crazy Horse and Custer.* New York: Random House.

Bartlett, Richard A. 1992. *From Cody to the World: The First Seventy-Five Years of the Buffalo Bill Memorial Association.* Cody, Wyoming: The Buffalo Bill Historical Center.

Benjamin, Walter. 1969. *Illuminations.* Trans. Harry Zohn. New York: Harcourt, Brace & World, Inc.

Besaw, Mindy A. 2010. Letter to Allan Mardon in Allan Mardon, *The Narrative Art of Allan Mardon,* 9. Tuscon: The Larsen Group LLC.

Bighead, Kate. 2004. "She Watched Custer's Last Battle," as told to Thomas B. Marquis, in Paul Andrew Hutton (Ed.), *The Custer Reader,* pp. 363–377 Norman: University of Oklahoma Press. (Orig. pub. 1992.)

Blish, Helen. 1967. *A Pictographic History of the Oglala Sioux.* Lincoln: University of Nebraska Press.

Boehme, Sarah E. 1997. *Whitney Gallery of Western Art.* Cody, WY.

Bradley, Douglas E. 1991. *White Swan: Crow Indian Warrior and Painter, October 13–December 15, 1991* (catalog). Notre Dame: The Snite Museum of Art, University of Notre Dame Sesquicentennial Publication.

Brindza, Christine C. 2010. "Truth, Myth and Imagination: Art of the Battle of Little Bighorn." *Points West: Magazine of the Buffalo Bill Historical Center.* Summer, 4–9.

Brown, Dee. 1970. *Bury My Heart at Wounded Knee: An Indian History of the American West.* New York: Bantam.

Brown, Dee. 1974. *The Westerners.* New York: Holt, Rinehart and Winston.

Brust, James S., Brian C. Pohanka and Sandy Barnard. 2005. *Where Custer Fell: Photographs of the Little Bighorn Battlefield Then and Now*. Norman: University of Oklahoma Press.

Budweiser.com/index.aspx. 2007. "Budweiser History: 1850-2007." St. Louis: Budweiser Beer, Inc.

Catlin, George. 1880. *North American Indians: Being Letters and Notes on their Manners, Customs, and Conditions, Written during Eight Years' Travel amongst the Wildest Tribes in North America, 1832-1839*, Vol. 1. Repr., New York: Dover, 1973.

Cody, William F. 1879. *The Life of the Hon. William F. Cody, Known as Buffalo Bill, the Famous Hunter, Scout and Guide, an Autobiography*. New York: Indian Head Books.

Cody, William F. 1910/2001. *The Life of Buffalo Bill, Or, the Life and Adventures of William Cody as Told by Himself*. Pony Express Books. Repr. Santa Barbara: Narrative Press.

Connell, Evan S. 1984. *Son of the Morning Star: Custer and the Little Bighorn*. New York: Harper and Row.

Conquergood, Dwight. 1998. "Beyond the Text: Toward a Performative Cultural Politics" in Sheron J. Dailey (Ed.), *The Future of Performance Studies: Visions and Revisions*, pp. 25–36. Annadale, VA: National Communication Association.

Cowles, David C. 1982. "White Swan: Crow Artist at the Little Big Horn." *American Indian Art Magazine*, 7, 4 Autumn: 52–61.

Crawford, Jack. 1879. *The Poet Scout: Being a Selection of Incidental and Illustrative Verses and Songs*. San Francisco: H. Keller & Co.

Crow, John Medicine. 1999. "Custer and his Crow Scouts" in H. J. Viola (Ed.), *Little Big Horn Remembered: The Untold Indian Story of Custer's Last Stand*. pp. 105–123. New York: Times Books.

Custer, Elizabeth B. 1994. *Tenting on the Plains, Or, General Custer in Kansas and Texas*. Norman: University of Oklahoma Press. (Orig. pub. 1895.)

Custer, General George Armstrong. 1962. *My Life on the Plains, Or, Personal Experiences with Indians*, with an Introduction by Edgar I. Stewart. Norman: University of Oklahoma Press (Orig. pub. 1874).

Deloria, P. J. (1998). *Playing Indian*. New Haven, CT: Yale University Press.

Deloria, P. J. (2004). *Indians in Unexpected Places*. Lawrence: University of Kansas Press.

Deloria, Vine, Jr. 1969. *Custer Died for Your Sins: An Indian Manifesto*. Norman: University of Oklahoma Press.

Denzin, N. K. 1970. *The Research Act: A Theoretical Introduction to Sociological Methods*. Chicago: Aldine Publishing Co.

Denzin, N. K. 1995. *The Cinematic Society: The Voyeur's Gaze*. London: Sage Publications.

Denzin, N. K. 2003. *Performance Ethnography: Critical Pedagogy and the Politics of Culture*. Thousand Oaks, CA: Sage Publications.

Denzin, N. K. 2005. "Emancipatory Discourses and the Politics of Interpretation," in N. K. Denzin and Y. S. Lincoln (Eds.), *Handbook of Qualitative Research* 3rd. ed., pp. 933–958. Thousand Oaks, CA: Sage Publications.

Denzin, N. K. 2008. *Searching for Yellowstone: Race, Gender, Family and Memory in the Postmodern West*. Walnut Creek, CA: Left Coast.

Denzin, N. K. 2009. *Qualitative Inquiry Under Fire*. Walnut Creek, CA: Left Coast.

Denzin, N. K. 2010. *The Qualitative Manifesto*. Walnut Creek, CA: Left Coast.

Dickinson, Greg, Brian L. Ott, and Eric Aoki. 2005. "Memory and Myth at the Buffalo Bill Museum." *Western Journal of Communication*, 69 2 (April): 85–108.

Dippie, Brian W. 1974. "The Custer Battle on Canvas: Reflections and Afterthoughts." *Montana: The Magazine of Montana History*. 24, No. 1 (January): 55–67.

Dippie, Brian W. 1976. *Custer's Last Stand: The Anatomy of an American Myth*. Lincoln: University of Nebraska Press.

Dippie, Brian W. 1994. "Preface to the Bison Book Edition" in *Custer's Last Stand: The Anatomy of an American Myth*, Lincoln: University of Nebraska Press.

Dippie, Brian W. 1996. "'What Valor Is': Artists and the Mythic Moment" in Charles E. Rankin (Ed.), *Legacy: New Perspectives on the Battle of Little Bighorn*, pp. 209–230. Helena: Montana Historical Society.

Dippie, Brian W. 1998. "Introduction" in Robert M. Utley, *Custer and the Great Controversy: The Origin and Development of a Myth*, pp. 1–7. Lincoln: University of Nebraska Press.

Donovan, James. 2008. *A Terrible Glory: Custer and the Little Bighorn—The Last Great Battle of the American West*. New York: Little, Brown and Company.

Dorst, John D. 1999. *Looking West*. Philadelphia: University of Pennsylvania Press.

Everett, George. 2002. "Butte, Montana's Pioneer Artist Edgar S. Paxson." *Wild West Magazine*.

Fox, Richard A., Jr. 1997. "The Art and Archaeology of Custer's Last Battle," in Brian Leigh Molyneaux (Ed.), *The Cultural Life of Images: Visual Representations in Archaeology*, pp. 19–183. London: Routledge.

Godfrey, E. S. 2004. "Custer's Last Battle," in Paul Andrew Hutton (Ed.), *The Custer Reader*, pp. 257–318. Norman: University of Oklahoma Press (Orig. pub. in *Century Magazine*, January, 1892).

Gray, John S. 1991. *Custer's Last Campaign: Mitch Boyer and the Little Bighorn Reconstructed*. Lincoln: University of Nebraska Press.

Hassrick, Peter H. 1983. *The Way West: Art of Frontier America*. New York: Abradale Press/Harry N. Abrams, Inc.

Hassrick, Peter H. 2002. *Drawn to Yellowstone: Artists in America's First National Park*. Seattle: University of Washington Press.

Hassrick, Peter H. 2005. "Artists in America's First National Park." *Points West: Magazine of the Buffalo Bill Historical Center*, Spring:15–18.

Hassrick, Peter H. 2007. "Where is the Art in Western Art?" in Linda Caruso (Ed.), *Redrawing Boundaries: Perspectives on Western American Art*, pp. 9–11. Seattle: University of Washington Press. (In association with Institute of Western American Art, Denver Art Museum.)

Hedges, John. 2008. "Historical Society Acquires Little Bighorn Battle Artifact." *Carbon County News*, 87, 3 (Thursday, January 31): 8.

Heider, Karl G. 1988. "The Rashomon Effect: When Ethnographers Disagree." *American Anthropologist*, 90, 1 (March): 73–81.

Hollock, Julian Crandall. 1992. "The American West in the European Imagination." *Montana: The Magazine of the American West*, 42, 2 (Spring): 17–21.

Hutchins, James. 1999. "Edward S. Curtis and Custer's Crow Scouts," in H. J. Viola (Ed.), *Little Big Horn Remembered: The Untold Indian Story of Custer's Last Stand,* pp. 152–163. New York: Times Books.

Hutton, Paul Andrew. 2004a. "The Little Big Horn: Introduction," in Paul Andrew Hutton (Ed.), *The Custer Reader,* pp. 227–238. Norman: University of Oklahoma Press. (Orig. pub. 1992.)

Hutton, Paul Andrew. 2004b. " 'Correct in Every Detail': General Custer in Hollywood," in Paul Andrew Hutton (Ed.), *The Custer Reader,* pp. 488–524. Norman: University of Oklahoma Press. (Orig. pub 1992.)

Hutton, Paul Andrew. 2004c. "From Little Bighorn to Little Big Man: The Changing Image of a Western Hero in Popular Culture," in Paul Andrew Hutton (Ed.), *The Custer Reader,* pp. 395–423. Norman: University of Oklahoma Press. (Orig. pub. 1992.)

Johannsen, Albert. 1950. *The House of Beadle and Adams and Its Dime and Nickel Novels: The Story of a Vanished Literature.* Norman: University of Oklahoma Press.

Josephson, Matthew. 1962. *The Robber Barons: The Great American Capitalists, 1861–1901.* New York: Harcourt, Brace & World, Inc.

Kemmick, Ed. 2002. " 'Custer's Last Fight' sales to benefit battle memorials." *Billings Gazette*: Billingsgazette.com/newdex.php?display=rednews/2002/06/22/build/local/62-custer.inc

King, Charles. 2004/1890. "Custer's Last Battle," in Paul Andrew Hutton (Ed.), *The Custer Reader,* pp. 345–362, 377. Norman: University of Oklahoma Press. (Orig. published in *Harper's New Monthly Magazine* 81 (August 1890): 378–87.

Kirshenblatt-Gimblett, Barbara. 1998. *Destination Culture: Tourism, Museums, and Heritage.* Berkeley: University of California Press.

Lane, Harrison. 1973. "Brush, Palette and the Battle of Little Big Horn." *Montana: The Magazine of Montana History.* 23, 3 (July): 66–80.

Langellier, John P. 1999. "Custer: The Making of the Myth," in H. J. Viola (Ed.), *Little Big Horn Remembered: The Untold Indian Story of Custer's Last Stand,* pp. 186–219. New York: Times Books.

Langford, Nathaniel Pitt. 1972. *The Discovery of Yellowstone Park.* Lincoln: University of Nebraska Press. (Orig. pub. 1905.)

Loendorf, Lawrence. 2008. *Thunder and Herds: Rock Art of the High Plains.* Walnut Creek, CA: Left Coast.

Longfellow, Henry Wadsworth. 1878. *Keramos and Other Poems.* Boston: Houghton, Osgood and Company.

Luke, Timothy W. 2002. *Museum Politics.* Minneapolis: University of Minnesota Press.

Madison, D. Soyini, and Judith Hamera. 2006. "Performance Studies at the Intersection," in D. S. Madison and J. Hamera (Eds.), *The Sage Handbook of Performance Studies,* pp. xi–xxv. Thousand Oaks: Sage Publications.

Marcus, Greil. 2010. *Bob Dylan: Writings 1968–2010.* New York: Public Affairs.

Mardon, Allan. 2010. *The Narrative Art of Allan Mardon*. Tucson: The Larsen Group LLC.

Marquis, Thomas. 1931. *Wooden Leg: A Warrior Who Fought Custer*. Omaha: Midwest Company.

McCracken, Harold. 1952. *Portrait of the Old West, with a Biographical Check of Western Artists*. New York: McGraw-Hill.

Maclean, Norman. 2008. "The Custer Writings: From the Unfinished Custer Manuscript," in O. Alan Weltzien (Ed.), *The Norman Maclean Reader*, p. 365. Chicago: University of Chicago Press.

Mallery, Garrick. 1881. *Sign Language Among North American Indians Compared With That Among Other Peoples And Deaf-Mutes*. First Annual Report of the Bureau of Ethnology. Washington, D. C.

Michno, Gregory F. 1997. *Lakota Noon, the Indian Narrative of Custer's Defeat*. Missoula, MT: Mountain Press.

Miller, D. H. 1957. *Custer's Fall: The Indian Side of the Story*. Lincoln: University of Nebraska Press.

Molon, Dominic. 2010. "Revisiting the Studio in the Twenty-First Century: An Introduction to Production Site: The Artist's Studio Inside-Out," in *Production Site: The Artist's Studio Inside-Out*, pp. 5–7, 12–29. Chicago: Museum of Contemporary Art.

Nash, Gerald D. 1992. "European Images of America: The West on Historical Perspective." *Montana: The Magazine of Western History*, 42, 2 (Spring): 2–16.

Navy League of the United States. 2003 (July). "Anheuser-Busch teams with Intrepid Museum to establish Fallen Heroes scholarship fund." Provided by ProQuest Information and Learning Company. Copyright 2007 CNET Networks, Inc.

New, Lloyd Kiva. 1976. "Introduction," in Leslie Tillett (Ed.), *Wind on the Buffalo Grass: Native American Artist-Historians*, pp. viii–ix. New York: Da Capo Press, Inc.

Noyes, Al J. 1917. *In the Land of Chinook: or, The Story of Blaine County*. Helena: Montana State Pub. Ço.

Parramon, J. M. 1990. *The Big Book of Oil Painting: The History, The Studio, the Materials, the Techniques, the Subjects, the Theory and Practice of Oil Painting*. New York: Practical Art Books.

Paxson, William Edgar, Jr. 1984. *E. S. Paxson: Frontier Artists*. Boulder, CO: Pruett Publishing Company.

Pond, Fred E. 1919. *Life and Adventures of Ned Buntline*. New York: The Camdus Book Shop.

Philbrick, Nathaniel. 2010. *The Last Stand: Custer, Sitting Bull, and the Battle of Little Bighorn*. New York: Viking.

Radin, Paul. 1956. *The Trickster: A Study in American Indian Mythology*. London: Routledge & Kegan Paul Ltd.

Reddin, P. 1999. *Wild West Shows*. Urbana: University of Illinois Press.

Richardson, Laurel, and Elizabeth Adams St. Pierre. 2005. "Writing: A Method of Inquiry," in N. K. Denzin and Y. S. Lincoln (Eds.), *Handbook of Qualitative Research*, 3/e. pp. 959–978, Thousand Oaks: Sage.

Rosenberg, Bruce A. 1974. *Custer and the Epic of Defeat*. University Park: Pennsylvania State.

Russell, Don. 1968. *Custer's Last, or the Battle of the Little Big Horn*. Austin, TX: Amon Carter Museum of Western Art.

Ruskin, John. 1847. *Modern Painters*, 5 vols. New York: John Wiley & Sons.

Samuels, Peggy and Harold. 1976. *Samuels' Encyclopedia of Artists of the American West*, 1/e. New York: Doubleday.

Sather-Wagstaff, Joy. 2010. *Heritage that Hurts: Tourists in the Memoryscapes of September 11*. Walnut Creek, CA: Left Coast.

Scott, Douglas D. 1999. "Archaeologists: Detectives in the Field," in H. J. Viola (Ed.), *Little Big Horn Remembered: The Untold Indian Story of Custer's Last Stand*, pp. 164–179. New York: Times Books.

Scott, Douglas D., Richard A. Fox, Jr., Melissa A. Connor, and Dick Harmon. 1989. *Archaeological Perspectives on the Battle of the Little Bighorn*. Norman: University of Oklahoma Press.

Seton, Ernest T. 1897. *Seton Journals Vol. 6: Yellowstone Bears/Crow Indians*. Seton Memorial Museum and Library, Cimarron, New Mexico.

Shay, Becky. 2009. "82nd Airborne Makes Grand Entrance at Battlefield Site." *Billings Gazette*, 29 June: A1, 6A.

Simmon, S. 2003. *The Invention of the Western Film*. Cambridge: Cambridge University Press.

Smith, A. D. 2004. *House Arrest and Piano*. New York: Anchor Books.

Smithsonian Institution Research Information System (SIRIS): http://www.siris.si.edu/

Snow, Clyde Collins, and John Fitzpatrick. 1989. "Human Osteological Remains From the Battle of Little Bighorn," in D. D. Scott et al. (Eds.), *Archaeological Perspectives on the Battle of Little Bighorn*, pp. 243–282. Norman: University of Oklahoma Press.

Spang, Alonzo, Joseph Walks Alone, and Alberta American Horse Fisher. 1999. "Cheyenne Memories of Little Bighorn" in H. J. Viola (Ed.), *Little Big Horn Remembered: The Untold Indian Story of Custer's Last Stand*, pp. 33–56. New York: Times Books.

Stekler, Paul. 1994. "Afterword: Filming 'The Last Stand,'" in James Welch with Paul Stekler, *Killing Custer: The Battle of Little Bighorn and the Fate of the Plains Indians*, pp. 287–296. New York: Penguin.

Taft, Robert. 1946. "The Pictorial Record of the Old West, IV: Custer's Last Stand. John Mulvany, Cassilly Adams and Otto Becker." *Kansas Historical Quarterly* 14, 4 (November): 361–390. www.kancoll.org./khg/1946/46_4_taft.htm: pp. 1–43. Reprinted in Paul Andrew Hutton (Ed.). 2004. *The Custer Reader*, pp. 424–462. Norman: University of Oklahoma Press.

Taft, Robert. 1953. *Artists and Illustrators of the Old West: 1850–1900*. New York: Bonanza Books.

Tilden, Freeman. 1964. *Following the Frontier with F. Jay Haynes: Pioneer Photographer of the Old West*. New York: Alfred A. Knopf.

Tillett, Leslie. (Ed.). 1976. *Wind on the Buffalo Grass: Native American Artist-Historians*. New York: Da Capo Press.

Tilley, Christopher. 2008. *Body and Image: Explorations in Landscape Phenomenology 2*. Walnut Creek, CA: Left Coast.

Ulmer, Gregory. 1989a. *Teletheory: Grammatology in the Age of Video*. New York: Routledge.

Ulmer, Gregory. 1989b. " 'Derrida and the Little Bighorn': A Fragment," in Gregory Ulmer, *Teletheory: Grammatology in the Age of Video*, pp. 212–243. New York: Routledge.

Utley, Robert M. 1998. *Custer and the Great Controversy: The Origin and Development of a Myth*. Lincoln: University of Nebraska Press. (Orig. pub. 1962.)

Utley, Robert M. 2004. "The Little Bighorn," in Paul Andrew Hutton (Ed.), *The Custer Reader*, pp. 239–256. Norman: University of Oklahoma Press. (Orig. pub. 1992).

Viola, Herman J. 1999a. "The Trail to Little Bighorn," in H. J. Viola (Ed.), *Little Big Horn Remembered: The Untold Indian Story of Custer's Last Stand*, pp. 3–21. New York: Times Books.

Viola, Herman J. 1999b. "The Day of Death," in H. J. Viola (Ed.), *Little Big Horn Remembered: The Untold Indian Story of Custer's Last Stand*, pp. 22–31. New York: Times Books.

Viola, Herman J. 1999c. "Red Horse and the Battle Drawings," in H. J. Viola (Ed.), *Little Big Horn Remembered: The Untold Indian Story of Custer's Last Stand*, pp. 82–103. New York: Times Books.

Viola, Herman J., with Jan Shelton Danis. 1998. *It Is a Good Day to Die: Indian Eyewitnesses Tell the Story of the Battle of Little Bighorn*. New York: Crown.

von Schmidt, E. 1976. "Custer, Dying Again at that Last Stand, is in a New Painting." *Smithsonian*, June: 58–76.

von Schmidt, Eric. 1992. "Sunday at the Little Bighorn with George." *Montana: The Magazine of Montana History*, 42 (Spring): 50–61. Reprinted in Paul Andrew Hutton (Ed.). 2004. *The Custer Reader*, pp. 239–256. Norman: University of Oklahoma Press.

Waitley, D. 1998. *William Henry Jackson: Framing the Frontier*. Missoula, MT: Mountain Press.

Waldman, C. 1985. *Atlas of the North American Indian*. New York: Facts on File.

Wallace, Anthony F. C. 1999. *Jefferson and the Indians: The Tragic Fate of the First Americans*. Cambridge, MA: Belknap Press of Harvard University Press.

Warren, L. S. 2005. *Buffalo Bill's America: William Cody and the Wild West Show*. New York: Alfred A. Knopf.

Welch, James. 2000. *The Heartsong of Charging Elk*. New York: Doubleday.

Welch, James, with Paul Stekler. 1994. *Killing Custer: The Battle of Little Bighorn and the Fate of the Plains Indians*. New York: Penguin.

Weltzien, O. Alan (Ed.). 2008a. *The Norman Maclean Reader*. Chicago: University of Chicago Press.

Weltzien, O. Alan. 2008b. "Introduction," in O. A. Weltzien (Ed.), *The Norman

Maclean Reader, pp. vii–xxiv. Chicago: University of Chicago Press.
White Bull, Chief Joseph. 2004/1933. "The Battle of the Little Bighorn as told to Stanley Vestal," in Paul Andrew Hutton (Ed.), *The Custer Reader*, pp. 336–344. Norman: University of Oklahoma Press. Reprinted from *Blue Book Magazine* 57 (September 1933): 52–58, courtesy of Malory C. Ausland and Dorothy Callaway.
Whitman, Walt. 1982/1876. "From Far Dakota's Canons," in Walt Whitman, *Complete Poetry and Collected Prose*, pp. 592–593. New York: Library of America. (Orig. pub. in *New York Tribune*, July 10, 1876.)
Whitman, Walt. 1982. *Complete Poetry and Collected Prose*. New York: Library of America.
Whittaker, Frederick. 1876. *A Complete Life of Gen. George A. Custer*. New York: Sheldon & Company.
Yellow Bird, Michael. 2004. "Cowboys and Indians: Toys of Genocide, Icons of American Colonization." *Wicazo Sa Review*, 19 (Fall):33–38.
Zinn, Howard. 2003. *A People's History of the United States: 1492–Present*. New York: HarperCollins. (Orig. pub. 1980.)

Filmography

Bury My Heart at Wounded Knee. 2007. HBO Films, a Wolf Films/Traveler's Rest Films Production. Screenplay: Daniel Giatt; Director: Wes Simoneau; Cast: Aidan Quinn, Adam Beach, August Shellenberg, Eric Schweig, J. K. Simmons, Wes Studi, Colm Feore, Gordon Tootoosis, and Anna Paquin.
Last Stand at Little Big Horn: Sitting Bull and Crazy Horse Battle Custer. 1992/2004. Midnight Films for *American Experience*. Produced and directed by Paul Stekler; written by James Welch and Paul Stekler.
Little Big Horn: The Untold Story. 1999. A & E Television Networks, The History Channel.

INDEX

Page ranges for each of the plays are shown in boldface. Characters in plays are indexed by name only when that character quotes or paraphrases at length the actual person portrayed. See author's caveat on page 19.

Adams, Cassilly
  background of, 66
  painting by, in Buffalo Bill's Wild West show, 187–88, 198–99, 207–8
  See also *Custer's Last Fight* (Adams); *Custer's Last Fight* (Adams-Becker)
advertisements
  Custer's Last Fight (Adams-Becker) in, 16–17, 24, 32, 151, 200–203, 255n3
  Grand Canyon of the Yellowstone (Moran) in, 200–201
  Last Stand paintings in, 222
Alexie, Sherman, 104, 219, 240–41
alternatives, proposed
  for ending to "Custer's Last Rally," 215–17
  to idealized West, 238
  to presentation of Last Stand exhibits, 230–41
  to re-enactments of Custer's Last Stand, 16
Ambrose, Stephen, 41–42
American invasion of Iraq, 201
American Landscape (Scholder), 106–7, 235
Anheuser-Busch Corporation
  and *Custer's Last Fight* (Adams-Becker), 16–17, 24, 151, 200–203, 255n3
  InBev acquisition of, 260n6 (chap. 6)
art patronage, 200, 254n12
author's caveat, 19
author's dream, 225–27
author's memories, 13, 20–21

Bad Heart Buffalo, Amos, 117, 147–48, 148–49, 255n26, 259n2
Barnum, P. T., 192–93
battlefield markers, 49, 256–57n14
Battle of Greasy Grass
  aftermath of, 43
  and Declaration of Independence anniversary, 106–7
  as Native American name, 258n17
  Native American representations of, 11
  oppositions at work in representations of, 57–59

  timeline, Native American, 44–48
  timeline, semiofficial, 40–42
  as turning point in American history, 10
  white man's version one year later, 49–50
  white man's version the morning after, 50–53
Battle of Greasy Grass (Mardon)
  Besaw on, 236
  counter-images to pro-Custer paintings in, 224
  Custer in, 116, 214
  encampment depicted in, 166
  ledger art as model for, 13, 107–9
  Maehr's response to, 13–14
  Michno map as reference for, 108
  Native Americans in, 111, 115, 223
  organization of, 109–11
  point of view in, 215
  Seventh Cavalry in, 111
  story told by, 111–15
"Battle of Little Big Horn" (cyclorama), 203–4
Battle of Many Names, 59–60, 243–49
  See also Battle of Greasy Grass; Battle of the Little Bighorn
"Battle of Many Names, The" (play), 22, **31–61**
"Battle of Many Names" exhibit, 14, 23, 34–35, 115–16, 258n1
Battle of the Little Bighorn
  in American history, 10, 31–32
  as battle over history, 59–60
  common fallacy about, 31
  duration of, 256n10
  and The Great Sioux War, 34
  Native American artists' representations of, 118–20
  in Plains Indian history, 120–21
  politics of representation in paintings of, 10
  as prelude to Wounded Knee, 36–37
  reporting of, 54–56
  sites of, multiple, 42
  timeline for paintings of, 246–49
  timeline for Plains Indian Wars and, 243–45
  See also Battle of Greasy Grass; Last Stand entries

273

274   Index

Battle of Warbonnet Creek, 196
Battle on the Little Big Horn River (Cary), 56, 59, 64–65, 253n4
Battle on the Rosebud, 41
battle sites in Little Bighorn Valley, 42
Becker, F. Otto
    background of, 66
    lithograph of Adams's *Custer's Last Fight* by, 22, 24, 32, 65, 253n3, 255n3
    See also *Custer's Last Fight* (Adams-Becker)
Benteen (Captain in Seventh Cavalry), 50, 112–13
Besaw, Mindy A., 236, 261n9 (chap. 7)
Bighead, Kate, 114, 236
Bismarck Tribune (newspaper), 54
Biss, Earl
    General Custer in Blue and Green, 102–5, 115–16, 136, 214, 235, 254n17
    Scholder's influence, 258n9
blackface minstrelsy, 255n20
Bloody Knife, 112
Bonita, Pena, 237
Boston Company, 203–4
Bradley, Douglas, 146
Brindza, Christine C., 74, 106, 107, 234
Brown, Dee, 9, 13, 55, 223–24
Brown, J. Mitchell, 13
"Brush, Palette and Custer's Last Stand" (exhibit), 258n1
Buel, J. W., 64
Buffalo Bill Cody—King of the Border Men (Buntline), 190
Buffalo Bill Historical Center
    and dark tourism, 229–30
    death, violence, and genocide in paintings of, 230
    exhibit announcement for "Battle of Many Names," 35
    expansion of, 212–13
    imagining Last Stand exhibits presented differently at, 230–41
    and politics of representation, 10, 232
    See also "Battle of Many Names" exhibit
Buffalo Bill's Wild West show
    Adams's painting in, 187–88, 198–99, 207–8
    Congress of Rough Riders of the World and, 204–6
    Elizabeth Custer and, 203–4, 210
    Custer in, 214
    marketing for, 35
    minstrelsy in, 187–89, 224, 255n20
    Mulvany's painting as poster for, 208
    in Northern Plains Tribes timeline, 37
    re-enactment of Chief Yellow Hair's scalping in, 196–97, 208–10, 228
    re-enactment of Custer's Last Stand in, 10, 208–10, 222
    Sitting Bull (Tatanka-Iyotanka) in, 233
buffalo hunts, staged, 192–93
Buntline, Ned (Edward Zane Carroll Judson), 189–91, 206–7

Bury My Heart at Wounded Knee (Brown), 13
Bury My Heart at Wounded Knee (HBO movie), 254n15
Busch, Adolphus, 22, 32, 64–65, 200–203, 255n3
    See also Anheuser-Busch Corporation
Bush, George W., 201, 259n6

Carbon County Historical Society Museum, Red Lodge, 256n7
Cary, William de la Montagne, 56, 59, 64–67, 253n4
Catlin, George, 68, 223
Cheyenne people, 11, 15, 53, 132–33, 211
    See also Native Americans
Cody, William F. "Buffalo Bill"
    Custer and, 192–93
    Custer's death avenged by, 191, 194–98
    in "Custer's Last Rally," 186–87
    marketing for Wild West show, 35
    origins of nickname, 189
    scalping of Chief Yellow Hair by, 196–97
    timeline for, 251–52
    as white Indian, 191–92
    See also Buffalo Bill's Wild West show
Cody, Wyoming, 212–13
Cody High Style, The, 212
color lithography technology, 257n1
compass, in Mardon's painting, 114–15
Congress of Rough Riders of the World, 204–6
Cooke, Jay, 200, 261n1 (app. A)
Cooke, W. W., 169
Cook-Lynn, Elizabeth, 261n9 (chap. 6)
co-performance stories, 20
Coyote, the trickster, as recurring figure, 18
"Coyote Speaks out Against Revenge" (Alexie), 240–41
Crawford, Jack, 195
Crazy Horse, 36–37, 41–42, 113, 214, 258n7
critical museum studies, exercise in, 230–41
Crittenden, John J., 256n7
Crow people, 11, 15, 58, 146, 259n9
cultural sightings, 14–17
Custer, Elizabeth "Libbie," 43, 203–4, 210
Custer, George Armstrong
    agenda in honoring, 140
    attack on Indian villages, 120, 124, 129–31
    in Biss's painting, 116, 136, 214, 235
    in Buffalo Bill's Wild West show, 198–99, 214
    character of, 193–94
    in contemporary American imaginary, 14
    death of, 37–39, 47–48, 179–80
    on Indians' character, 40
    Indians' treatment of body of, 46, 51–52
    in Last Stand paintings, 11, 33, 158
    in Mardon's painting, 112–13, 116, 214
    in McDonald's Happy Meal, 14
    in *Night at the Museum: Battle of the Smithsonian* (movie), 14, 206–7
    omission of, in Red Horse drawings, 136–37

in postmodern Western landscape, 15
reputation of, 41
as symbol of American military power for post-Civil War America, 10
versions of, in paintings at Whitney Gallery of Western Art, 115–16
in von Schmidt painting, 159, 169
and Western minstrel show, 187–89
as white Indian, 191–92
Custer, Thomas W., 52, 169
Custer and 20,000 Indians (Scholder), 106–7, 235
Custer Battlefield Museum, Garryowen, Montana, 16–17, 32, 151, 181, 255n4, 257n11
Custer equestrian monument, 15
Custer family vacation package, 256n7
Custer films, 32
Custer Hill, 182
Custer National Forest, 255n22
Custer's Death Struggle (Steinegger), 64
Custer's Last Battle (Williams), 65
Custer's Last Charge (Elder), 64
Custer's Last Charge (Fuchs), 64, 257n7, 257n9
Custer's Last Charge (Waud), 64, 257n6
Custer's Last Fight (Adams), 22, 31, 64, 187–88
Custer's Last Fight (Adams-Becker)
 Anheuser-Busch Corporation and, 16–17, 24, 65, 151, 200–203, 255n3
 limited edition print, 16–17, 257n11
Custer's Last Fight on the Little Big Horn (Barnsley), 64
"Custer's Last Rally" (Buffalo Bill's Wild West show), 208–10
Custer's Last Rally (Mulvany), 64, 208–10, 255n28
"Custer's Last Rally" (play), 23–24, **185–217**
Custer's Last Stand (Paxson)
 as basis for Scholder's *American Landscape*, 107
 Custer as depicted in, 116, 214
 horror in, 228
 Maehr's response to, 13–14
 point of view in, 215
 purchased by Whitney Gallery of Western Art, 258n5
 von Schmidt's placement of figures compared to, 169
 in "Whose Custer" (play), 23
Custer's Last Stand (Remington), 65
Custer's Last Stand (von Schmidt), 153–55
"Custer Suite" (Nieto), 136
Custer tourism, in Greater Yellowstone region, 34–35, 57–58
Cyclorama of Gen. Custer's Last Fight (Pierpont), 64

"Death of Custer, The" (Crawford), 195
Death of General Custer (Buel), 64
deaths in Battle of the Little Bighorn, 39, 41, 256n12, 261n2 (app. A)
Deloria, Vine, Jr., 9, 48, 256n5
"Derrida at the Little Bighorn: A Fragment" (Ulmer), 20
Dippie, Brian W., 152
Disney, and Wild West shows, 213
Dorman, Isaiah, 114
dramatis personae, 11, 27–30
dreams
 Alexie's, 219, 240–41
 author's, 225–27
 von Schmidt's, 152

Eagle Lance (Amos Bad Heart Buffalo), 117, 147–48, 148–49, 255n26, 259n2
"Educating the Wild Child" exhibit, Auckland, New Zealand, 224
Elder, John, 64
Erdrich, Louise, 261n8 (chap. 6)
ethnographic writing and performance, 19

Far West (steamboat), 54
First Nation. *See* Indian entries; Native Americans
folk song movement, 156
Fouch, John, photograph by, 53
Fox, Richard, 123
French, Thomas, 125
Fuchs, Feodor, 64, 66, 257n7, 257n9

Gall, 42, 111
"Garryowen" (Moore), 162–63, 192, 256n8, 260n1 (chap. 5), 260n5 (chap. 5)
Garryowen, Montana
 Custer Battlefield Museum, 16–17, 32, 151, 181, 255–56n4
 origin of name, 256n8
"General Custer" doll, 14–15
General Custer in Blue and Green (Biss), 102–5, 115–16, 136, 214, 235, 254n17
genocide at Battle of the Little Bighorn, 107, 128, 152, 183, 230
Godfrey, Edward S., 51, 65, 257n15
gold discovery, Black Hills, 34
Grand Canyon of the Yellowstone (Moran), 200–201
Great Philadelphia Exposition, 54
Great Sioux Wars, The, 34, 36–37

Haynes, E. Jay, 253n3
He Dog, 147
Heinz, H. J., 257n9
Here Fell Custer (von Schmidt)
 autoethnography, 151–52
 encampment depiction in, 166–67
 in "Killing Custer" (play), 23
 location of, 255n27
 lyrics of "Garryowen" on, 260n5 (chap. 5)
 National Park Service and, 117, 260n1 (chap. 5)
 Native Americans as depicted in, 180–81

276 Index

placement of figures in, compared to Paxson's painting, 169
point of view in, 163–65, 183–84
steps involved in creation of, 177
"Here Fell Custer: An Autoethnography of a Painting" (play), 23, **151–84**
Hickok, Wild Bill, 190–91

InBev, 260n6 (chap. 6)
Indian, as term, 254n10
Indian camp of seven circles, 110, 112–13
Indian Memorial Center, 259n6
Indian north, 114–15
Indian reservations, 239
Indian warriors, 182
  See also Native Americans

Kellogg, Mark, 54, 114, 236
Kemmick, Ed, 32
"Killing Custer" (play), 23, **117–49**
Kortlander, Christopher, 256n4

Lakota people, 11, 15, 37–38, 43, 53
  See also Native Americans
Lame White Man, 49
"Last Stand, The" (play), 24, **219–41**
Last Stand, The (Zogbaum), 65
Last Stand painters, 37, 66–68, 184, 221, 223
  See also individual painters
Last Stand paintings
  accuracy in, 108, 169, 172–73
  in advertisements, 222
  author's thesis and purpose in interpreting, 11–12
  back story to, 37
  in "Battle of Many Names" exhibit, 23, 34–35
  and Custer mythology, 11, 33, 68, 139
  as custodians of myth, 228
  as fictional history of white men, 14, 23, 33–35, 39–40, 184
  iconography of the Wild West in, 232
  memory and loss reflected in, 227–29
  Native Americans in, 11
  racism in, 239
  realist military aesthetic in, 21, 184, 221
  themes central to romantic mythology in, 238
  timeline for, 64–65
  time required for creation of, 160
  See also titles of individual works
Last Stand(s)
  early paintings of, 63–66
  as form of genocide, 107, 128, 152, 183
  four, 112–13, 115
  Native American vs. official version of, 60–61
  rescripting, 220–25
  as social construction, 220
Least Heat-Moon, William, 139
ledger art
  Bad Heart Buffalo and, 147–48
  compared to Western figurative art, 222
  as counter-resistance narrative, 221
  as model for Mardon's painting, 13, 107–9
  on National Park Service website, 167
  Red Horse and, 11, 23, 123–29
  as term, 254n16
  White Swan and, 23, 117, 142–46, 153, 160, 178
Little Big Horn (film), 20
Little Big Horn Associates (LBHA), 15
Little Bighorn Battlefield National Monument, 35, 151, 181, 255n27, 259n10
Longfellow, Henry Wadsworth, 121–22, 223

Maehr, Naomi, 13–14
Maeher, Sylvia, 13
magnetic north, 114–15
Marcus, Greil, 253n8
Mardon, Allan, 115, 236, 259n21
  See also Battle of Greasy Grass (Mardon)
masks, in performing the text, 18
McCracken Research Library, 261n8 (chap. 7)
McDonald's, 14–15, 257n6
Medicine Coulee, 112
memories, as social constructions, 139–40
memories, the author's, 13, 20–21
memoryscapes, 229–30
Michno, Gregory F., 108
Milwaukee Lithographing Co., 65
Minneconjou, 37
minstrelsy, 187–89, 224, 255n20
Monahsetah, 193
Moore, Thomas, 256n8, 260n5 (chap. 5)
Moran, Thomas, 68, 200
Mulvany, John
  background of, 67
  Custer's Last Rally, 64, 208, 255n28, 257n9
  on historical detail, 157
Museum of Native American Art, Buffalo Bill Historical Center, 234
Museum of Plains Indians, 234
museums, critical studies exercise, 230–41
myths
  challenges to, 220
  Custer's martyrdom, 11, 33, 68, 106, 139
  Last Stand paintings and, 228, 238
  no survivors, 37–38
  realist narratives and, 182

National Park Service, and von Schmidt's painting, 23, 117, 151, 167, 181
Native Americans
  artwork by, ignored, 148–49
  battlefield markers for fallen warriors, 49, 256–57n14
  Battle of Greasy Grass depictions by, 11, 118–20, 123
  Battle of Greasy Grass in history of, 44–48, 120–21
  in battles of Greasy Grass and Wounded Knee, 58, 60–61

in collective white imagination, 14, 16, 22
Custer's attack on villages of, 120, 124, 129–31
deaths of, 39
as depicted by Last Stand painters, 223
in Mardon's painting, 111, 115
in official Last Stand stories, 220
pictographic narrative in culture of, 127, 221
rituals of revenge and mourning, 42, 45–46, 51–52, 55–56, 121, 126
as term, 254n10
villification of, 10, 40, 54–55
in von Schmidt's painting, 180–81
See also individual names
New, Lloyd Kiva, 119
New West, beginning and end of, in 19th century, 17
New West Museum, 237
Nieto, John, 136
Night at the Museum: Battle of the Smithsonian (film), 14, 206–7
9-11 parallels to the Battle of Greasy Grass, 121
"No Remorse" (play), **31–61**
north direction, Indian vs. magnetic, 114–15
Northern Plains Tribes, 36–38, 58–59
Nye-Cartwright Ridge, 112

Omohundro, Texas Jack, 190–91

Paxson, Edgar Samuel, 67, 157, 258n5
See also *Custer's Last Stand* (Paxson)
Peace Monument, Custer Battlefield Museum, 32, 257n11
"Peace Through Unity" (Indian Memorial), 167
performance ethnography, 20
performing the text, 18–20
photographs, 53, 237, 253n3
pictographic narrative, 127, 153–54, 168, 221
See also *ledger art*
Pierpont, E., 64
Plague of Doves, The (Erdrich), 261n8
Plains Indian Wars timeline, 243–45
Plains Tribes, 36–38, 58–59, 120–21
point of view
in Mardon vs. Paxson painting, 215
in Red Horse's drawings, 118, 165
in von Schmidt's painting, 163–65, 176, 183–84
of white painters, 221–22
Points West (magazine), 261n7 (chap. 7)
politics of representation, 10, 21, 57–59, 232, 239

race relations, making a difference in, 25
racism
artistic realism and, 184, 220, 222
exposure and criticism of, 21
in Last Stand paintings, 239
perpetuation of, in re-enactments of Custer's Last Stand, 188–89

Rain in the Face (Red Star), 122–23, 235
Rashomon (Kurosawa), 257n17
Rashomon effect, 57–59
realism, as ideology, 159–60, 182
realist aesthetic in Western figurative art, 21, 184, 222
Red Horse, drawings by
aesthetic of, 128–29, 178
Battle of Greasy Grass, 11, 23, 123–29, 131–33
first-hand observations in, 137, 234–35
in "Killing Custer" (play), 117
Lakota and Cheyenne warriors in, 132–35
Mardon's painting compared to, 107–8, 166–67
Native Americans honored in, 136–38
omitted from "The Battle of Many Names" exhibit, 35
organization of, 127
as pictographic narrative, 64, 65, 153–54
point of view in, 118, 165
production and reproduction of, 254n14
Seventh Cavalry attack on Native American village, 129–31
Smithsonian Institution and, 124
Red Star, Kevin, 122–23, 136, 235
re-enactment of Chief Yellow Hair's scalping by Cody, 196–97, 208–10, 228
re-enactments of Custer's Last Stand
alternatives to, 16
as annual events, 182, 213, 238
in Buffalo Bill's Wild West show, 10, 208–10, 222
power endowed by, 139
racism perpetuated in, 188–89
as ritual, 187
as story of theft, genocide, violence, and tyranny, 239
Remington, F., 65
Reno, Marcus, 41–42, 47, 110–13, 142–43
Richards, W. T., 255n3
rituals of revenge and mourning, Native American, 42, 45–46, 55–56, 121

Scholder, Fritz, 106–7, 115–16, 136, 235, 258n9
Searching for Yellowstone (Denzin), 261n5 (chap. 7)
September 11 parallels to the Battle of Greasy Grass, 121
Seventh Cavalry
Adams's painting presented to, 65, 202
agenda in honoring the fallen of, 140
attack on Native American villages, 120, 124, 129–31
in Battle of Greasy Grass semiofficial timeline, 41–42
burial of dead, 49, 53
genocide as mission of, 183
Indians' treatment of dead soldiers, 42, 121, 126

278 Index

in Mardon's painting, 111
regimental song for, 260n1 (chap. 5)
in von Schmidt's painting, 180–81
War Department monument for, 259n6
Shields, Pamela, 237
Short Bull, 147
Sitting Bull (Tatanka-Iyotanka), 35–37, 41, 113, 115, 233
"Sitting Bull War" (play), 211
Smithsonian Institution, and Chief Red Horse drawings, 124
Smithsonian of the West. *See* Buffalo Bill Historical Center
soldiers. *See* Seventh Cavalry
Spotted Wolf-Yellow Nose, 123
Standing Bear, 123
Steinegger, Henry, 64, 67
Stekler, Paul, 9
"Sunday at the Little Big Horn with George" (von Schmidt), 161–63
survivors of Battle of the Little Bighorn, 31–33, 37–38, 137, 234–35

Taft, Robert, 9, 32
textual performance, resistance model, 20
Tillett, Leslie, 120, 147
timelines
    for William F. "Buffalo Bill" Cody, 251–52
    for Last Stand paintings, 64–65
    Native American, for Battle of Greasy Grass, 44–48
    for Northern Plains Tribes, 37–38
    for paintings of Battle of Many Names, 246–49
    for Plains Indian Wars and Battle of Many Names, 243–45
    semiofficial, for Battle of Greasy Grass, 40–42
Tomb of the Unknown Soldier, Custer Battlefield Museum, 32, 257n11
Tonto, as recurring figure in plays, 18
tourism, dark, 229–30
tourism, in Greater Yellowstone region, 34–35, 57–58
treaty agreements between U.S. government and Lakota and Cheyenne people, 211
"Truth, Myth, and Imagination: Art of the Battle of Little Bighorn" (play), **230–41**

Ulmer, Gregory, 20
Utley, Robert, 33–34

von Schmidt, Eric
    autoethnography of painting by, 151–52, 161–63
    background on, 156–57
    on composition, 176–78
    dream of, 152
    genocide masked by, 152
    on historical detail, 157–61
    importance of, 184
    on landscape accuracy, 172–73
    making sense of, 174–76
    painting by father of, 153–55
    on painting Indians, 170–72
    photograph as Indian model, 171
    on point of view in Red Horses's drawings, 118
    See also *Here Fell Custer* (von Schmidt)
von Schmidt, Harold, 153–55
Voss, Henry, 169

War Department monument for Seventh Cavalry, 259n6
Warren, Louis S., 9
Waud, Alfred R., 64, 67, 257n6
Weir Point, 113
Welch, James, 9, 55–56
West, idealized
    indigenous narratives and representations as alternatives to, 238
Western American art, 19th-century, 168, 200, 254n11–254n12
Western figurative art
    realist aesthetic in, 21, 184, 221
Western history, proposal for disruption of, 138–41
Western minstrel shows, 187–89, 224, 255n20
White Bull, 123
white Indians, 191–92
whitening process, 60
White Swan, ledger drawings and paintings by, 23, 117, 142–46, 153, 160, 178
Whitman, Walt, 59, 223
Whitney Gallery of Western Art, Buffalo Bill Historical Center, 13, 212–13, 229, 256n6, 258n5
    See also "Battle of Many Names" exhibit
"Whose Custer" (play), 23, **91–116**
"Whose Last Stand" (play), 22, **63–89**
Wild West, as entertainment, 15, 222, 229, 238
Wild West shows, 16, 213, 224
    See also Buffalo Bill's Wild West show
Wind on the Buffalo Grass (Tillett), 147–48
Wooden Leg, 167
Wounded Knee, 13, 36–37, 39, 58, 254n15

Yates, George W., 169

Zinn, Howard, 59–60
Zogbaum, Rufus, 65

ABOUT THE AUTHOR

Norman K. Denzin is Distinguished Professor of Communications, College of Communications Scholar, and Research Professor of Communications, Sociology, and Humanities at the University of Illinois, Urbana-Champaign. One of the world's foremost authorities on qualitative research and cultural criticism, Denzin is the author or editor of almost fifty books, including *The Qualitative Manifesto*; *Qualitative Inquiry Under Fire*; *Reading Race*; *Interpretive Ethnography*; *The Cinematic Society*; *The Voyeur's Gaze*; and *The Alcoholic Self*. He is past editor of *The Sociological Quarterly*, coeditor (with Yvonna S. Lincoln) of four editions of the landmark *Handbook of Qualitative Research*, coeditor (with Michael D. Giardina) of six plenary volumes from the annual International Congress of Qualitative Inquiry, coeditor (with Lincoln) of the methods journal *Qualitative Inquiry*, founding editor of *Cultural Studies/Critical Methodologies* and *International Review of Qualitative Research*, and editor of three book series. This book is a sequel to Searching for Yellowstone (Left Coast, 2008), which explored similar themes regarding the New West through the lens of the history of Yellowstone National Park.